The New Barons
Union power in the 1970s

STEPHEN MILLIGAN

THE NEW BARONS

Union power in the 1970s

TEMPLE SMITH · LONDON

For Briony

First published in Great Britain 1976
by Maurice Temple Smith Ltd
37 Great Russell Street, London WC1
© 1976 Stephen Milligan
ISBN 0 85117 101X
Typesetting by D P Media Ltd, Hitchin
Printed in Great Britain by
Billing & Sons Ltd,
Guildford, London and Worcester

Contents

Introduction

Trade unions in Britain have emerged in the last ten years as a major, perhaps the major, political force. In many ways they have now acquired more power and influence than political parties. In February 1974, this new power ignited a political explosion that removed one government from office and brought in another more in sympathy with union aspirations. But long before, the public sensed that their future was being decided in union headquarters rather than in the House of Commons. In June 1972, for example, a Harris poll asked:

Do you think trade unions nowadays have more power to affect the wellbeing of the country than the government has?

Yes 66%, No 21%. (Trade-union members: Yes 67%, No 26%).

Thus it is that the unions and their leaders have become the barons of our times: enjoying immense power but based on a questionable degree of popular support in the country. This book is intended to explain how the unions came to enjoy this power, and the factors that determine the unions' politics. It is, for the most part, a descriptive book – although in the final two chapters I suggest some personal prescriptions for future policy. The opening section attempts to explain the traumatic change in union power between 1965 and 1975, and the middle section describes and explains the character and traditions of the principal barons.

I should like to thank all those union leaders and others in the trade-union movement who have been so helpful to me both in the course of the preparation of this book and in my work as labour correspondent on the *Economist*.

I should also like to thank my friends who have helped in the preparation of this book, especially my colleagues at the *Economist*, and in particular Norman Macrae, Brian Reading and Robert Moss who have all helped me by their comments and criticisms.

I am grateful too to Gallup Polls and the Opinion Research Centre for their help.

Permission to quote from the following books is hereby acknowledged: Mrs Sonia Brownell Orwell for permission to quote from *The Road to Wigan Pier* by George Orwell (Secker & Warburg); Joseph Goldstein, *The Government of British Trade Unions* (Allen & Unwin).

One textual note: I have frequently referred to 'left-wing' and 'right-wing' positions and people in the unions. These are inevitably slightly loose words, but I use them to refer to typical union politics. Thus 'left-wing' usually refers to Tribunite/Marxist politics and 'right-wing' to social democrat/right-wing Labour Party politics. I have also used the words 'moderate' and 'militant'. These are even less precise, and refer to industrial attitudes rather than political attitudes. Thus if Frank Chapple calls a strike, he may be acting as a militant even though his politics are right-wing. Normally, of course, left-wingers in the unions tend also to be the militants, and right-wingers tend to be the moderates.

I should also like to thank my publisher, Maurice Temple Smith, for his help and advice which has frequently made my comments more constructive and precise.

PART ONE
The rise of the barons

1 Yesterday's legacy

Trade unions are a British invention. The world's first proper trade unions were formed in Britain in the eighteenth century, although trade unionism did not develop as a serious force until the second half of the nineteenth century. But even today, foreign trade-union movements look to British unions as a model of development.

This does not, of course, mean that British unions are the best in the world. But union movements abroad have learnt much from Britain's experience. The German trade unions, for example, are probably the most logically structured in the west, because they were formed after the second world war on a system designed by Vic Feather, later to be General Secretary of the British Trades Union Congress.

History explains many of the eccentricities that characterise Britain's unions. To understand the attitudes of unions in the 1970s, we must also understand the attitudes of unions in the 1770s and the 1870s.

Why were unions formed?

Every group of people in society with identifiably common interests will tend to combine especially when (a) they can identify themselves as the victims of shared injustice and (b) they realise that, together, they can exert more power in society. So it is hardly a surprise that trade unions have been formed in every free western society. But the character of a trade-union movement is determined by the shape of these two conditions. A union movement which is formed because it perceives great shared injustices and great potential collective power will tend to be more Marxist and more militant.

In the United States, a prosperous society with almost infinite land supply did not breed such a union movement. Most workers thought their salvation lay in their own hands. Labour was in short supply, so wages were high even without unionisation. In such a new society, common interests among working people were not clearly identified. Those workers who were dissatisfied with industrial life on the east coast could always head west and, in any case, most of them were angered less by American injustice than by the European injustice they had left behind. And the continued waves of immigration created class divisions between nationalities and between new and old immigrants far stronger than Europe's divisions between the boss class and the working class. In the brash, unsettled life of the new world, the transition from worker to boss was easier and more common. That is why today's American trade unions are so weak and so anti-communist. Only twenty-two per cent of Americans belong to a union and the American Federation of Labor – Congress of Industrial Organisations (AFL-CIO), the American trade-union centre, sponsors both Democrats and Republicans at elections.

These conditions applied to few European nations, where most unions originated in conditions more favourable to Marxism, especially in southern Europe, in the grimmest period of the industrial revolution. However, the development of unions was complicated by religious divisions, and a strong, united trade-union movement emerged only where the beliefs of liberal Protestantism did not conflict with the practice of trade unionism, as in Britain.

The other unions of northern Europe – in Germany, Sweden, Denmark and Norway – grew in conditions similar to those of Britain. In the 1930s, they were as militant and as radical. But then their histories diverged. In Germany the old unions were destroyed by Hitler, and in Scandinavia the political system adjusted to union power. Scandinavian employers developed equal power, and almost permanent social-democrat government drew the teeth of the unions. The smallness of these countries also tended to lessen the divisions. Small countries are naturally more cohesive: thus in Ireland the trade-union movement, which is similar to Britain's, is much less anti-establishment.

The conditions under which British unions emerged were substantially different from the conditions that prevailed elsewhere. They did not develop either as capitalist unions as in the United States, or as fully-fledged Marxist unions like so many of the movements in southern Europe, notably in France and Italy. Instead they emerged as a curious hybrid.

The first record of wage bargaining in Britain is in 1696, when twelve feltmakers are recorded as having negotiated with their employers to avoid a wage cut. Some writers have tried to find earlier records and suggest that Britain's unions really originated back in the Middle Ages as the craft guilds. The guilds were, of course, formed for the same reasons as unions, but there is no traceable link between a guild and a trade union.

Trade unions did, however, spring up first in the same skilled industries which once produced the guilds. And they did not spring up in those industries where the conditions of work were the most abominable. As Sidney and Beatrice Webb put it in their classic history of British trade unions:

> It is often assumed that trade unionism arose as a protest against intolerable industrial oppression. This was not so. For fifty years from 1710 there was an almost constant succession of good harvests . . . the curriers, hatters, wool-staplers, shipwrights, brushmakers, basketmakers and calico-printers, who furnish prominent instances of eighteenth-century trade unionism, all earned relatively high wages. (*History of Trade Unionism* (1894 revised 1920)

One of the first industries to develop unions was London printing. The practice of forming 'chapels' (the name used for union branches in printing and journalism) began in the early eighteenth century. Benjamin Franklin ran into trouble in 1724 when he tried to take a job at a unionised London printing works.Franklin found that his pages were transposed and type was mixed up.

The very fact that unions developed so early meant that they could not be Marxist from the outset. Karl Marx was not even born when these unions began to grow. Indeed, at first, the unions had little to do with wage bargaining. Many of them were merely 'friendly societies' which provided insurance against sickness, old age and death at a time when there was no form of national health service or social security benefit.

Later developments dwarfed the unions' welfare role, but it still remains an important part of union business today. In 1971, for example, the General and Municipal Workers' Union (GMWU) spent £3.3 million on funeral benefits, considerably more than its total spending on strike pay.

As the Webbs showed, trade unionism grew more because of

the perception of bargaining power than because of the perception of injustice, which augured for a non-revolutionary approach. At first, they also developed without any political ties. Such was the basis for the pragmatic apolitical approach, which has always been an important plank in British unionism.

Unfortunately, Britain's ruling classes did not appreciate the need or the means to help the growth of moderation in the unions in the late eighteenth century. They associated the unions with the terror and anarchy that spread through industry and agriculture. Riots, arson and machine destruction were quite common, and politicians who had witnessed the storming of the Bastille, felt they needed to take tough action.

In 1784, Lord Melbourne, the Home Secretary, prosecuted six farmworkers from the village of Tolpuddle in Dorset, as an example. There was no proof that the six had been responsible for any violence but they were charged with having 'administered and taken unlawful oaths for seditious purposes'. The evidence against them was thin, but they were convicted and sentenced to seven years' transportation to Australia.

Such a savage sentence may have been sensible as a deterrent to violence – like the sentence imposed on the Shrewsbury pickets after the violence of the 1972 building strike – but in this case, the men were almost certainly not guilty. This injustice was all too apparent and seemed to symbolise the one-sided view the government took of trade-union activity.

The story of the Tolpuddle Martyrs has since been invested with much emotion (few unionists know that the 'martyrs' were freed two years later and given a free pardon) but it does illustrate how the law was twisted against the unions.

The 'example' of the Tolpuddle Martyrs did not stop the violence, and ministers believed that more general action needed to be taken against unions. Quite apart from the violence, they reckoned that the growth of unions would have bad economic effects by limiting the supply of labour. So, in 1799, a new Combination Act was passed which introduced yet tougher penalties against unions, ranging from three months in jail to two months' hard labour. This act did nothing but harm. It produced 'mutual irritation and distrust' according to a report by a Commons committee in 1824. In the same year, the Act and all such preceding laws were repealed. But even so, the legal rights of the unions were kept at a minimum. Repressive legislation continued to help the growth of resentment and class feeling in the unions just as it did under the Industrial Relations Act between 1971 and 1974.

More violence broke out in the 1860s. In Sheffield, a long and bitter campaign by cutlery unions against non-union members reached a dramatic climax in 1866 when union militants bombed and wrecked one worker's home. Once again, the government of the day felt some counter-action was needed, but they were not quite sure what. So it did what governments always do in such moments: it set up a Royal Commission. The original intention behind the commission was to conduct a McCarthy-style witch-hunt to find the troublemakers. But that was not how it turned out. Establishment thinking was turned on its head by the so-called junta of trade-union leaders, led by Robert Applegarth, the able leader of the engineers who showed that it was in the interest of the nation to strengthen the big responsible unions – like the engineers. So in the end, the commission's report recommended not more, but fewer, legal shackles

The extension of the franchise in 1867 encouraged both Liberals and Tories to curry favour with the working class, and both Gladstone and Disraeli passed legislation to help the unions. The 1871 Trade Union Act and the 1875 Conspiracy and Protection of Property Act did much to establish the unions as reputable organisations. Indeed, Disraeli believed, rather optimistically, that his laws would 'gain and retain for the Conservatives the lasting affection of the working classes'.

In 1868, the first Trades Union Congress met, but the member unions were all 'trade' unions, that is, craft unions based on particular skills. The unions that catered for unskilled labourers and the industrial unions which catered for all workers in particular industries did not develop until the late nineteenth century and the early part of the twentieth century.

It was in the development of these other unions that Marxism began to creep in. The most striking example was in the docks. The 1889 dock strike, led by the legendary orator, Ben Tillett, demonstrated to the dockers their new industrial power and created unionism in the docks at a stroke. These new unions were led and formed from above.

The leaders of this 'new unionism' were not the conservative tradesmen of the past. They were radical socialists, who saw

that the unions must be involved in politics. It was in these
years that the left-wing character of today's unions was established.

Politics came next

The old-style union leaders were not bothered about politics.
Many of them were Tories or Liberals. But the anti-union bias
of the law dragged the unions into politics. In the 1874 election,
the unions posed candidates with a series of test questions to see
which they should back. Normally they backed Liberals, but a
few Tories won union support.

In 1871, the TUC set up a parliamentary committee, but
once it had achieved the reforms in union law, it had little to do.
The politicisation of the unions only resumed in the 1890s. In
1889, the TUC agreed to combine with the new socialist
societies to set up a conference to consider Labour representation in parliament – although not without opposition. The
miners, who already sponsored their own MPs, opposed the
plan. Indeed, only half of the TUC unions turned up at the
conference. But it met and voted to create the Labour Representation Committee, later to become the Labour Party.

The first issue to which the nascent Labour Party addressed
itself was not nationalisation or income redistribution but the
old issue of unfair labour laws. In 1901, a railway company
successfully extracted large damages from the railwaymen's
union, which had called a strike. This decision (The Taff Vale
judgment) seemed yet again to remove the right to strike. In
1906, the Liberal government passed the Trade Disputes Act
which gave the unions almost untrammelled freedom and
ensured that their right to strike would not be challenged again.

Between 1908 and 1926, a near-revolutionary fervour grip-
ped the trade unions. In this period, an average twenty-four
million days were lost in strikes each year (twice as many as the
average in the recent bout of militancy between 1968 and
1974). Membership of TUC unions rocketed from 1.56 million
to 6.51 million between 1906 and 1920. Inflation accelerated,
especially during the war. And syndicalism and related radical
ideas took a grip on the trade-union consciousness. But all this
was dissolved by the defeat of the 1926 general strike and the
seven-month miners' strike that followed it. The general strike
was called to back the miners' fight against wage cuts, but it

collapsed after nine days. The miner's strike went on but at the end the miners had to settle for even worse terms than they could have obtained when the strike was called.

After 1926, the unions moved sharply to the right. There were no more grand national strikes, and in the years of depression the unions were more worried about survival. The moderate right-wing leadership dominated Britain's unions until the mid-1960s, when a new wave of militancy swept through the Labour movement. In both 1971 and 1972, more days were lost in strikes than in any year since 1926.

The history of Britain's union movement in the twentieth century is the history of the struggle between the Marxists and the moderates. Each faction has been dominant at different times, but neither can claim to own the unions. It is the alternation of power between the two factions which has produced so many of the paradoxes of the modern unions we know today.

An aphorism frequently quoted by union leaders themselves is that they want either 'capitalism without profits' or 'socialism without discipline'. It is this pursuit of the irreconcilable that has led to so much of the anarchy and contradiction that prevails within Britain's unions. We now turn to consider how those forces have reacted to produce the turbulence of the 1960s and 1970s.

2 The swing to the left

After the cataclysm of 1926, Britain's unions adopted a new role. They turned their backs on the revolutionary ideas of the previous twenty years for a more prosaic existence. They lived in a world where they were officially recognised and accepted. The first world war had brought the unions much closer to government and the centres of power. After 1919, the creation of Whitley councils (now known as national joint industrial councils) for collective bargaining formalised and extended the influence of trade unions. They rarely had to battle against employers who would not recognise unions and the law no longer bore on them so heavily. The Labour Party had become a party of government, and the trade unions realised that they could achieve their political objectives through the ballot box and their economic objectives at the bargaining table. On top of this, the great depression and mass unemployment did not strengthen the left in the union leadership of the time. They weakened it. The unions did not seek radical solutions – instead they put their faith in democratic political solutions.

This condition prevailed through the second war and beyond. The post-war Attlee government fulfilled many of the unions' most cherished political aims, and Keynesian demand management by both parties led to an almost golden age of low unemployment and steady growth. The men who dominated the unions in these days were all unemotional right-wingers: Tewson at the TUC, Deakin at the Transport and General Workers Union (TGWU) and Carron at the Amalgamated Union of Engineering Workers (AEU).

The thirteen-year rule by the Tories between 1951 and 1964 produced no counter-reaction from the unions. The unions did not actively cooperate with the Tories, but then their cooperation was hardly needed. Inflation, although persistent, showed no tendency to grow out of hand, and growth, although low, was as high as Britain had ever achieved before. The level of strikes in Britain was low by international standards – some industries like mining were dogged by poor industrial relations, but there was no hint of the use of the strike weapon as a political tool. And while unemployment hovered around two per cent, the left-wingers in the unions interested themselves in non-economic issues like nuclear disarmament. Union membership stagnated and union affairs disappeared from the headlines.

The collapse of the moderates

The 1960s was a catalytic decade throughout the world. It was a period when the post-war generation became adult and when so many of the unquestioned beliefs of the war generation began to be questioned. Everywhere authority was challenged; in the church, in schools, in universities, in politics and in the trade unions. The growth of education, the spread of television and the mass media created a complete new spectrum of expectations and thus frustrations.

The groundswell did not hit the unions until the second half of the 1960s and it did not produce its effect until the 1970s.

It is an over-simplification to describe the change as a 'swing to the left', but it is perhaps the best shorthand description of the following events. Between 1966 and 1972, the number of days lost in strikes rose in each successive year. In 1972, the total was 900 per cent higher than in 1966. In 1966, just 530,000 workers were involved in strikes. By 1972, the total had jumped to 1,722,000. Between 1966 and 1972, the willingness in the trade unions to support incomes policy disintegrated. In 1966, the unions had supported Mr Wilson's wage freeze. By 1972, they were opposed to any restraint on free collective bargaining. In 1966, the unions supported British entry into the European common market. By 1972, they were implacably opposed. Those are but a few of the measures of the 'swing to the left'.

The explosion in strikes was a world-wide phenomenon. The number of days lost in strikes in the forty-six countries that submit annual returns to the International Labour Office in Geneva averaged 68 million a year between 1963 and 1967, but shot up to 126 million in the next five years, 1968 to 1972.

It is hard to find any general thesis to explain this world trend. But the surge was most strongly pronounced in Britain, so that Britain moved sharply up the world strike league table. And some of the factors that applied in Britain also applied in other countries.

In Britain, six critical explanations seem to underly the change between the mid-1960s and the mid-1970s:

1   The character of the new men who took power in the unions in this period.

2   The effect of accelerating inflation, which tended to induce a greater sense of relative deprivation amongst most people and hence more support for militancy.

3   The failure of conventional economic policy, notably as run by the 1964-70 Labour government, to raise living standards.

4   The growth of decentralised power in the unions and the rise in influence of the militant shop stewards.

5   The counter-productive effect of both Labour and Tory attempts to legislate to control the right to strike (see Chapter 5) and the success of left-wing opposition to these attempts.

6   The repeated victories for unions that called major strikes.

The most significant changes in leadership were the election of Hugh Scanlon as President of the engineers to succeed Sir William Carron and the election at the TGWU of Jack Jones and, before him, Frank Cousins. This meant that for the first time since the war the two biggest and most powerful unions were led by avowed militants. But the change was also reflected in many other elections, with the emergence of leaders like Bill Kendall, Alan Fisher, Ray Buckton and Lawrence Daly.

The general secretaryship of the TUC stayed in moderate hands, but that was only because the TUC succession is near automatic. The general council of the TUC remained more right-wing than the average trade-union activist, but most union executives became more left-wing and more politically conscious.

The increased politicisation of the trade-union leadership might be seen as a consequence of greater education of the post-war generation. But this was not so. Most of the new union leaders of the 1960s and 1970s were educated before the war and left school at the age of fourteen. Some of them may have become militant as a result of their experiences in the 1930s, but then they might equally be expected to be less militant on account of the improvements they had since experienced.

They certainly did not have any connections with the New

Left that reared its head in the universities in the 1960s. The politics of the New Left belonged to a generation that did not know the 1930s, and centred on idealistic, non-economic issues. The change in the unions' leadership was both a cause and a result of the new mood of militancy.

The second reason for the new militancy, inflation, was perhaps the most important – although again inflation was both a cause and a consequence of militancy. Trade-union militancy accelerated wage inflation and this in turn produced faster price inflation which in turn further encouraged trade union militancy.

Inflation leads to militancy, even if it is accompanied by a rise in real incomes. This is because the effects of inflation are asymmetrical. People feel they are becoming worse off in times of high inflation, even though their wages are actually outpacing prices. This is mainly because wage increases take place infrequently, while prices rise every day.

If a man is given a wage rise in, say, January, he assumes that his labour is worth the real value of his wages at January pricesm So if his wages are increased by thirteen per cent to £40 a week, he assumes that this means he is worth £40 a week. Now, suppose prices rise in the next year by six per cent. The economist observes that in that year, the man's real income has increased by seven per cent, and supposes that he should feel better off. But opinion polls show that this is not what happens. In 1972, for example, real incomes rose by nine per cent, easily the fastest rise in any year since the war, but most people still reported that they felt worse off over the year.

Our hypothetical man assumes that his labour is worth £40 a week at January prices. He does not imagine that his rise is partly intended to discount the price rises in the year ahead (which it will also help to cause). In every month after January, his wages buy less and less as prices rise: so he can legitimately say that his standard of living is falling through the year. Most of us simply do not see the link between our own wage rises and price rises (although we are all bright enough to understand the link between *other* people's wage rises and price rises).

Inflation also means that everyone becomes more conscious of his relative income. When we read in the papers of massive wage rises for other people, we naturally begin to make comparisons. It is a human tendency in making comparisons to find that other people seem to be doing better than oneself. The more conscious one becomes of other people's incomes, the more one begins to feel that one deserves a rise oneself. This trend may have been accelerated by long-term influences: better education and communication (more people watch the news on TV, which has become more detailed in recent years, and so they hear more about other people's incomes).

This increased consciousness of relative income also tends to provoke increased debate about the distribution of income. There is more resentment against those at the top of the income scale, and, as Latin America and Weimar Germany found, hyperinflation bred Marxism and Fascism.

The rise in militancy began in the traditionally militant industries and then spread to the less militant. The traditional militants became dissatisfied first and their success provoked emulation among the next most militant group of workers. Thus in 1970 and 1971 there were strikes among normal militants like the dockers and the Ford car workers. In 1972, it was the miners and the railwaymen who led the main strikes (both middle-of-the-road unions). In 1973 it was gasmen, civil servants and hospital workers who struck, none of whom had ever been on strike before. In this way, militancy slowly percolated through the spectrum of moderation.

An important factor is that militancy spreads by example. More and more people have come to realise that militancy pays. In recent years nearly every strike secured a rise above the going rate (with the exception of the postmen in 1971 and all those who struck during the Government's 1973 stage two policy).

Inflation also tends to strengthen trade unions, because it is usually associated with fear and insecurity. This encourages workers to seek the protection of membership of a union. Unions with more members have a higher penetration rate and a higher income, which allow strikes to be called more easily. Moreover, nearly every union which calls a strike finds that this tends to accelerate recruitment. The National Union of Public Employees, for example, made record gains in membership after the 1970 dustmen's strike and the 1973 hospital strike. This means that militancy tends to be self-perpetuating.

Thus, the sharp and unprecedented acceleration in inflation, which began after the 1967 devaluation, was one of the main reasons for increased union militancy. We shall see in Chapter 13 that the external boost to domestic inflation, which devaluation (and the following rise in taxation) provided, was the impulse which allowed the vicious wage-price spiral to begin turning.

Between 1967 and 1970, the militancy-inducing effects of faster inflation were intensified by a squeeze on real income. The combination of large rises in taxation, price inflation and wage restraint meant that net real incomes rose by an average of only 0.7 per cent a year between 1964 and 1970. This squeeze came at a time when expectations had never been greater, partly as a result of awareness of foreign growth rates, partly as a result of greater advertising and communication, and partly as a result of the promises made by the politicians. In 1960, the average wage-earner lost eight per cent of his earnings in tax and other deductions. By 1970, this had risen to twenty per cent. The table shows that the rate of increase of real net pay in the 1960s was half the average rate of the 1950s.

How taxes bred militancy in the 1960s

% rates of compound growth in incomes, male manual workers	Gross pay	Gross real pay	Net real pay
1948-52	6.9	0.6	0.7
1952-56	7.2	3.6	3.5
1956-60	5.0	2.9	2.1
1960-64	5.5	2.2	1.3
1964-68	6.6	2.5	0.5
1968-70	10.0	3.6	1.3

Source: *Department of Employment Gazette;* and *Do Trade Unions Cause Inflation?* (Dudley Jackson et al, Cambridge, 1973)

When all wage restraint was lifted in 1970, wages roared ahead and militancy, bottled up by the three-year squeeze, exploded. This led to sharp price rises in 1971, and gave another twist to the wage-price spiral. Although real income expanded swiftly in 1970, 1971 and 1972, this was now overshadowed by the other militancy-inducing effects discussed above. Militancy also tended to grow because of the ratchet effect. Since most strikes were successful, any previously moderate group which decided to strike tended to be encouraged by the experience and was more likely to strike again in the future.

The final factor in the growth of union militancy was the change in their internal power structure. Throughout the 1960s, more and more wage bargaining was carried out at individual factories, rather than by national negotiations. This was one of the main findings the Donovan Commission produced to explain the new tensions in British industrial relations. This change meant that decision-taking within unions was being transferred from union officials to shop stewards.

Shop stewards have traditionally been more militant than union officials. Indeed, the shop-steward movement was founded by a revolt against union officialdom on Clydeside during the first world war. Partly, this may be because few shop-steward elections are contested and since militants are keen to become stewards, they more often do so. This applies less to union officials, who are usually appointed rather than elected, and who often have to face more competition for their posts. (The job of union official is more attractive because it is paid and carries greater power and status.) It may also be because shop stewards are naturally mainly concerned with maximising pay rates in their own factory and so are not constrained by the broader policy considerations that bear on full-time officials.

Many unions have tried to 'democratise' their decision taking, by holding delegate or shop-steward conferences before deciding industrial policy. All three of the biggest unions have moved in this direction in recent years. Yet the activists who attend such conferences are often more militant than the union's officials.

Do the communists matter?

Although this has not been the critical factor, the trade-union movement's shift to the left owes not a little to the activities of the extremist left-wing organisations. The oldest of these is the Communist Party.

Its influence cannot easily be dismissed, for it has played a prominent role in most of the big union-Government confrontations of recent years. The struggle at Upper Clyde Shipbuilders was led by a communist, Jimmy Reid (although he left the party in 1974). The five dockers imprisoned for flouting the law in the summer of 1972 were led by a communist, Bernie Steer. The building militants who forced their union to continue the 1972 strike were led by communists like Peter Carter. The most prominent influences in the 1973-4 miners' dispute were the Scottish, Welsh and Kentish miners' representatives, dominated by Communist Party members. (The President and most of the executive of the Scottish miners at the time belonged to the Communist Party.) Six of the 24-strong National Union of Mineworkers (NUM) executive were communists and all supported a strike. And many of the top shop stewards in the car industry in this period (e.g. Dick Etheridge at British Leyland's giant Longbridge plant and Jock Gibson at Chrysler's Ryton plant) were communists.

Many of today's leading trade unionists like Len Murray, Hugh Scanlon, Lawrence Daly, Frank Chapple, Clive Jenkins, Tom Jackson, Dick Briginshaw and George Smith were all members of the Communist Party at one time.

At the same time, there is a Communist Party member on nearly every union executive in Britain (including, in 1975, such moderate unions as the Union of Post Office Workers (UPW) and the National Union of Teachers (NUT).

The Communist Party is the only effective organisation within the trade union movement that tries to control the outcome of elections, and its success over the years has been remarkable, thanks to the widespread apathy among trade union members towards elections (see Chapter 16).

Yet since the last war the membership of the Communist Party has been in steady decline. At its peak during the war years it claimed 50,000 members, but since then it has been falling by an average of 6 per cent a year although there was a rise between 1971 and 1973 – at the peak of the swing to the left in the unions. In 1975, the membership was only 29,000 The Young Communist League, the party's youth organisation, is in even worse straits: in 1975 it boasted only 2,800 members against 3,500 four years before.

In general elections, the party's performance has gone from bad to catastrophic. In October 1974, it scored an all-time low of 17,426 votes, 47 per cent fewer than in the February 1974

election. The Party is also short of cash. Its income as of 1974
was some £130,000, of which only £2,000 was left to pay the
party's general secretary, and a similar sum for other officials.
The party's general secretary is Gordon Mclennan, a charming
easy-going Scot who is a keen golfer. He gives the impression
that he would not look out of place fingering cucumber sandwiches at a vicarage tea party. In fact, he is as tough a Stalinist
as they come.

In the 1950s and the 1960s, it was not respectable for trade-
union leaders to be Communist Party members, and several
unions proscribed communists from holding office. But most
unions have relaxed their rules and in 1972, for example, the
TUC relaxed its ban on trade-council delegates belonging to
the Communist Party.

On balance, it is still probably a disadvantage to be a communist in the top hierarchy of the trade union movement, but
membership can be useful in winning elections in the lower
ranks, and on occasions essential. The communists exercise
their main influence through their daily paper, the *Morning Star*
(once the *Daily Worker*). This has a wide circulation and is read
by the majority of leading trade unionists – partly because it is
much more sympathetic to militant trade unionism than any
other daily, and partly because its coverage of union affairs is
extremely good.

There is no evidence that foreign communist powers donate
much money to help the British communists, although they like
to finance free trips and holidays for trade-union leaders. A visit
to the party's headquarters in London's Covent Garden is
enough to relieve any worries of funds being poured in to back
industrial agitation. It is a pathetic sight. Ironically, it stands
opposite Moss Bros., the symbol of upper-crust London, and it
has only the tiniest of nameplates outside.

Inside the wallpaper is peeling, the light bulbs hang without
lampshades and there is no carpet on the floor. The furniture is
limited to a few bare chairs, desks and filing cabinets. Only the
constantly ringing telephones remind one that the party is still
alive.

The party's industrial work is left in the hands of Bert Ramelson. Ramelson is a forceful speaker and a powerful writer. His
knowledge and influence run deep, and he has a good understanding of the way British trade unions operate. He keeps in close

touch with all the militants, and is to be seen at the TUC congress
hurrying to and fro, lobbying and organising.

His strategy is sophisticated. He does not aim to stir up trouble
in industry for the sake of causing trouble. That would only
alienate workers from the Communist Party. What he aims to do
is to stir up trouble on what he calls 'legitimate issues'.

The communists wait until some genuine grievance crops up.
Then they step in and stir it up. Their hope is that (a) the workers
will see that the communists really are trying to pursue their
intersts and (b) that in the course of the trouble, the workers will
become radicalised and realise that their long-term grievances can
only be resolved by supporting the revolutionary Marxist ideology of the Communist Party.

This strategy means that in any given strike it is impossible to
determine whether it is caused by communist agitators or whether
it is caused by a real grievance. It is usually a mixture of the two.
And it is impossible to persuade the workers that they are being
led on if there is a genuine grievance at the root of the strike. For
management, it is usually better to remove the grievance than to
try to discredit the communists.

The Communist Party played a key role in trying to move the
TUC to the left, through a front organisation set up in 1966, called
the Liaison Committee for the Defence of Trade Unions.
Although it included several non-communist militants, the majority belonged to the Communist Party. Its strength was that it
included many powerful conveners (top shop stewards) who
could easily mobilise rank-and-file support.

The liaison committee brought pressure to bear on the trade-
union movement in a variety of ways. Some were public: like large
demonstrations and parliamentary lobbies. Others were private:
such as organising letter-writing to the union executives supposedly from rank-and-file members. The committee also helped
to give union executives the impression that their members were
moving to the left, by sending in suitable resolutions for debate at
conference.

But the liaison committee came into its own in the controversy
over the reform of industrial-relations law. It organised big rallies
to discredit Mr Wilson's reform plans and later, it organised a
series of one-day strikes against the Tories' Industrial Relations
Act, enthusiastically supported by the engineering union.

The communists are not the only organisation on the left fringe of the trade-union movement. In recent years, a host of new leftist groups have sprung up, mainly made up of enthusiastic Marxist students just down from university. They are revolutionary, but, understandably, feel that the communists have been discredited. They like to attack the communists for their 'Stalinism', their rigidity and their conservatism. They believe that the communists' tactic of only exploiting so-called 'legitimate issues' reveals them as a non-revolutionary party. Instead they want to see plenty of spontaneous trouble. They like to picket official union meetings with placards demanding a general strike.

The communists reply by pointing out that there is no chance of achieving mass support for regular general strikes, and therefore there is little point in advocating them. They refer contemptuously to these leftist groups, like the International Socialists and the Workers' Revolutionary Party as 'infantile' and 'non-working class'.

Yet the younger militants find both the IS and the WRP more attractive than the communists, and are joining them in increasing numbers. Both the IS and the WRP now have their own newspapers. But their members are more middle class than the communists and have less claim to be the working-man's militant.

The IS is strongest in the white-collar unions. IS members have set up 'action groups' in the National and Local Government Officers' Association (NALGO), the Association of Scientific, Technical and Managerial Staffs (ASTMS), the Association of Professional, Executive, Clerical and Computer Staff (APEX) and the teachers' union, and have already managed to elect several of their supporters to these unions' executives. But they have not developed anything to match the Communist Party's electoral machine, and their impact is, as yet, marginal in the big manual unions.

The IS was founded in the early 1950s, following the dissolution of the short-lived Revolutionary Communist Party, by Tony Cliff. It made little headway until the late 1960s when it cashed in on the upsurge of student militancy.

By 1974, it claimed only 3,300 members, and probably only 1,000 of those were industrial workers. Its weekly paper, *Socialist Worker*, however, sells around 38,000 copies. It is now edited by Paul Foot, nephew of Michael Foot and one of the best investigative journalists in the country.

The IS seems to be aware that its only progress so far has been in a few white-collar unions, and in 1974 it decided to launch an attack on some of the big manual unions, like the Amalgamated Union of Engineering Workers (AUEW), TGWU, NUM and the Union of Construction, Allied Trades and Technicians (UCATT). In June 1974, 70 AUEW members of IS met and set up a thirteen-man committee to supervise coordination of their effort in the union. But they realised they did not yet have much support and they decided not to put up a candidate for the AUEW election for general secretary in the autumn of 1974.

The Socialist Labour League is another far-left Trotskyite group, but it only has some 1,000 members, all of whom are tightly screened before admission. It has its own small network of shop stewards and operates under a front name, the All Trades Union Alliance.

The International Marxist Group, which won fame through its colourful leader, ex-president of the Oxford Union, Tariq Ali, claims 5,000 members but it does not pretend to have any industrial influence. The Communist Party of Great Britain (Marxist-Leninist) is the official Maoist organisation, and only has a paltry 300 members, but unlike most of the others does have a member, Reg Birch, on an important trade union executive (the AUEW) and on the TUC general council.

The growth of these fringe groups has cut into the communists' recruitment.

By contrast, there is only one right-wing pressure group inside the unions. This is IRIS (standing rather unhelpfully for Industrial Research and Information Services). IRIS was founded in 1956 with the aim of safeguarding unions' constitutions and protecting them from 'insidious encroachments' from communists and fellow-travellers. One of its founders was C.W. Hallet, then the right-wing secretary of the AUEW. His aim was to defeat the left by building 'IRIS cells', which would be a focus for right-wing trade unionists.

IRIS played an important part in the Gaitskellite fight against extremism in the Labour Party, and in exposing the ETU scandal. It may also have helped to stop the move to the left within the AUEW, temporarily.

But IRIS's virulent anti-communism became less and less popular as the trade-union movement shifted leftwards in the late 1960s and early 1970s. It publishes a regular bulletin attacking the left wing and exposing their misdeeds. But its power is far less than the communists', although its well-informed chief organiser, Andy McKewon, is an influential figure among right-wingers in the AUEW.

Will the unions ever swing right?

The growth of militancy and left-wing politics inside the unions during the last decade is not an irreversible trend. In 1975, there were signs of a swing back to the right. Jack Jones led the TGWU back towards moderation, and in the AUEW the moderates began to win back seats in elections. Many militant leaders in other unions also began to advocate more moderate policies – partly through fear of unemployment, partly to help a Labour government, and partly because they realised the excesses of previous wage demands.

Since we have to struggle to explain the causes of the great swing to the left over the last decade, it would be foolish to be too confident in predicting the future trend. I fancy that the swing to the left will resume before long when living standards have again been cut and when the desire to help a Labour government weakens. But this swing will in turn be reversed if the government adopts some of the remedies which I discuss in the final chapter.

3 The surge in inflation

The swing to the left in the unions had much to do with the growth of inflation, partly because inflation itself was a radicalising force and partly because it drove unions and governments into conflict. This chapter seeks to explore the causes of the dramatic rise in inflation in the years from 1964 to 1975 and the extent to which the growth of trade-union power caused that inflation.

Inflation is not a new phenomenon. Since price statistics have been collected from 1661 on, there have been inflationary bouts, but most were short-lived. Only in eight periods before 1933 did prices rise for more than three years in a run, and six of these were in wartime. Over the long run, there was no inflationary trend. One estimate showed that in 1933 the level of prices was actually slightly below the level in 1661. But since 1933 prices have never fallen and have shown a steady tendency to rise.

The conventional explanation for modern inflation is straightforward enough: since 1933, governments have learned from Keynes how to manage the economy so as to avoid serious slumps and to keep unemployment low. This was achieved, by chance, through the high level of public spending in the war, and then in the post-war period by deliberate policies of deficit finance. The result of this apparent conquest of unemployment was that the post-war economy was run with booming, or near-booming, demand. This led to rising prices, as did booms before 1933, but without the falling-price slumps that used to punctuate the pre-1933 booms.

Demand-management policy in the 1950s and 1960s did not succeed in squashing the economic cycle. So the level of unemployment oscillated, although only by small amounts, between one and two per cent. The rate of inflation tended to follow these movements, although the average rate also tended to rise over the long term.

This correlation when mapped out looks like a curve, showing that prices rise faster when unemployment falls (the Phillips curve). The correlation is characteristic only of 'demand-pull'

When did wages cause inflation?

The percentage rise in final output prices due to

	Wages and salaries	Profits, rent, self-employed income	Imports	Taxes*	Residual error	Output prices	% due to wages and salaries
LABOUR RULE Planning. Oct 1964– June 1966	3.0	−0.1	0.3	0.8	0.1	4.1	73
Freeze July 1966– Sept 1967	0.9	0.8	−0.2	0.7	0.7	2.9	31
Hard Slog Oct 1967– June 1969	1.4	0.7	1.4	1.0	0.4	4.9	29
Election spree July 1969– June 1970	4.4	0.2	1.0	0.9	0.1	6.6	67
TORY RULE Selsdon Heath July 1970– Dec 1971	3.4	2.2	0.1	0.0	1.9	7.6	45
Post-miners Jan–Sept 1972	5.1	3.1	1.3	0.1	−2.3	7.1	72
Heath pay controls Oct 1972– Dec 1973	4.0	1.2	6.8	−0.3	−0.4	11.3	35
LABOUR RULE Social contract Jan 1974– Feb 1975	13.9	0.7*	4.9	−0.9	3.0*	21.6	64

* Indirect taxes less subsidies

Sources: National income and expenditure statistics, *Economist*
8 September 1973, p. 12; *Political Quarterly*, autumn 1975.

inflation (that is, inflation caused by excess spending), for a rise in unemployment reflects a drop in spending. By contrast, 'cost-push' inflation is produced by pressures which have nothing to do with the level of demand, such as import costs, trade union militancy, monopoly pricing or higher taxation.

In this first phase (pre-1966) of the new inflation, demand-pull was a more significant factor than cost-push. But cost-push pressures had already, if imperceptibly, grown more significant since the war. They formed the bedrock of the new inflation, and ensured that inflation continued even when demand pressure slackened. In the middle 1960s, they suddenly grew much stronger, for reasons explained below. They were responsible, it seems, for the transition to the second phase of the new inflation and for its continuation.

Phase two: the new inflation

The surprising characteristics of the second stage (1965-75) of the inflation were (a) that the rate of inflation began to accelerate sharply and (b) that it seemed only marginally affected by the level of demand in the economy, i.e. there was little Phillips-style correlation. Thus, for example, between mid-1974 and mid-1975, inflation hit a record twenty-five per cent although industrial production had been falling for twelve months and unemployment was at a record post-war high. This suggests that this phase of inflation cannot be explained purely in terms of demand-pull. The same is true throughout most of the world. Inflation accelerated in thirteen of the sixteen major OECD nations between the period 1964-8 and 1969-73, although unemployment rose in all but two countries. What is more, there was nil correlation between the acceleration of inflation and the change in unemployment.

'Cost-push inflation therefore seems to fit the facts better in this period. The table opposite shows how costs rose in the nine periods up to the summer of 1975. This does not prove which cost rises caused inflation because one cost rise causes another, and unless there is a redistribution within the economy all costs are likely to rise by the same amount over the long run. However, it provides a clear indication of which costs accelerated when.

The figures in brackets indicate the proportion of the rise in all output prices caused by each item. The pattern is fairly clear. Except in periods of statutory wage control (1966-9, 1972-4), wages have tended to be the leading factor in cost-push. It can be argued that the wage explosions were merely the reactions to wage control: but note that wages were making the running in 1964-6, before any statutory wage controls had been applied. It is difficult to argue that profits have been a main factor in cost-push inflation, except for the brief period after the Tories came to power in 1970. For most of the period, profits' share of national income had been falling steadily, except for occasional spurts. Taxation and import costs have been more important. The 1964-70 Labour government imposed heavy extra taxation (and higher national insurance contributions) as the table shows. This directly pushed up retail prices by nearly one per cent a year, but also cut sharply into real incomes and provoked higher wage demands.

The effect was particularly traumatic between 1967 and 1969, when the value of average real take-home pay remained exactly static. The rise in wages was entirely eaten up by higher deductions and higher prices. The 1967 devaluation – forced on the government by their earlier failures to control inflation – bumped up prices sharply through import costs.

Thus in the period between 1966 and 1969 the unions can hardly be blamed for inflation. But between July 1969 and October 1972 wages took up the running again. This can be 'blamed' either on Labour's tax policies which created a pent-up demand for rises in real income, or on the absence of an incomes policy, or on the militancy of the unions.

After November 1972, the Heath incomes policy had a dramatic effect on all the components of inflation – except for import prices. In the next two years, the rise in import prices, triggered partly by the devaluation of the pound and by the world commodity boom, was indisputably the principal cause of inflation. In October 1973 the quadrupling of oil prices added a new twist to the spiral.

But after February 1974, when a Labour government was returned, the pattern changed. The rise in commodity and import prices came to an end, and the rate of inflation was again determined by internal factors. As the table shows, wages once more roared out of control, most especially after July 1974 when the Labour government formally ended the Heath incomes policy. In the following year, the wage explosion almost doubled the rate of British inflation at a time when in nearly every other western country inflation was slowing down.

This forced the Labour government, in conjunction with the TUC to introduce a semi-statutory pay policy limiting all rises to £6 a week from August 1975.

The conclusions from this seem to be (1) wage rises are not the exclusive cause of inflation, but (2) except in periods of incomes policy, wage rises are the driving force behind inflation.

Even if we can agree that wages have been the principal domestic cause of Britain's inflation (and the principal reason why British inflation has exceeded other western nations' inflation rates in the 1970s), it does not necessarily follow that the trade unions' excessive wage claims are responsible. It could still be true that excessive wage rises are the consequence of excessive demand in the economy (as in the conventional post-Keynesian theory).

There are some clear examples of this: during the first year of the Heath incomes policy, pay rates on building sites rose by an estimated fifty per cent – way above the pay limits. This was not due to union wage demands – much of the industry is non-unionised, and anyway officially bargained wage rates were kept within the limit. It was caused by the desperate shortage of labour in a building boom. Such wage rises can be attributed to pressure of demand rather than to union wage claims. But the 'excess demand' theory does not explain why general wage inflation persists in periods of high unemployment.

The school of monetary economists led by Professor Milton Friedman, and represented in Britain by Enoch Powell and Sir Keith Joseph, explains all inflation in terms of the pressure of demand – although they equate demand with monetary demand as measured by the money supply. Their argument (much simplified) is as follows:

1   There is a clear correlation between the growth of money supply and inflation – especially in Britain in 1972-4.

2   This is not surprising because prices cannot rise unless more money is provided for people to buy goods or unless fewer goods are bought, i.e. demand contracts and unemployment rises.

3   Most governments react to wage demands or worsening terms of trade, by printing more money and extending credit to ensure that unemployment does not result: most notably in

Germany in 1923, when hyperinflation resulted directly from excessive printing of money (at a time when unemployment was much lower than in most countries).

4   Therefore the answer is simple. Governments should let the money supply expand at a steady rate consistent with industrial growth. Excess wage demands need not cause inflation, although they will cause unemployment. But after a while that unemployment will put an end to excess wage demands.

I do not want to dwell on the arguments for and against monetarism at length – that would require a book on its own – save to record some general observations. It is not at all surprising that there should be a long-term correlation between price levels and money supply. The original 'quantity' theory of money specifies the tautology that: $M \times V = P \times T$. (M = money supply, V = the speed with which money changes hands, P = average price level, T = the number of transactions in the economy.) If V and T are constant, then an x per cent rise in money supply must create an x per cent rise in prices.

However, the evidence clearly suggests that V and T are not constant in the short run. For example, in the year to July 1975, the money supply under the broad definition M3 (i.e. all forms of money including current and deposit accounts at banks) only rose by 8.4 per cent while output prices rose by 24.8 per cent. The extent of the correlation also varies sharply according to the definition of money supply. Between 1972-4, M3 appeared to rise dramatically, but the narrowly defined M1 (which excludes deposit accounts) rose far more slowly, and its rate of increase slowed sharply between the second quarter of 1972 and mid-1974 – the period when inflation was accelerating.

The long-term correlation is clearer, but this is only to be expected and proves little. In certain sectors, money in the form of excess credit clearly does act as a direct cause of inflation – most obviously in the great boom in property prices between 1971 and 1973 – caused directly by the free availability of mortgages and the easy lending policies of banks.

The monetarists, however, can fairly argue that although money supply may not be the root cause of inflation, governments perpetuate inflation by allowing the money supply to expand to maintain employment. This was evidently the case in the German hyperinflation of 1923.

In a narrow sense this is true, but it is not necessarily a

particularly useful explanation. The more important question is: Why were governments forced to do that? The money supply may be the petrol that drives the perpetual inflation machine, but governments need to know how the motor works and why the ignition key was turned on. However, although the money supply theory may not add much to our understanding of the motor that drives inflation, its implied cure for inflation – higher unemployment – is more relevant. I shall discuss this later.

To date, governments have chosen to react to cost-push inflation by monetary and budgetary measures to maintain full employment. As I have argued above, the most dominant element in cost-push in recent years has been the growth of wages, independent for the most part of the level of demand.

Can unions be held responsible? Not all wages and salaries are bargained by unions: indeed half the labour force is non-unionised. But collectively bargained wage increases inevitably induce other wage rises in non-unionised sectors. It would be extraordinary if the process of collective bargaining was in vain, i.e. if it did not lead to higher wage rises than under pure market forces. After all, the main object for union negotiators is to achieve bigger rises than their members would otherwise get.

There has been little research in Britain on the comparative pay of unionised and non-unionised workers, but a good deal of work has been done in the United States. The first major inquiry by H. Gregg Lewis on evidence from the late 1950s suggested that comparable unionised workers earned between ten and fifteen per cent more than non-unionised workers. Later researchers produced a wide variation of estimates of the differential. The most recent estimates suggest that when the variables of age, education, region and occupation are held constant, the effect of belonging to a trade union raises earnings by twelve per cent. The effect, however, was much higher for craftsmen averaging twenty to twenty-five per cent and in some jobs up to forty per cent. But all the researchers agree that unions do raise wages above the market level (see Paul M. Ryscavage, *US Monthly Labour Review*, December 1974). Further support for this is supplied by the evidence from periods when free collective bargaining is suspended: i.e. under incomes policy. As we have seen, there was a dramatic decline in wage inflation when free collective bargaining was suspended. A similar pattern applied in the United States under the Nixon incomes policy: the average wage-rate increase in contracts signed in 1971, before the incomes policy began, was 8.1 per cent. This dropped to 6.4 per cent in 1972 and 5.2 per cent in 1973 under the incomes policy, even though demand was booming.

This is a sample of the evidence that free collective bargaining has been the most persistent inflationary force in Britain. Until recently, the unions have explicitly denied this. Speaker after speaker at union conferences and at the TUC has consistently attacked the theory that wages are responsible for inflation. Often the union assertion was modified to the unarguable proposition that 'it is untrue that only wages are to blame for inflation'. But even so, few union leaders wished to admit that wage rises were in any way a causal factor – for if they accepted such an argument, they accepted that they, as union leaders, were causing inflation. The argument struck at the heart of the objectives of trade unionism.

The 1973 TUC economic report provides a good illustration of the arguments presented to show that wages were not to blame for inflation. It did not maintain that wages had no part in causing inflation, but it asserted that 'the prime responsibility for price inflation could not be laid at the door of the trade unions'. It argued that wage costs compose only forty per cent of the ingredients of retail prices – and that the other ingredients, like profits, imports and expenditure taxes, had risen just as much. The TUC's figures, however, were based on the components of the prices of manufactured goods. In fact, wage costs comprise over sixty per cent of the cost of all output prices. The argument also ignores the fact that an inflationary rise in wages is likely to lead to a rise in all other costs. (If it did not, we could all increase our pay and automatically be better off.) Higher wage costs push up the cost of public spending, so requiring higher taxes. Higher wage costs reduce the real value of profits, so forcing businesses to seek higher margins. Higher wage costs also reduce the value of the pound, and thus raise the price of imports.

The second line of argument advanced by the TUC was that Britain's unit wage costs since 1970 had not risen substantially faster than in other major industrial countries. This was of course true, but nearly every other major industrial nation was increasing its productivity faster and so could afford higher wages. In Britain, productivity was rising far slower, so that similar wage increases were more inflationary.

By 1975, union leaders were more ready to admit that wages had become – at least temporarily – the dominant cause of inflation. As the table on page 32 shows, the facts could hardly be denied. 1974-5 was a year of almost unrestricted free collective bargaining. Import costs did not rise sharply, profits were stagnant, there was no excess demand, money supply was tightly contained – and yet inflation roared up to twenty-five per cent – almost twice as high as the year before.

That was why Jack Jones, the TGWU general secretary, told the 1975 TUC congress that wage demands had become 'out of all proportion: going up to forty, fifty and even sixty per cent'.

Why union power grew

If the argument above is accurate, it appears that union behaviour changed radically some time in the mid-1960s. Free collective bargaining, stable prices and full employment proved fairly compatible between 1945 and 1965 – although prices were never completely stable. What changed?

I have already outlined some of the explanations behind the rise in militancy in the previous chapter: the change in leadership, the switch in power within the unions, the failure of government's economic policies and the self-feeding militancy caused by inflation. But this militancy would never have developed if it had not revealed a new and hitherto unknown power to the unions. In the majority of major national strikes between 1965 and 1975, the striking union was the clear winner – from the 1966 seamen's strike to the 1974 miners' strike. Many of these strikes were carried out in direct opposition to government policy and, in nationalised industries, against the full resources of government. Yet all but the 1971 postmen's strike led to union victories. A similar pattern prevailed in private industry. A rough-and-ready estimate between 1970 and 1972 showed that workers involved in major national strikes won an average rise of twenty-nine per cent against the industrial average of twenty-four per cent in the same period. If non-strikers, say, won a rise of twenty-three per cent this would imply that, unless a strike lasted more than three weeks, a striker would recoup the money lost on strike within the year in the shape of the extra wage rise won because of the strike. The success of strike action inevitably bred more strikes in unions not known for their militancy. In the 1970s, there were plenty of groups of workers who went on strike for the first time: such as gasmen, hospital workers, civil servants, local government officers and bakers.

Many of these groups discovered that the interdependence of all sectors of the modern economy gave them more power than they had ever realised. Only groups producing products which were not needed for other production processes (teachers, postmen, etc.) found that their power was smaller than they imagined. Many others – like the miners, power workers, car component workers, and oil tanker drivers – found that if they struck, whole sectors of the economy could grind to a halt. The new industrial power of the miners is perhaps the best example. It was generally reckoned before the 1972 miners' strike that their industrial power was extremely weak: it was a revelation to everyone (including the miners' leaders) when they brought the country to its knees in six weeks.

The increase in the ratio of capital to labour in industry also gave the unions new power. An industry with high capital overheads stands to lose more from a strike and suffer less from conceding a high wage rise. So increased mechanisation and automation actually helped the bargaining power of unions.

Britain's unions have always enjoyed exceptional power in major industries thanks to the closed shop: the system whereby all workers have to join a union. This means that when a major industrial union calls a strike, it can be sure of 100 per cent support from its members. In most countries outside Britain the closed shop is regarded as a threat to individual rights and is illegal. The tradition of solidarity and mutual support between unions has also been a continuing source of strength. Thus during the 1974 miners' strike all other unions supported the miners. None of these factors were new in the 1960s and 1970s, but they created the power potential which the unions found, to their surprise, they commanded.

The collapse of commercialism in the nationalised industries played an important role in increasing the unions' sense of power. In an effort to keep the prices down, successive governments forced nationalised industries into loss-making and destroyed the notion that nationalised industries have to be

profitable. Unions in the nationalised industries, realising that
there was no financial constraint, naturally pressed for high
wage rises. Since roughly half of all workers covered by nation-
ally bargained wage deals work in the public sector, the apparent removal of financial sanctions proved a powerful incentive
to higher wage demands.

Another factor, cited by Sir Fred Catherwood when he was
Chairman of the National Economic Development Council as a
possible explanation for the shift in the balance of industrial
power, was the growth of international competition through
the fall in tariffs and the expansion of trade over the last decade.
Sir Fred argued that this meant that strike-bound companies
were more vulnerable because they could lose a permanent
slice of their market to a competitor. British Leyland, for example, adopted a policy of double-sourcing (i.e. having more than
one supplier of each component) after a rash of strikes in the car
component industry in 1971. Such fears could induce managers
to give in to strikes more readily. But the trend in competition
has not been one way: although there has been a rise in transna-
tional competition, there has been a fall in domestic competition in most manufacturing industries thanks to the steady
concentration in ownership.

Are strikes subsidised?

Another explanation frequently advanced by right-wing
analysts is that union power has increased thanks to the provision of social-security benefits to strikers. The provision of aid
to strikers is not new. Relief to strikers' families was available as
long ago as the early nineteenth century, although a striker
would have had to be liable to prosecution as 'an idle and
disorderly person' under the Vagrancy Act before his family
was entitled to relief. But since the 1948 National Assistance
Act, strikers' families have been able to claim social security as
a matter of right, although strikers themselves have only been
able to receive benefit in cases of urgency and have no statutory
right to benefit. The Act was replaced in 1966 by a new Social
Security Act, but the principles were not substantially altered.
The 1971 Social Security Act, introduced by the Tories,
modified the provision of help by reducing the amount of
income 'disregarded' in calculating a family's need from £4.65
to £1.

The table shows that the proportion of strikers who were able to claim benefit has risen in recent years and that the rate of take-up has also risen. But the average amounts paid out have not risen in relation to average earnings. Between 1955 and 1972, the average weekly payments to strikers' dependants and to strikers rose by 187 per cent and 246 per cent, while average industrial earnings rose by 261 per cent. The higher total amount of benefit paid out may simply be the result, not the cause, of the increase in strikes.

How the state helped strikers

Year	Eligible strikers as % of all strikers	% of eligible strikers who got social security	Average payment (£) dependants	strikers
1955	21.0	13.5	2.55	1.01
1956	9.1	7.9	2.71	1.63
1957	15.6	19.8	2.24	1.51
1958	18.4	12.2	2.57	2.05
1959	23.1	5.3	2.88	1.49
1960	13.3	7.3	3.66	1.74
1961	17.4	7.1	4.11	2.01
1962	0.9	15.1	4.20	2.12
1963	5.8	8.7	4.25	2.88
1964	4.8	11.0	4.46	3.01
1965	15.0	4.4	5.21	3.93
1966	13.5	11.0	5.58	2.76
1967	10.6	25.3	6.01	1.77
1968	4.6	18.4	5.86	2.75
1969	25.2	16.1	6.01	3.24
1970	31.0	18.4	5.96	3.01
1971	29.4	36.8	7.08	3.18
1972	44.5	32.5	7.32	3.48

Source: *British Journal of Industrial Relations*, March 1974.

As the law stands, few strikers can claim any social security for themselves. For example, in the 1972 national dock strike, only six (unmarried) strikers were able to claim help. In the 1971 Ford strike, only seventeen unmarried strikers got help. The only substantial claims are granted to strikers with families with no other sources of income. Besides this, social security is seldom paid out until a strike has been going for at least two weeks. The result is that most strikers and their families are

ineligible for any sort of help. Thus even in 1972, a year of many
long strikes, less than fifteen per cent of the strikers claimed any
benefit. Even in the long coal strike that year, half the miners
never received a pennyworth of aid for themselves or their
families.

There is virtually no correlation between the relative changes
in the value of social-security benefits and the incidence of
strikes. Thus the value of benefits available to strikers rose
sharply between 1957 and 1961 from nineteen per cent to thirty
per cent of average earnings, yet there was no upward trend in
strikes. During the sharp rise in strike activity between 1967
and 1970, the relative value of benefits declined from thirty-
four per cent to twenty-seven per cent of average earnings.

Nor has there been any relation between the average length
of strike and the availability of social security. Some of the
longest strikes occurred in the nineteenth and early twentieth
centuries when little help was available for strikers or their
families. In 1926, for example, the miners stayed on strike for
seven months.

Tax rebates are another source of income to strikers, but
their availability does not seem to have been considered in the
timing of strikes. Rebates are worth most for strikers in the last
quarter of the tax year (the first quarter of the calendar year),
but an analysis of the period 1956-70 showed no change in the
seasonal incidence of strikes.

All this does not imply that a tougher policy (perhaps the
introduction of loans to replace social security) might not
reduce the number of strikes, but it does suggest that the
availability of social security and tax rebates has not been a
major cause of the increased strength of the unions.

A study of building workers during their ten-week strike in
1972 revealed how insignificant social security can be as a
source of income during a strike. The author interviewed thirty
workers on strike and found that their income came from the
sources shown in the table below. This shows that the major
source was savings (on average, each striker spent £150 of
savings during the strike) and income from wives. Social security only provided sixteen per cent of the strikers' income.

The 1971 Act did make one change which, unintentionally,
has made strikes less painful for union treasuries. By lowering
the 'disregard' (the amount of income not taken into account in

How strikers survive

Average amounts of income received from various sources by
the building strikers.

Source of income		Average amount per week	Percentage of total
Strike pay		£ 0.50	2
Income tax rebates		£ 3.00	10
Second jobs		£ 1.00	4
Wife's earnings		£ 5.00	17
Family allowances		£ 1.50	5
Supplementary benefit		£ 4.80	16
Personal savings		£13.00	45
Other[1]		£ 0.20	1
	Total	£29.00	100

[1] Includes picket duty payments, payments from hardship fund and payments from collections by sympathisers.
Source: *British Journal of Industrial Relations*, Vol. XIII, No. 1, March 1975.
Research note by W.J.Cole.

calculating a family's need), it hoped to get unions to bear more
of the cost of strikes – because it was believed that strike pay
would then have to replace social security. However, many
unions have taken advantage of the rule to stop paying strike
pay altogether (since many of their members would be no
better off if they got it) or at least to pay it out much more
selectively. This may have been a marginal incentive to unions
to be more strike-happy. The miners' union, for example, in
1972 spent its £100,000 strike fund to pay squads of flying
pickets rather than to dish out cash to all its members.

The mechanism of wage inflation

The characteristic pattern of wage inflation in Britain is that
one union or group of unions succeeds in winning a wage rise
above the going rate because it has a claim to 'special treatment'. This then breeds an endless succession of wage claims
from unions demanding parity with the unions who have
broken through.

'Comparability' is the most important element of any union
wage claim, because expectations of most workers are defined
in terms of what other people are earning. The traditional

format of most wage claims is first to demand compensation for the rise in the cost of living over the previous period, second, to demand the same rises as other unions have won, and third, to demand extra compensation because of low levels of pay or high productivity or the unsocial nature of the work. But too often when special rises are awarded these are soon quoted as arguments for rises for other workers to whom these factors do not apply. For example, in 1971, power workers won over twenty per cent because of their excellent record of co-operating with employers to boost productivity; in 1972, miners won a twenty-five per cent rise because they were adjudged to have fallen behind other workers; in 1975, low-paid council workers were given an extra big rise of over thirty per cent. But all these rises were quoted by other unions, although their circumstances were quite different.

Special rises due to productivity improvements have led to much confused thinking. The productivity agreement was a great vogue of the 1960s. Both the Prices and Incomes Board and the Wilson government saw productivity agreements as a means to tie wage rises to higher output. The first few major agreements, notably the Fawley oil refinery deal, seemed very promising. Unions agreed to end restrictive practices, output rose and so did wages. Then the government tried to encourage further such agreements by excluding them from the limits of incomes policy: this created a surge of bogus agreements to circumvent the limit – notably in the engineering industry. At the same time, a presumption developed that workers in any industry were entitled to win higher-than-average wage rises if productivity rose – even if they had had nothing to do with it, i.e. if it had been achieved by the installation of new machinery.

If the full rewards of productivity improvements are given only to those who work in the industries where productivity is growing, that leaves no scope for improvement in incomes of other workers in other sectors unless they demand (as they properly do) equal rises. But this is bound to be inflationary because the total national pay bill will advance by the rate at which productivity is improving in the most advanced sectors which will be more than the national average. Aubrey Jones, former chairman of the Prices and Incomes Board (PIB), has argued that the 'root cause of the new inflation is the social tendency of wages to follow the rate of increase in productivity

4   The State reply: Incomes policy

If free collective bargaining is inflationary, governments need
to interfere with it to stop inflation. This can be achieved either
directly, through incomes policy, or indirectly by altering the
nature of bargaining through industrial law reform, or perhaps
by creating more unemployment. This chapter analyses the
attempts to counter inflation by incomes policy.

There have been four major separate incomes policies since
the war: the 1948-51 (Labour), 1966-9 (Labour), 1972-4 (Conservative) and 1975-? (Labour); all of these except the first were
backed up by law. In between there has been a series of
attempts at voluntary incomes policies.

The first incomes policy was perhaps the most successful
ever. It began in February 1948 when Attlee called for voluntary restraint on profits, prices and wages. He did so without
even consulting the TUC general council (imagine that happening now!) but the council promptly endorsed the policy. A
conference of all trade-union executives was called in London
in March, which voted by five million to two million to back the
policy. In 1949, when Britain faced a new threat to sterling, the
iron Chancellor, Sir Stafford Cripps, asked the TUC to back
even tougher wage restraint. The TUC agreed to a total wage
freeze.

The policy worked remarkably well for two years: wages rose
by only 2.4 per cent a year, well within the rise in productivity.
But then it broke down because of the rise in import prices after
the 1949 devaluation and the Korean commodity price boom.
At the 1950 TUC congress in Brighton, a motion declaring that
there was now 'no basis for a restraint on wage applications'
was opposed by the general council but carried by the congress:
an ominous precedent for later incomes policies. After that
wages roared away, reaching an annual rate of 10 per cent in
1951.

The success of the policy, while it lasted, was due to a
combination of factors: the unions were strongly supporting a

Labour government which had implemented a radical programme, they were still afraid of an economic collapse which
could lead to 1930s-style unemployment again, and they saw
the situation developing as a short-term crisis where the help
was needed. But the union support could not last when prices
took off.

Then the Tories were returned to power. They wanted no
truck with incomes policy – but they were very lucky. The end
of the Korean war commodity price boom dramatically cut the
price of imports and the Tories were able to cut taxes. Thus,
temporarily, all inflationary pressures were eased and the
steam went out of the wage explosion. But not for long. By 1956,
the Tories were again worried by escalating wages, so they tried
to copy Labour's 1948 policy and asked the TUC for voluntary
restraint. But the TUC had no motive to help the Tories and
promptly refused. Instead wages were slowed by a recession
(between January 1955 and March 1959, industrial production
did not rise at all in a period when it rose by a quarter in most
other industrialised countries) and by a 'confrontation': in
1958, the government resisted a strike by London busmen and
won. As a result, inflation ground to a halt. Retail prices were
no higher in May 1960 than in April 1958. But the slowdown
was brief.

By 1960-1, excess demand and a major victory for the
National Union of Railwaymen who were granted a big wage
rise by the Guillebaud award (which created the principle of
comparability in the public sector), sent the wage-price spiral
into action again. The Tories then introduced a pay pause (July
1961) with the aim of giving an example to private industry by a
clampdown on wages in the public sector. Pay rates did slow,
but mainly because of rising unemployment. The Tory policy
won little public support, particularly when it was harshly
applied to the nurses. The pay pause was followed by a 'guiding
light' policy which laid down pay rise norms for negotiators.

In 1964, Labour returned – determined to introduce a more
workable incomes policy. The party had the advantage of a
better relationship with the unions and Mr (later Lord) George
Brown persuaded unions and management to sign the 'Decla-
ration of Intent' which promised voluntary price and wage
restraint in return for faster growth. This laid down a norm for
wage rises of 3-3½ per cent which the TUC promised to vet.

The TUC called a congress of trade-union executives as it had done in 1948. This met in April 1965 and voted to support the policy after powerful speeches from George Brown and the TUC general secretary, George Woodcock. The general council argued:

> The justification for trade union participation in an incomes policy lies in the contribution that it will make to the attainment of economic and social policies which will lead to more substantial and lasting benefits for members.

But union support was not so strong as it was in 1948 even though the policy was far weaker. The full congress in September 1965 only backed the policy by 5.3 million to 3.3 million.

The TUC set up a special committee to vet wage claims. It examined six hundred claims in just nine months and often gaily ploughed through fifty claims an hour. The committee approved many claims that were way above the government's target and only questioned a handful. Its effect on the course of wages was negligible. By 1966, wage rates were rising at an annual rate of eight per cent compared with the five per cent rate before the policy began.

In July 1966, a sterling crisis forced Labour to abandon voluntary restraint. It deflated demand and froze all wages and prices for six months. The TUC congress supported the freeze, but only by the knife-edge margin of 4.5 million to 4.2 million. (The TGWU led by Frank Cousins, voted against the policy.) This was the last occasion on which the TUC supported any form of statutory incomes policy until the 1975 Blackpool congress.

The freeze worked wonders. Inflation was chopped back to a mere three per cent a year by April 1967. But then the problem began. Predictably, the TUC's patience collapsed. Just as in 1950, the general council still supported incomes policy but it could not convince congress. By a majority of over one million the congress condemned 'intervention in collective bargaining as a solution to the country's economic problems'. The government ended the freeze, but in August 1967 passed a new law giving itself the power to delay any price or wage rise for up to seven months. On top of this, deflation began to bite. Wages and prices moved ahead but not out of control. The unions, although opposing the government, did not try to smash the policy, but strike activity increased steadily.

The next wage explosion began when the Labour government abandoned any attempt at incomes policy in late 1969. By the time the Tory government led by Mr Heath won power in June 1970, inflation was roaring away again. In October 1970, hourly wage rates were twelve per cent up on the year, more than double the five per cent rise in the year to October 1969.

Why incomes policy returned in the 1970s

After 1970, incomes policy went out of fashion. The Tories had never liked it because it reeked of state intervention. Labour disliked it because it brought the party into conflict with the unions. But the unavoidable fact that free collective bargaining was inflationary forced both parties to eat their words in turn.

The first man to eat his words was Mr Heath. His government began by dismantling all the apparatus of pay control, notably the Prices and Incomes Board. In 1970-1, his government had no policy on incomes at all. But rapid escalation of wages followed – so a rough-and-ready 'confrontation' policy was adopted. The government hoped to stand up to excessive wage claims and slowly de-escalate wages on the 'n minus one' formula: the aim was to cut successive wage settlements by one per cent. This policy had an early success: two major strikes, by power workers in late 1970 and postmen in 1971, were defeated (although the power workers were awarded such a high rise by a committee of inquiry that this proved a pyrrhic victory for the Tories). The postmen struck for seven weeks, after rejecting an eight per cent pay offer: they had to settle for a mere nine per cent. The success of this confrontation (although ministers did not see it as such), plus rising unemployment, helped slow down wages through the rest of 1971.

Then the policy collapsed in ruins at the hands of the miners. The full story of that battle is told in Chapter 8, and suffice it to say that the government decided to resist the miners' claim but were utterly humiliated. After a six-week strike, Mr Heath had to surrender to the full miners' claim, costing some twenty-five per cent. This time neither a tough government nor record unemployment (which touched one million in the month the miners' strike began) could stop wage inflation taking off. Other unions, like the railwaymen, insisted on similar wage rises to the miners'. So, with all reluctance, Mr Heath began to turn his mind back to incomes policy.

In the late summer of 1972, Mr Heath summoned the TUC and Confederation of British Industry (CBI) leaders to a series of talks at Chequers and 10 Downing Street to thrash out a voluntary agreement on pay and prices. The TUC was reluctant to participate from the start: particularly since it had been deeply antagonised by the battles over the Industrial Relations Act earlier in the summer. For two years Mr Heath had ignored the TUC and there was no love lost between the two. On 12 July, at a meeting of the TUC's economic committee, several union leaders led by Hugh Scanlon and Dick (later Lord) Briginshaw, argued that no talks should be held with Mr Heath unless he promised to suspend the Industrial Relations Act. But Jack Jones, who was already playing a moderate role behind the scenes, argued that they could talk to Mr Heath under the auspices of the National Economic Development Council, to which both ministers and union leaders already belonged. Accordingly, the talks began the following week.

Both sides were agreeably surprised by the mood at the talks. Mr Heath found the union leaders workmanlike and sometimes easier to get on with than the CBI team. Everyone accepted the need to achieve growth and to cut unemployment and inflation. Thus both sides began to feel that an agreement might, after all, be possible. Ministers and, in private, union leaders like Sidney Greene, Vic Feather and Jack Jones waxed enthusiastic. Mr Jones suggested that any wage-rise limit should be based on a flat-rate formula (just as he did in 1975). But the union leaders also wanted a range of concessions on other issues like the Industrial Relations Act, property speculation, food subsidies and price controls. After a while, Mr Heath's patience began to wear thin because nothing definite seemed to be emerging. On the union side, there was no coordinated approach. Hugh Scanlon never showed any enthusiasm, and early on, in the lobby at 10 Downing Street, he told his union colleagues that they should walk out unless they could extract an immediate promise to scrap the Industrial Relations Act. Before this could be discussed, the union men were summoned into Mr Heath's study on the second floor, and Mr Scanlon never repeated his suggestion.

Eventually, Mr Heath submitted a plan to limit all wage

rises to £2 a week on the principle advanced in private by Jack
Jones, designed to help the low-paid most of all. Price rises
would have been voluntarily restrained to four per cent a year.
When the plan was put to the TUC team their first reaction was
favourable. The TUC general secretary, Vic (now Lord)
Feather told a reporter outside Downing Street that the proposals 'offer a good deal of fair play to a good many people'. But
Mr Feather found he had little support back at TUC headquarters, and Mr Jones was not prepared to carry his private
support for incomes policy into the open. The TUC economic
committee and later the general council replied by demanding
more concessions on other issues: growth, taxes, rent rises, food
subsidies, threshold clauses. dividends. pensions and house-
building.

Agreement proved impossible, and on 5 November Mr
Heath introduced a ninety day wage freeze. Like Mr Wilson's
1966 freeze, this proved a great success. Although the TUC
opposed it, it did not organise any strikes to smash the freeze:
indeed strikes plummeted and the rate of wage inflation slowed
sharply. This was followed by a mild relaxation in 'stage two'
when all pay rises were limited to a formula (suggested by the
CBI) of £1 plus four per cent a week. This also worked well –
again the unions opposed it, but in practice adopted a policy of
'reluctant acquiescence'. Then from 5 November 1973, the
policy entered its second year under 'stage three'. This was
more flexible, in line with private union arguments put to Mr
Heath and his colleagues. Once again, the unions declared
their formal oppositon in public but tacitly prepared to cooperate. All the signs were that there would be few clashes with the
government. But then fate took a hand. The Yom Kippur war
in the Middle East led to the Arabs' decision to quadruple oil
prices. This undermined the stage three policy, first by boost-
ing prices and second by giving the miners extra power (aggra-
vated by the temporary oil embargo).

In fact, Tory ministers had feared that the miners might
attempt to wreck the policy so they had deliberately designed it
to give the miners more than average. Soon after the stage three
policy was announced, the National Coal Board (NCB) offered
the miners the maximum allowable. But, for reasons explained
in Chapter 8, this tactic failed, and thanks to mismanagement
by the NCB, ministers and the moderates in the National

Union of Mineworkers, the dispute developed into a full-scale strike. With great reluctance and only after heavy pressure from cabinet colleagues, Mr Heath called an election on the issue in February 1974. He lost narrowly although the Tories won a higher share of the votes than any other party.

The social contract

Labour party policy pursued an erratic course during the equally erratic years of Tory rule. But immediately after the party's defeat in 1970, Labour strategists concluded that their main failure had been their inability to win support from working-class voters – many of whom had abstained in the 1970 election. They also thought that the split between the unions and the previous Labour government had done much to cause this disillusion. So an immediate effort was made to improve links with the unions. Labour leaders found it easy enough to join with the TUC in opposing the Tories' Industrial Relations Act, and this bred a new relationship. This took concrete form with the creation of the TUC-Labour Party liaison committee, which met regularly to discuss policy. In July 1972, the committee agreed on the need to repeal the Industrial Relations Act, but it did not agree to any strategy for dealing with inflation.

When Mr Heath introduced his incomes policy, Labour leaders did not criticise the principle, but instead preferred to criticise detailed weaknesses and unfairnesses. However in February 1973, the liaison committee did agree on economic policy. This agreement included nineteen major points but the policy for inflation only called for effective price controls and food subsidies. It made no mention of wages. Yet this agreement was the basis of the social contract, which later became the centrepiece of Labour's plan to tackle inflation. The theory was that if government introduced social and economic policies which were fair and just, the unions would respond by lowering wage claims as their side of the contract.

But the nature of the social contract was still extremely vague by the time of the February 1974 election: so much so that Hugh Scanlon told Robin Day on BBC television: 'We are not agreed on any specific policy as of now' (19 February 1974).

The social contract only became a practical policy when the Labour government took power. At first, Labour decided to

retain the stage-three policy and the pay board, set up by Mr
Heath, for several months to allow an alternative policy to be
devised.

The Labour Party manifesto had been studiously vague on
wages policy. It merely committed itself against statutory pay
controls and 'to create the right economic climate for money
incomes to grow in line with production'. Michael Foot, the
new employment secretary, concentrated on the repeal of the
Industrial Relations Act – so little thought was given to pay
policy. But by early summer, talks began between ministers
and union leaders on the voluntary social contract that would
follow the abolition of pay controls. The TUC agreed to produce wage bargaining guidelines and published a document
entitled 'Collective Bargaining and the Social Contract'. This
suggested the following woolly and wordy guidance to
negotiators:

(i)   although the groundwork is being laid for increasing consumption and living standards in the future, the
scope for real increases in consumption at present is limited,
and a central negotiating objective in the coming period will
therefore be to ensure that real incomes are maintained;

(ii)   this will entail claiming compensation for the rise
in the cost of living since the last settlement; taking into
account that threshold agreements will already have given
some compensation for current price increases;

(iii)   an alternative approach would be to negotiate
arrangements to keep up with the cost of living during the
period of the new agreement;

(iv)   the twelve-month interval between major
increases should in general continue to apply;

(v)   priority should be given to negotiating agreements
which will have beneficial effects on unit costs and efficiency,
to reforming pay structures, and to improving job security:

(vi)   priority should also be given to attaining reasonable minimum standards, including the TUC's low pay
target of a £25 minimum basic rate with higher minimum
earnings, for a normal week for those aged 18 and over;

(vii)   a continuing aim is the elimination of discrimination against particular groups, notably women; improving
non-wage benefits such as sick pay and occupational pension

schemes; and progress towards four weeks' annual holiday;

(viii)   full use should be made of the conciliation, arbitration and mediation services of the CAS to help towards a quick solution of disputes.

This advice was so vague that almost any interpretation could have been put on it. But even so, some unions like the engineers and the civil servants objected to any form of wage restraint and determined to vote against the social contract at the 1974 Brighton congress. Ken Gill of the Amalgamated Union of Engineering Workers (AUEW) moved the opposition but was eventually persuaded to withdraw the motion in order 'to help Labour win the general election' of October 1974 – as he later explained to the 1975 congress. Thus the social contract was carried without opposition. The pay board had been finally abolished in July.

If the guidelines of the contract had been interpreted severely – so that all pay rises were either tied to the rise in retail prices in the previous year or the coming year – it would have de-escalated inflation. But they were not. Neither the TUC nor the government had any means of monitoring the policy. The TUC did call in several unions and ask them to lower their claims. The TUC reckons this had some effect – notably in the builders' settlement (they only got a seventeen and a half per cent wage rise, but this was mainly due to the slump in building and the fear of unemployment). The TUC also claimed that it had helped avoid another miners' strike – but the miners settled for a rise worth around thirty-five per cent (including all fringe benefits).

The TUC's job was made harder by the surge in wages caused by thresholds. These were a leftover from the stage-three policy which had allowed every wage agreement to provide for an extra forty pence a week (roughly one per cent of wages) for every one per cent by which inflation in the year to November 1974 exceeded seven per cent. Thanks to the surge in inflation caused by the continued commodity and oil price boom, eleven thresholds were triggered, adding £4.40 to most paypackets. But thresholds cannot be blamed for all of the surge in this period: if they had not existed, unions would have insisted on reopening and renegotiating their existing wage contracts.

Wage inflation continued to rise, way in advance of prices, through late 1974 and the first half of 1975. By April, average earnings were 30.5 per cent up on the year before although retail prices had only risen 21.7 per cent in the same period.

The failure of the mark-one social contract had been evident to TUC leaders from early in 1975, but there was an obvious reluctance to take any action. Many felt that the wage explosion was temporary: caused by the aftermath of the end of pay controls, the resolution of anomalies that had arisen during controls and, above all, the impact of thresholds. But these arguments wore thin as it became clear that there was no slowdown in wage demands in 1975. In February, Len Murray and David Lea, head of the TUC economic department, put a paper to the TUC economic committee which considered ways of tightening up the contract and the possibility of the re-introduction of wage-vetting. But it rejected.

No further moves were made until after the budget. But then Mr Healey asked the TUC to consider plans for a tougher mark-two social contract. In mid-May, Jack Jones publicly launched a scheme for pinning all pay rises to a flat-rate sum. It was the same idea that he had put to Mr Heath three years before.

The debate about the mark-two social contract was still proceeding at a leisurely pace when a major run on sterling suddenly forced ministers and union leaders into action. The principle of the flat-rate pay rises for the mark-two contract had been agreed at a meeting of the TUC general council on 25 June, by a twenty-one to six majority. Mr Jones laid it on the line. He warned the council of a 'massive withdrawal of funds by foreign bankers' and of 'a right-wing coalition which would impose a statutory incomes policy, cut living standards and raise unemployment' unless they backed the pay limit plan. Hugh Scanlon spoke against Mr Jones on the grounds that the TUC would do better to leave 'unpleasant fiscal and economic decisions' to the government. But even at this stage, the TUC was still thinking in terms of the continuation of the old-style contract without vetting or sanctions.

On Monday 30 June, the Governor of the Bank of England appears to have warned Mr Healey, then Chancellor, that a massive run on sterling was imminent because a major American bank controlling substantial oil-state funds was about to withdraw them from sterling. Mr Healey, who had been in favour of a statutory policy from an early stage, decided to make an immediate statement. On Tuesday 31 June, he tried to persuade the cabinet to accept legislation to provide for a ten per cent limit on all forms of income, but left-wing ministers secured a week's grace to see if some voluntary agreement could not be secured from the wreckage of social contract mark one. Mr Healey told the Commons on the Tuesday that if voluntary agreement with the TUC could not be reached within the week, the government would introduce a statutory pay policy.

The TUC quickly decided to try and reach agreement with ministers on the basis of the Jones flat-rate plan. Negotiations were brief, but the TUC submitted a detailed plan for pay limits based on a rise of £6.50 a week for everyone (roughly equal to ten per cent of the national pay bill). There was some haggling over the figures: at one point Mr Jones was even ready to accept a £4.50 limit, but eventually £6 was agreed. On Wednesday 9 July, the TUC general council voted by nineteen to thirteen to back the policy.

Inside the cabinet, there was a protracted row over how sanctions should be applied to those who broke the policy. But it agreed to begin by applying sanctions only to employers, through price controls and limits on state aid, and to keep in reserve powers to compel registration of all pay settlements and to impose tougher sanctions. This policy was announced on 11 July, just eleven days after negotiations had begun. It was approved at the TUC Blackpool congress in the first week of September by a vote of 6.9 million to 3.4 million.

So began the latest British attempt to control free collective bargaining, although this time with more determined trade-union support than at any time since 1948. The unions were prepared to forego their principles in 1975 (a) because they realised that the level of wage claims had become 'fantastic', as Mr Jones put it, (b) because they realised that inflation was causing massive unemployment, and (c) because they saw this as the only way to preserve a Labour government in power – a government which was carrying out almost every policy the unions wanted. But there was still considerable opposition within the TUC – both from the far-left unions like the engineers who thought the policy was helping to prop up capitalism and from unions representing higher-paid workers.

In June 1976, the TUC agreed to another year of restraint with a limit on wage rises of close to 3 per cent. But it is far from clear whether the policy can last for long.

Does incomes policy work?

A simple test of the efficacy of incomes policy is to measure the average rate of wage inflation before and after the policy and compare it with the rate of wage inflation during the policy. On this test, the voluntary policies of 1964-6 and 1974-5 were a total flop and all statutory policies were a success – at least in the short run. For example, in the year to July 1966, earnings rose by 7.4 per cent but by only 3.1 per cent in the following pay-controlled year. In the year to November 1972, earnings rose by 16.5 per cent but in the following pay-controlled year by only 12.4 per cent.

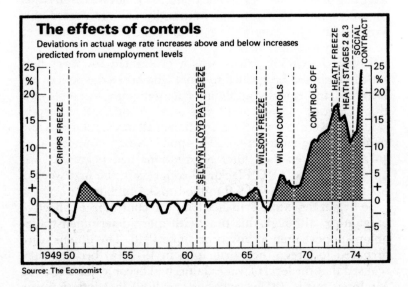

The effects of controls

Deviations in actual wage rate increases above and below increases predicted from unemployment levels

Source: The Economist

These figures, however, do not necessarily measure the effect of incomes policy because wages might have slowed down in any case. A more sophisticated analysis adjusts the wage figures according to the level of unemployment. The chart shows the deviation in actual wage increases below and above the levels expected from the past relationship between demand and unemployment. These reveal that most periods of formal or statutory incomes policy did slow down wage inflation below the trend – but that they were followed by periods of excess deviations in the opposite direction, i.e. a wage explosion. This can be interpreted by the anti-incomes-policy school to show that the policy has no permanent effect, or by the pro-incomes-policy school as an illustration of the disastrous effect of abandoning incomes policy. The second interpretation seems more persuasive to me. The only indisputable evidence is that wages rise slower in periods of incomes policy.

It should be noted, however, that most incomes policies are introduced in times of maximum stress when other factors are often adverse. The Attlee policy, the 1966-9 Wilson policy and 1972-4 Heath policy were all damaged by a surge in import prices. In view of this, it was remarkable how successful these policies proved. If there had been no incomes policy in operation in Britain in 1973, the import price surge would have almost certainly fed straight into wages and doubled the rate of inflation. As it was, Britain's internally-generated inflation fell to one of the lowest rates of any country. The table below is based on OECD figures for the year to the second quarter of 1973. 'Home-made inflation' is calculated by deducting the effect of import price rises on inflation from the recorded rise in retail prices.

A year of success

% changes between second quarters 1972-3

Country	Effect of imports on home prices	Consumer price rise	Home-made inflation
Britain	6.1	9.5	3.4
Sweden	2.3	6.2	3.9
Canada	2.2	6.5	4.3
USA	0.9	5.6	4.7
Netherlands	2.8	8.7	5.9
Switzerland	1.5	8.0	6.5
France	0.7	7.3	6.6
Denmark	1.9	8.9	7.0
Norway	0.8	8.0	7.2
Germany	0.9	8.2	7.3

Critics of incomes policies, however, point to other snags. They argue (a) that they lead to misallocation of resources by interfering with market forces, (b) they lead to conflict between government and unions and more industrial unrest, and (c) they interfere with individual freedom.

Let us examine these allegations in turn. There can be little doubt that argument (a) is accurate, especially when incomes policies are accompanied by price controls as they usually are. A prize example is the over-investment in power-generating capacity in 1972-4 because of the underpricing of electricity. There are fewer examples of misallocation in the labour market, because employers who are short of labour can normally find ways of busting the policy to provide the wages necessary to attract the labour they need. An exception was London Transport in 1973, when it had to cut services because it could not raise its pay rates sufficiently to attract labour. But if it is true that the alternatives to income policy are faster inflation or higher unemployment, then incomes policy may lead to less misallocation than either of the alternatives.

Argument (b) is simply false. A study of strikes in Britain between 1950 and 1967 showed that there were on average some forty fewer strikes a year in periods of incomes policy than in periods of free collective bargaining. In the twelve months following the introduction of the Heath incomes policy in November 1972, days lost in strikes were down seventy-seven per cent on the previous twelve months. In the United States, the Nixon incomes policy cut days lost in strikes by twenty-eight per cent between 1970 and 1971, and another forty-three per cent between 1971 and 1972. The fall in strikes both in Britain under the Heath policy and in the United States under the Nixon policy occurred in periods of falling unemployment when the incidence of strikes normally rises. (A study by the Massachusetts Institute of Technology in the period 1950-69 found a clear link between low unemployment and strikes.) Of course, those who advance argument (b) think of Mr Heath's confrontation with the miners as an example of the ills of incomes policy. But that confrontation would have happened even if there had been no statutory incomes policy: indeed it would have been more necessary. After all, the period without statutory policy between 1970 and 1972 also led to a confrontation with the miners.

The effect of incomes policy on social justice is more debatable. Most incomes policies of recent years have been designed to give bigger rises to the lower-paid through the use of a partial flat-rate limit – but this has not always been successful because many lower-paid workers were not in a strong enough bargaining position to achieve their full entitlement. But the low-paid would have suffered even more under a continued free-for-all in which only the strongest benefited.

There are many ways in which the operation of Britain's incomes policies could be improved, which I shall develop in Chapter 16 – but there seems to me little doubt that incomes policy has been a more effective weapon against inflation than most of its critics admit.

5   The State reply: Legal restraint

The growth of union power, the increase in strikes and the surge in wage inflation suggested an alternative state response in the 1960s: the use of legislation to limit the right to strike. The arguments in favour of this approach seemed strong. Since the 1906 Trades Disputes Act, unions could not be held responsible for almost any damage caused by strikes. British unions could not only strike when they chose, but could break contracts freely entered into, without being liable to any penalty. They were also able to force all workers in a company or industry to join a union and abide by its rules – regardless of whether they wished to do so – under the 'closed shop' system. The generality of these privileges was unmatched in any other western country. With the increase in the extent of the damage that strikes could cause, it seemed increasingly arguable that unions should be more accountable for the use of their power.

It was with such arguments in mind that Harold Wilson set up a Royal Commission under Lord Donovan in 1965 to investigate the reform of industrial relations in Britain. Oddly, the commission was set up before the real extent of trade-union power had become evident and before the principal growth in strike activity had begun.

The commission reported in 1968. Its broad conclusion was that the voluntary non-legalised system of industrial relations was a strength not a weakness, and it contented itself with recommending a number of useful and uncontroversial reforms. It did, however, recommend one important limit on the right to strike: that the right should be confined to registered unions. This would have removed legal protection for unofficial strikes – which the commission found accounted for ninety-five per cent of strikes. And it recommended that all unions should be compulsorily registered.

The commission reckoned that this might assuage the main problem with industrial relations in Britain in the 1960s, which was the incompatibility of the formal structure of unions and bargaining with the informal structure of the localised plant-by-plant bargaining system that had been spawned in the previous decade. It did not see any need to give governments the power to order ballots of strikers or cooling-off periods. The recommendations of the commission probably represented the maximum that could be achieved in reform by legislation. But at the time the problem seemed to require a more dramatic approach, and Andrew Shonfield's minority note to the commission's report provided a powerful statement for the case for more extensive legal regulation. He accused his fellow-commissioners of producing a report 'which barely concerns itself with the long-term problem of accommodating bodies with the kind of concentrated power which is possessed by trade unions to the changing future needs of an advanced industrial society'. He argued that society's increasing vulnerability to strikes necessitated more legal regulation.

The Shonfield view was in tune with the mood of the Wilson government. Ministers knew that there was widespread public dissatisfaction with the power of the unions and support for legislation to control it. They also wanted to show that the Labour Party was not a prisoner of the unions and was sufficiently independent to control union power in the wider interests of society.

So, in 1969, Barbara Castle presented a white paper entitled *In Place of Strife* which proposed several remedies quite different from Donovan's. It rejected the Donovan plan for curbing unofficial strikes, but included provisions to give the employment secretary powers to call a twenty-eight-day cooling-off period in unofficial strikes where proper procedures had not been observed, and to call a ballot of all workers involved in official strikes.

This caused a great deal of fuss. The unions rose in anger and dubbed these powers 'penal clauses'. Mr Wilson declared that 'the passage of this bill is essential to the continuation of this government in office. There can be no going back on that.' And the Tories claimed that the plan was quite inadequate.

Later experience under the Tories' Industrial Relations Act showed that the cooling-off period and the strike ballot were ineffective weapons. In the United States, strike ballots called by the state have always backed the strike although cooling-off periods have produced settlements without a resumption of the

strike in fifty per cent of cases. But in 1969 these powers
appeared to raise a great issue of principle.

Opposition from the TUC and many Labour MPs forced the
Wilson government to drop the penal clauses. Instead, in June
1969, the TUC offered the government 'a solemn and binding
undertaking' to strengthen its own powers to control strikes: (a)
by changing its own rules to give it power to intervene in
unofficial strikes, and (b) to forbid strikes caused by inter-
union rows until they had been investigated by the TUC.

The undertaking proved almost worthless (although it marginally reduced the number of inter-union strikes in the following years); but it served the convenient political purpose of
giving the government an excuse to withdraw its penal clauses.
In the spring of 1970, the government introduced its emascu-
lated Industrial Relations Bill, but this did not reach the statute
book before the dissolution of parliament and the return of a
Tory government.

The Tories had been thinking seriously about trade-union
law reform ever since they had lost the 1964 election. They had
managed to pressure Wilson into setting up the Donovan
Commission, but they were critical of the Donovan findings. In
April 1968, under the hand of earnest Robert Carr, they published *Fair Deal at Work*. This pamphlet laid down the strategy
which formed the heart of the Industrial Relations Act, which
became law four years later. The motivation behind the Tories'
thinking, as with Labour's, was a feeling that union power had
become excessive. It was precisely because the unions were
aware of the politicians' motivation that they believed that the
legislation both parties wanted had to be fought tooth and nail.

The Tory strategy had many significant differences from the
abortive Labour plan. Its anti-strike clauses were tougher,
allowing employers to sue unofficial strikers, and it gave more
protection to the individual union member from union 'bully-
ing'. But, like the Castle plan, it included most of the non-
controversial Donovan reforms such as protection against
unfair sackings.

When the Industrial Relations Act became law in early 1972,
it banned every strike if it was an 'unfair industrial practice' (a
UIP) – a completely new concept. The principal UIPs were:

All unofficial strikes and strikes by unregistered unions

(except if long notice was given).

The breaking of a legally binding agreement, e.g. by striking before an agreement expired. (All agreements were assumed to be legally binding, unless they specified that they were not.)

Sympathy strikes. This covered any strike by employees on an issue not connected with their employer, say, in support of a strike at another factory.

Strikes to force employers to infringe workers' rights, e.g. to make an employer sack a non-union man.

Strikes to force an employer to recognise a union while the Commission on Industrial Relations was investigating.

It also set up the National Industrial Relations Court, as an adjunct of the High Court, to deal with the major cases under the new Act. The NIRC sat in a windowless room in London's Chancery Lane, presided over by another earnest man, Sir John Donaldson. Sir John had been a keen Tory activist in his younger days. This proved to be an unfortunate background.

The initiative to take a union (or strike leaders) to court resided solely with employers (except under the emergency procedures): so the operation of the Act depended on the willingness of employers to take offenders to court. Moreover, they could only take the union itself or a strike leader to court. Nothing in the Act made it illegal to take part in a strike: so the Act's operation also depended on employers being able to identify strike leaders. Although the Act gave the employer theoretical power to deal with strikes, in practice the employer was faced with big problems if he wanted to put the law into action.

Unlike Labour, the Conservatives accepted the Donovan plan to restrict the right to strike to registered unions. So all unofficial strikes became UIPs. Registration was not a new idea: before 1971 most unions were registered with the Registrar of Friendly Societies.

Registration under the Industrial Relations Act was not so easy to get. Registered unions had to have fair rules covering entry of new members, conduct of elections and discipline. The most controversial requirement of the new registration system was that the rules had to say who could call a strike, and when.

This greatly angered the unions. They have always maintained that strikes may be called by anyone, because circumstances are not always foreseeable.

The aim of restricting the freedom to strike to registered unions was, first, to crack down on unofficial strikes, and, second, to pressure unions to register and so compel them to have fair rules. There was extra pressure on unions to register, because unregistered unions did not get any of the other rights given to unions under the Act.

In the Labour plan, the main weapon against strikes was to be the power given to the employment minister to intervene and order cooling-off periods or strike ballots. These powers were also included in the Tory Act, in a more limited form. They could only be used in the event of a 'national emergency'. These powers were only used once.

The Act also aimed to outlaw the closed shop, and replace it with the new 'agency shop'. In an agency shop, every worker had to belong to the union or pay an equivalent of the union subscription, unless he was a conscientious objector, in which case he could opt out.

There were several significant new rights for workers and unions, provided by the Act. Workers or unions could take employers to court for the following:

> Breaking a legally binding agreement. An employer who changed the wages and conditions specified in such an agreement, before a contract expired, was committing a UIP.
>
> Unfair sackings. It was a UIP if an employer sacked a man because, for instance, he was an active trade unionist.
>
> Disobeying a court order to recognise and negotiate with a trade union.
>
> Refusing to employ a worker because he was a trade unionist, or, equally, because he was not.

The Act succeeded in a number of non-controversial areas. The remedies provided to workers who were unfairly sacked worked well, and according to several surveys encouraged employers to reform their disciplinary procedures. Perhaps as a result, the number of strikes over dismissals fell sharply. This showed that it was possible for the law to replace industrial action as a means of resolving disputes. Some twenty thousand claims were brought under this section of the Act although few unions except ASTMS made much use of it.

Altogether NIRC handled just over 1,000 cases but only 162 related to the controversial UIP section of the Act. Here, its record was dismal.

Why the Industrial Relations Act failed

The principal reason for the failure of the key sections of the Industrial Relations Act was the decision of the unions to fight and resist it at every stage. The Tories expected union opposition of the kind that other countries like Sweden had experienced when they had reformed labour law, but they did not believe that the unions' opposition would last. The Act had been carefully designed to impose tough penalties on unions who did not cooperate and did not register, and also to give the unions a few carrots in the form of new legal rights against employers.

These penalties and incentives might have been enough to persuade a trade-union movement which was still in its infancy to cooperate. But the British trade-union movement was already mature. It had fought and won its battles for power: it was already strong and unified. So it had no need for legal help. In the United States, the 1935 Wagner Act gave the country's weak unions important legal privileges which helped their development at the same time as imposing limited restrictions. As a result, the unions came to depend so much on legal procedures for winning recognition from stubborn employers that they did not wish to overturn the applecart even after the 1948 Taft-Hartley Act substantially increased restrictions on unions. In Britain, the unions had developed not with the help of the law but in direct opposition to it. From Tolpuddle to Taff Vale, the law appeared to hinder the growth of trade unionism.

Union hostility was inevitable, but the unions might have ended their policy of non-cooperation if events had been different. The TUC began by seeking talks with the government on the bill, but these were abandoned when Mr Carr made it clear that what he called 'the eight pillars' of the bill were non-negotiable. The TUC decided to adopt a non-cooperation policy at a special congress in March 1971. But its original policy was comparatively mild: in particular, unions were advised, not instructed, to deregister. And Vic Feather, the TUC general secretary, made it clear that the TUC accepted the rule of law. He told the congress:

> The general council have no sympathy with the objectives of this law; and they make this abundantly clear in their report. And although in this Act the government is in danger of bringing the concept of law itself into disrepute . . . we say that no trade unionists must contribute to a process of debasing principles of law. The fact that a law is offensive to a particular grouping of peoples does not entitle that grouping, no matter how vast and how important it is, deliberately to break the law. Trade unionists are not, either individually or collectively, above the law or outside the law and have never wished to be so.

At this time, it seemed likely that the TUC opposition would prove to be a bluff. Many unions reckoned that they had no alternative but to register – and even left-wing unions like the TGWU secretly began to consider how they would have to change their rules in order to register. But the September congress of TUC unexpectedly struck another blow against deregistration when an AUEW motion, which called for the TUC to instruct all unions to deregister, was carried by the narrow majority of 5.6 million to 4.5 million, against the opposition of Vic Feather and the general council. This was a decisive change of policy. Yet even so, in October twenty-four unions representing 2.5 million members had postponed a decision on registration, and twenty-two unions with 400,000 members had decided to register. No one thought the TUC would dare to expel all these unions – particularly since the twenty-four undecided unions included such giants as the General and Municipal Workers Union (GMWU), the Electrical, Electronic and Plumbing Trade Union (EEPTU), ASTMS, NALGO, the Union of Shop, Distributive and Allied Workers (USDAW) and the National Union of Seamen (NUS).

But each of the major waverers decided to deregister for the most ironic of reasons: they discovered that the Act's penalties were not really very severe. Both NALGO and the GMWU, for example, were assured by employers that deregistration would not disrupt existing bargaining arrangements and that they would suffer little. Others like USDAW and ASTMS only decided to deregister when they realised that the TUC might be serious in threatening expulsion. As a result, the TUC was brave enough to expel thirty-two unions who still defied the deregistration instruction, because they did not include any giant unions: the only unions with over 100,000 members who were expelled were the NGA and COHSE (the Confederation of Health Service Employees).

One plank of union opposition was broken: the TUC later allowed member unions to attend NIRC, but in every other respect, the non-cooperation policy succeeded. As a result, the Act was doomed. The unions' opposition stimulated fear among employers and the vast majority of managers decided not to use the Act to help solve their industrial relations problem. Only thirty-three employers applied for legal relief against strikes – and most of them provoked more strikes than they solved.

Employers did not use the law to break open the closed shop: indeed, the closed shop survived almost intact for the four million workers who were covered by it. Employers did not use the law to create more logical bargaining structures – indeed the law actually encouraged more multi-unionism by giving power to anti-TUC unions like the Telephonists' Staff Association in the post office. Employers did not seek to enforce contracts (and, indeed, could hardly do so because the unions insisted on adding the clause 'This is not a legally binding agreement' to every deal).

At first, employers' leaders had been great enthusiasts for the Act. Campbell Adamson of the Confederation of British Industry (CBI) happily proclaimed the Act as 'the greatest landmark in our industrial history' – although on the eve of the February 1974 election he denounced the Act. However, even from an early stage, the CBI wanted to take the initiative out of individual employers' hands. It suggested that the new Registrar should have the job of taking unofficial strikers to court. By the autumn of 1973, a CBI report admitted: 'The unions have managed to frustrate the purpose of the Act and the present position is detrimental to good industrial relations'.

The Act did give the government one power of its own: to apply for a cooling-off period or a strike ballot in emergency strikes. But this power proved to be useless when it was tried during the 1972 railway dispute. The dispute started at a time

when the government was desperately trying to recover lost
ground after its defeat by the miners. The railway unions had
been offered eight per cent. They refused it. Then they were
offered nine per cent. They refused it. Then they were offered
eleven per cent. They refused again. So an arbitrator was called
in and he recommended a compromise twelve per cent. The
unions refused it again.

This was too much for ministers to stomach. They had not
dared to use the emergency power against the miners' strike,
but they thought that they might work with the more law-
abiding railwaymen. So Maurice Macmillan, the new employment secretary, applied to NIRC for a cooling-off. This was
granted and the railwaymen obeyed the court order and
returned to work. But as soon as the order expired, the railwaymen planned to go back on strike – so the cooling-off
achieved nothing. The government reacted by asking for a
ballot of all railwaymen. This was carried out, but the railwaymen voted by a crushing six to one majority to back their
unions against the government – and indeed they would have
been foolish not to do so, because they could see that such a vote
would almost certainly increase the pay offer. The pay offer was
indeed raised to the fourteen per cent that the unions had
originally demanded. The use of the powers had been a total
flop.

There is no reason to expect a law which can delay strikes or
call ballots to take the heat out of wage demands. Such powers
might be useful in occasional strikes (where there has been
some misunderstanding), but they will not serve as a substitute
for incomes policy. Indeed, by alienating the unions, many of
the powers in the Industrial Relations Act hindered the
development of incomes policy.

The final collapse of the Act's authority followed quickly on
the heels of the railway dispute. The struggle moved to the
docks, the home of some of the most militant workers in the
country.

The battle began with an action brought against the Transport and General Workers Union (TGWU) by Heatons, a
Liverpool container firm. Increasing numbers of cargoes were
being handled in massive containers, which were unloaded and
loaded at depots away from the docks. The dockers feared that
this containerisation might threaten their jobs, and began

blacking containers. Samuel Heaton, the blunt boss of Heatons, went to NIRC to argue that this was an unfair industrial practice, since the men who were blacking him were not even his employees. NIRC agreed that this was so and ordered the TGWU (to which the dockers belonged) to stop the blacking

The TGWU tried to persuade the men to do so, but failed, and the blacking went on (although it was not clear that the TGWU tried very hard). NIRC maintained that the TGWU must be held responsible, since one of the declared objects of the act was to make trade unions more responsible for the actions of their members.

NIRC fined the TGWU £5,000 for contempt of court, but the TGWU ignored it. NIRC replied by levying a fine of £50,000. At this stage, the TGWU decided to appeal. When the Court of Appeal heard the case, they decided to reverse the NIRC's decision. To the TGWU's joy, its cheque for £55,000 was promptly returned. Heatons then appealed to the House of Lords. While the Heatons row was simmering through the summer months, a parallel dispute was taking place around the ramshackle wharves in the East London docks. Dockers had picketed container depots at Chobham Farm and elsewhere to protest at containerisation, and brought these depots to a standstill.

The first action against these pickets was actually brought by the workers in the container depots (who also belonged to the TGWU). NIRC granted an injunction against three pickets, but they were not arrested because of an intervention by the Official Solicitor – a mysterious lawyer whom no one had ever heard of before – who persuaded the court that there was not enough evidence to prove that the three had broken the injunction. But the showdown was not long delayed. Another depot hit by picketing, Midland Cold Storage, brought a better-documented action agaist seven dockers. NIRC issued an injunction to stop the picketing, which was ignored, so it ordered the arrest of five of the pickets, including communist Bernie Steer. They were marched off to Pentonville jail on 21 July.

The trade union movement was outraged. Workers in the docks, Fleet Street and other militant industries immediately walked out. The TUC met and decided to call a general one-day strike. A massive industrial crisis was threatened, and there seemed no way out either for the government or NIRC or the pickets. All eyes turned to the Official Solicitor: could he pull another rabbit from his hat? For three days, nothing happened. It was assumed that he could think of nothing to say. Then on Wednesday, he applied to NIRC for a hearing, to appeal against the jail sentence.

His grounds for appeal were slim, but on the very same day (and much earlier than expected) the House of Lords delivered its verdict on the Heaton case. The Lords ruled that the original NIRC decision had been right and orderd the TGWU to hand the £55,000 back again. The significance of it was that it enabled Sir John Donaldson to argue that the interpretation of the law had been changed again: and a union could be held responsible for the actions of its shop stewards. So, Sir John argued, the union, not the pickets, should be held responsible, and he ordered the release of the pickets. The five men were let out of Pentonville and carried shoulder-high through a cheering crowd of trade unionists, like modern-day Tolpuddle Martyrs.

Sir John's decision was a political finesse, which avoided a general strike. It was hardly good law. Even if the case against the pickets did not stand up after the Lords' decision – which was extremely dubious – the pickets were not jailed for the original offence but for contempt of court. The Lords' decision did not reduce the extent of their contempt. And although the decision averted an immediate crisis, it showed that NIRC could be successfully defied. The authority of the National Industrial Relations Court was never the same again.

The containerisation issue was eventually fought out in the old way – by a long and damaging dock strike.

In many ways, the docks dispute showed that the aims of the Industrial Relations Act were just and fair. The picketing of the container depots was quite indefensible. One group of well-paid workers was deliberately trying to bully another group of less well-paid workers and throw them out of work even though they were evidently more efficient.

But the argument about the IR Act was never about justice: it was about practicality. Its aims of introducing more rationality into industrial relations were splendid but they could be of no use if they provoked such a countervailing union reaction. It is hard to imagine any other circumstances in which the TUC could have been persuaded to support a small group of communist-led agitators in the docks. So although the Act attacked injustice, it had the effect of creating union support for injustice.

After NIRC's surrender in the docks dispute, there was no further attempt to challenge the unions directly. The AUEW confidently refused to obey any NIRC orders although it was involved in a series of cases. NIRC found the AUEW guilty of contempt when it refused to admit Jim Goad into the union. The union was fined and the money sequestered from AUEW funds, but the AUEW still refused to kowtow to the courts and threatened national strike action. But a showdown was avoided when Mr Goad's employers gave him the sack. Once again, union non-cooperation had paid off. It paid off again for the AUEW in the summer of 1974, when an anonymous donor stepped in to pay a massive fine imposed on the union.

The worst consequence of the Act was that it gave more power to the elbow of the militants in the union. In the AUEW, for example, those who opposed the union's rigid policy were discredited and moderates everywhere found that they had been weakened and undermined. Perhaps this should not be so surprising. Previous repressive legislation, as we saw in Chapter 1, only helped to strengthen the left-wingers in the unions.

The failure of the Act was not inevitable. If the TUC opposition had been as flexible as it once looked like being, if employers had been more cooperative and if NIRC had not been weak-willed at the moment of crisis, it might have survived. But it would never have got to grips with the fundamental imbalance of power in industry that had been created by the 1970s.

In 1974-5, the Labour government repealed the Act and also introduced an Employment Protection Act which extended trade-union bargaining rights. A Central Arbitration Committee (CAC) – part of the Advisory, Conciliation and Arbitration Service set up by Labour in 1974 – was given the power to make legally enforceable awards to help unions. The CAC can make bosses recognise unions and also has the power to force a boss into paying more to bring his pay into line with his competitors for similar work when there is no negotiated agreement. These new legal extensions of union power were in direct contrast to the five-year attempt to limit union power, although one day it may be possible to graft other powers on to institutions like CAC with sanctions against unions as well as bosses.

It is now pointless to advocate the reintroduction of major new legal restrictions on union power: they would in any case be swept away by an even tougher union reaction than met the Industrial Relations Act. Some day in the future, in a changed political and industrial climate, it may be possible to legislate again. But for now, legislation to restrict union power is a pointless, barren policy.

The closed shop

One of the aims of the Industrial Relations Act was to eliminate the closed shop, that is the system by which workers are forced to join a union if they want to keep their job. The closed-shop system is almost unique to Britain, because in most European and American legislation the system is outlawed.

In a closed shop, a worker must belong to the closed-shop union before he can be employed. In its milder form, the union shop, the rules allow non-union men to be employed provided they join the union once they start work. In Britain today, some four million workers are effectively forced to join a union because they are employed in closed or union shops.

The unions see these restrictions as an important buttress of their power. A closed-shop system maximises the union's power and membership and it also helps to exclude those who are not regarded as suitable for the work, for example, workers who (in the union's view) are inadequately trained. Some employers also find advantages in the system. Most would prefer their labour force to be non-unionised, but if it is unionised, the closed-shop system can simplify life. A closed shop stops the spread of multi-unionism because other unions cannot start recruiting. A closed shop also gives the union power over its members and thus acts as a deterrent to wildcat strikes.

Yet at the same time the closed shop is a clear violation of the rights of the individual. It effectively deprives him of his free-dom not to belong to a union, or indeed to belong to a different union. It may also deprive him of a job which he is quite capable of doing. In the celebrated case of the 'Ferrybridge Six' workers in a power station were sacked in 1975 because they would not join the main electrical union when the closed shop was introduced. They discovered not only that they would lose their job, but also that they would not be entitled to normal unemployment pay if they could not find another job.

Yet what can be done about it? The IR Act made a direct attempt to eliminate most closed shops and to replace them with 'agency shops', which provided safeguards for individuals who had good reasons for not joining a union. But this effort was an almost total failure: hardly any closed shops were broken up. The power of the unions, the weakness of the employers and the natural trepidation of cowed individuals meant that only a handful used the law.

There was a great deal of fuss when the Wilson government reinstituted the legality of the closed shop in its first (1974) Trade Union and Labour Relations Act, but the effect of the change was small – although it did accelerate the development of new closed shops, especially in nationalised industries.

The Wilson government showed no concern to leave any protection for the individual in closed shops (most notably in Fleet Street where the employment secretary, Michael Foot showed no qualms about the freedom of editors not to join the National Union of Journalists). But its reinstitution of the legality of the closed shop made less difference than it appeared. Oddly, Foot did accept that workers who had religious objections to joining a union should be free not to do so: a curious dimension of 'acceptable freedom' in a secular society.

Most union members do not support the closed-shop system. For example, in August 1973, a Gallup poll asked trade-union members:

In a factory which has a union, should the workers who are not members be free to stay out of the union if they are getting union rates of pay, or should it be compulsory that they join the union?

Free to stay out	53%
Compulsory to join	45%
Don't know	1%

In October 1975, a survey conducted by Market and Opinion Research International published in the *Economist* asked for reaction to the statement: Everyone who works should have to belong to a trade union'. The replies from trade-unionists were:

Agree	47%
Disagree	48%
Don't know	5%

Thus the closed-shop system is not supported by most union members, violates individual rights, and tends to lead to a misallocation of labour. These indictments, in my view, outweigh the advantages of stable industrial relations which accrue from the system. Yet at present there is no way of eliminating it. All that any government can hope to do, in the present circumstances, is to reintroduce some of the safeguards which were inserted by the Opposition parties in the first Trade Union and Labour Relations Act but are due to be removed by Foot's second Trade Union and Labour Relations Bill.

PART TWO
Inside today's unions

6 The roots of power

So much for the generalities. We now turn to look at the individual unions and the colourful men who run them. This chapter is intended as a prelude to explain the division of unions and the characteristic units within unions.

There were over three hundred unions in Britain in 1975, of which only 111 belonged to the TUC, but these accounted for 10.36 million workers, forty-one per cent of the working population. Within the TUC, the eleven giant unions accounted for over half of total union membership. The biggest twenty unions in 1975 are shown in the chart, which also indicates how each had grown or contracted over the previous five years.

There are four basic types of union: general, industrial, craft and white-collar, although these divisions are becoming increasingly blurred. The craft unions are the oldest form of union, and are perhaps the only true 'trade' union. Most were formed in the nineteenth century and will only admit members who have a particular skill. Thus the Amalgamated Society of Beamers, Twisters and Drawers (Hand and Machine), for example, has only 949 members. Most of the craft unions are small and no longer dominate the TUC.

The craft-union system has frequently been criticised because it leads to demarcation disputes. It emphasises skill specialisation, which militates against the flexibility and interchangeability needed by modern industry. The existence of separate unions for separate skills tends to create extra resistance when skills are outdated by technological progress: notably in industries like shipbuilding and printing. It also tends to create needless complication and rivalry in wage-bargaining, because companies or industries have to bargain with many different unions. Yet craft unions are perhaps the most natural forms of trade union, a grouping in which the common interests of members are most obvious. And they cannot be abolished or amalgamated by a fiat of convenience.

Everyone agrees that the 'industrial' union which recruits all

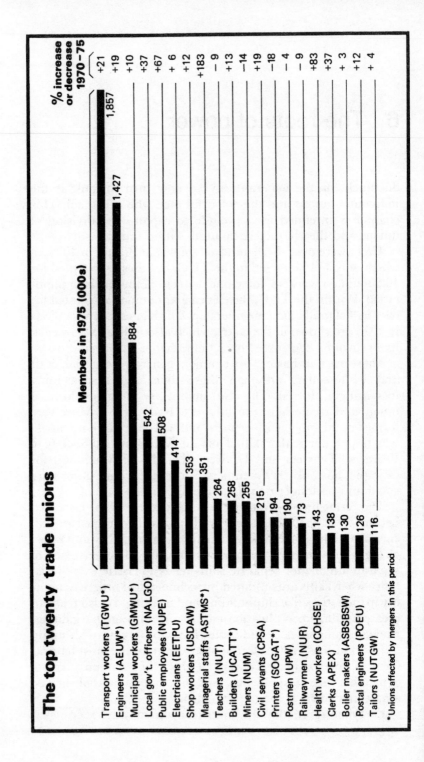

The top twenty trade unions

Members in 1975 (000s)

Union	Members in 1975 (000s)	% increase or decrease 1970–75
Transport workers (TGWU*)	1,857	+21
Engineers (AEUW*)	1,427	+19
Municipal workers (GMWU*)	884	+10
Local gov't. officers (NALGO)	542	+37
Public employees (NUPE)	508	+67
Electricians (EETPU)	414	+ 6
Shop workers (USDAW)	353	+12
Managerial staffs (ASTMS*)	351	+183
Teachers (NUT)	264	– 9
Builders (UCATT*)	258	+13
Miners (NUM)	255	–14
Civil servants (CPSA)	215	+19
Printers (SOGAT*)	194	–18
Postmen (UPW)	190	– 4
Railwaymen (NUR)	173	– 9
Health workers (COHSE)	143	+83
Clerks (APEX)	138	+37
Boiler makers (ASBSBSW)	130	+ 3
Postal engineers (POEU)	126	+12
Tailors (NUTGW)	116	+ 4

*Unions affected by mergers in this period

workers, skilled and unskilled, within one industry is the most convenient and logical combination.

Vic Feather advised West Germany after the war that the best system for that country's new unions would be to create a small number of industrial unions. But this system could not be imposed unilaterally on all Britain's non-industrial unions.

One of the earliest industrial unions in Britain was formed by the miners in 1888. They were followed by the railwaymen in 1913. Other industrial unions include the UPW (post office), NUPE (public employees) and UCATT (construction).

There are only two pure 'general' unions, the TGWU and GMWU, although many unions are becoming more general. They will admit anyone (including white-collar workers for whom both have created special sections). Both were founded in the 1920s. The AUEW (engineers) and USDAW (shop, distributive and allied) are both semi-general unions – recruiting over a wide range of industries, but not as general as the TGWU and the GMWU.

The white-collar unions are more recent creations, and many of them have only sprung up in the last twenty years. Some are general white-collar unions like Clive Jenkins' Association of Scientific, Technical and Managerial Staffs (ASTMS). Others are industrial white-collar unions like the National Union of Bank Employees.

Today all general unions are still as general as ever, but the exclusive unions are becoming less so.

Union leaders are no longer so concerned to preserve the craft or industrial purity of their union. Their real concern today, is to maximise the size of their membership. More members cannot be recruited if a union insists that all its members must be beamers and twisters.

In recent years, the more general or open unions have been growing faster than the closed unions. Their growth has precluded the creation of new unions: computer operators, for example, have no craft union to represent them – they have merely been absorbed in general or white-collar unions.

The power complex

The power structure of every union is different, and each is proud to have its very own constitution and rule-book. As we saw in Chapter 5 the suggestion that the Government should have the right to regulate the union's rules was deeply repugnant to trade union traditions.

None the less, there are similarities between unions. The basic unit of most unions is the branch. The membership of a branch may be anywhere between fifty and one thousand members, and it will normally cover a geographical area.

The officers of a branch are almost always part-timers, elected by show of hands, often without opposition. In the old craft unions, the doorkeeper is also a traditional post. His job is to check that everyone who attends is a bona fide member. Originally, his role was to stop company spies getting into the branch to hear the union's plans.

Shop stewards are separate from the branch officers. They represent members at their place of work, and are responsible for dealing with the management in the factory. They are elected by the workers in the factory but, as in the branch, there is usually little opposition and voting is by show of hands.

Shop stewards can and often do call a strike: although the strikes called by stewards are often unofficial, that is, they do not have the approval of the union.

The main job of shop stewards is not to call strikes, but to act as go-between for managers (or foremen) and the workers. In a large factory, there are often several unions to represent the workers. In the Ford Motor Company, for example, there are eleven separate unions. In this situation, a large group of stewards elect a leader, known as the convener.

There are around three hundred thousand shop stewards in Britain today. They are often at loggerheads with the official union bureaucracies. The stewards resent the attitude of union officers, who are often out of touch with what is actually happening in the factories. At the same time, the union officers resent the growing power of the shop stewards, and the often irresponsible way they use it. Yet Britain's shop-steward system also means that workers are more directly and effectively represented than in most countries.

The pyramid of the union structure is based on the branch, not on the shop stewards. The next level above the branch is the district. In big unions, there are two tiers (district and region) between branch and national level. Each union district or region is normally organised by a committee (elected by the branches), serviced by full-time officers. These committees are of varying power, but are usually quite important: particularly in the engineers' union and the GMWU. They have money to spend, and control the union's local political funds. They also have the power to call strikes in the area, and can discipline branches. Quite often, the national executive may have to confirm a strike ordered by a district committee, even if it really disapproves of it.

Next comes the National Executive. This is the cabinet that rules the union. Some are elected directly by members, region by region, as in the engineering union. Others are simply delegates from the regional committees (as in the GMWU). Others are elected by the annual conference (as in the UPW).

Executives meet regularly. They decide union policy on all major matters, subject only to the policy laid down at the union's annual conference. The men on the executive are sometimes all full-time officials drawing their salaries from the union's coffers, as in the engineers. Sometimes, they are all part-timers, drawing no salary, as in the TGWU and NUPE. More often, there is a compromise between full- and part-timers.

The chief executive of the union is either the general secretary or the president. In most unions, the general secretary acts as the union's chief, and the post of president is honorary. Often, the president is just expected to chair meetings of the executive and deliver a rousing address to the annual conference. Some unions have completely dispensed with the office of president. Only in the NUM and the AUEW is the president the chief. In the miners union, the president has only a slight edge on the general secretary.

Curiously, however, although the general secretary is the union's leader, he normally has no vote on the executive. This is because unions regard their general secretary merely as a civil servant, not as a leader.

The last piece in the jigsaw is the annual conference. This is the ultimate government of a union, although since it usually only meets once a year, it cannot have much influence on day-to-day policy making. Branches or regions send delegates to the conference which is held in some seaside resort in summertime. In an average union, the conference consists of perhaps a hundred delegates.

Some of the debates range over internal union affairs like the constitution, membership fees, mergers and the union news-paper. The others are about specific industrial problems (wages, holidays, pay systems and bonuses), or wider political issues. Unions delight in long arguments about the common market, defence, the economy or taxation.

In 1968, the National Union of Railwaymen held their annual conference in Penzance at the time of a big pay dispute on the railways. British Rail chiefs flew down to hammer out a deal in a Penzance hotel. Next morning, they had to sit through three hours of heated debate on Vietnam before the delegates got round to considering the new pay offer. Occasions such as this when conferences are directly involved in wage negotiation are rare. But the mood of a conference can be a good guide to union negotiators. The 1971 conference of the miners was very militant, and persuaded the union's leaders to take a tough stand in the pay talks and the strike that followed.

Union conferences do not normally elect officials, although there are exceptions, like the UPW. But they do have a few formal jobs, such as hearing appeals. Members who have been sacked or maltreated, officials who have got a rough deal from the executive or even branches which have been trodden on can appeal to the conference. Normally, a committee is set up to hear these appeals.

How unions are financed

Finance is no longer as critical as it used to be. This is because the ability of unions to dish out strike pay during strikes is now seldom a key factor in the success of a strike: (a) because strike pay rates (usually around £5 a week) are now minute in com-parison with normal earnings, and (b) because the operation of social-security rules (see Chapter 4) has meant that it is often pointless for unions to pay strike pay. Many of the big strikes in the 1970s were successful although no strike pay was paid – as in both the 1972 and 1974 coal strikes.

Yet finance is still important if a union is to fulfil all its other functions, and the lack of finance has caused many of the inadequacies of British unionism. British unions' income has not kept pace with inflation and is now tiny by international standards. A 1972 TUC survey found that the TUC subscrip-tion, then 12p a year per member, compared with 66p in Italy, £24 in Germany and £48 in Sweden.

The principal source of union income has always been members' subscriptions – in 1973, eighty-nine per cent of their income came from this source. Investment income is a bonus for unions, but only forms a substantial part of income in the old craft unions, who have built up large assets shared by a steadily declining membership. The National Union of Dyers, Bleachers and Textile Workers, for example, only relied on subscriptions for forty-nine per cent of its income in 1970.

The finances of most unions have dropped deeply into the red over the last decade because costs have consistently risen faster than contributions, the level of spending on strikes has soared (although fewer unions now pay strike pay, this trend has been outmatched by the sheer rise in strikes) and because investment income has failed to keep pace with inflation. The table below shows how the gap between income and spending steadily narrowed until 1973, when there was a brief improvement thanks to subscription increases and fewer strikes.

INCOME PER MEMBER

	1963	1968	1970	1971	1972	1973
Contributions	£3.57	£4.36	£4.72	£5.30	£6.10	£6.60
Investment	)		.77	.65	.42	.55
	)					
	) .51	.84				
Other sources	)		.14	.13	.30	.26
Total income	£4.08	£5.20	£5.63	£6.08	£6.82	£7.41

EXPENDITURE PER MEMBER

	1963	1968	1970	1971	1972	1973
Administration	£2.11	£2.99	£3.26	£3.85	£4.91	£4.42
Strike pay	.06	.14	.39	.48	.69	.34
Unemployment	.06	.05	.06	.14	.09	.03
Accident and Sickness	.25	.48	.42	.38	.31	.37
Superannuation	.34	.32	.30	.31	.28	.30
Death/Funeral	.12	.15	.15	.11	.11	.12
Total of above expenditure	£2.94	£4.11	£4.58	£5.27	£6.39	£5.58
Excess income over above expenditure	£1.14	£1.09	£1.05	.81	.43	£1.83

Source: TUC annual report 1975.

The failure of unions to make subscriptions keep pace with inflation is understandable: like every voluntary organisation, unions try to minimise subscriptions in order to maximise

membership. Union leaders cannot raise subscriptions at a
stroke: they have to get approval from their annual conference
and this can often be difficult. In relation to earnings, the
failure has been spectacular. In 1938, the average worker was
forking out 1.5 per cent of his gross pay to the union. By 1971,
this had fallen to 0.35 per cent. Again there has been great
variation between unions. Between 1960 and 1970, the NUR
raised their subs by a whopping 28.2 per cent, but the National
Graphical Association actually let theirs fall by 2 per cent.

Most unions expect their general secretary to act as treasurer, but few general secretaries have the time, or the expertise,
to do the job properly. The bigger unions employ a full-time
treasurer, but he is seldom allowed much discretion in investment policy.

Union investment policy has normally been extremely conservative. Before 1939, most unions thought it best to keep all
their money in bank accounts. Indeed, as recently as 1960, the
old Plumbing Trade Union kept eighty-nine per cent of its total
assets in a bank account. Unions gradually moved towards
investment in fixed-interest stocks after the war, but kept clear
of equities until the 1960s.

In 1961, the Trade Union Unit Trust was set up to provide
an easy means for unions to invest in equities. It was administered by the merchant bankers Hill Samuel. But it attracted
only a small fraction of total union funds. However, this ultra-
conservative policy paid some benefits when the stock market
crashed in 1973-4. A few unions now employ professional fund
managers, like Rothschilds, to run their investment, but most
unions are more than a little suspicious of the well-dressed,
fast-talking men of the City.

Like the Church Commissioners, the unions like an ethical
investment policy. They do not like to invest, for example, in
any company with South African connections. This led to a
major row between the TUC and the TUUT trustees who saw
no reason to sell shares in companies like Barclays Bank and
ICI just because they had links with South Africa. This row
induced the TUC and several other unions to sell their TUUT
units.

The British unions have not been interested in gaining power
over companies by investing in their shares, unlike the Danish
unions, for example, who want to set up a national trade union

fund to be invested in industry and financed by a levy on all private companies. (However, ASTMS owns one share in every public company where it has members, and so has access to financial reports.)

Some unions, like the engineers, have invested heavily in property, but few proclaim the fact. Not many unions have made attempts to make money by general entrepreneurship, although in 1972 the TGWU paid £100,000 into a £350,000 venture with British Road Services and Trust Houses Forte to build motels for lorry drivers on motorways. Such forays into business, so common among American and German unions, have not caught on in Britain.

On the other side of the balance sheet, union spending has risen fast in the last few years, mainly because of the rise in the number of strikes. In 1972 for instance, the Amalgamated Union of Engineering Workers spent £2½ million on strike pay, almost five times more than it spent in 1970. The TUC survey, quoted above, revealed that by the end of 1972 twenty unions with a combined membership of two and a half million were in a 'financially precarious position'. The level of *per capita* assets is another measure of relative union wealth. Between 1960 and 1970, the real value (after taking into account the rise in the cost of living) of *per capita* assets decreased in twenty-one out of thirty-nine major unions.

How much do union leaders earn?

British union leaders are not rich or well-paid. Their salaries are low by international standards (in 1972, for example, eleven American union leaders earned over £20,000 a year, led by Frank Fitzsimmons of the Teamsters who netted a cool £55,000 a year) and low by the standards of British management. But they are not low in comparison with the average earnings of their members or of MPs – which are equally valid comparisons. It is right that trade-union leaders should do their jobs out of dedication rather than for money, and there is no reason to suppose that better pay would induce better men to seek union careers.

However, union leaders are inexcusably secret about their pay. They insist on full disclosure from companies about how much directors are paid, yet no trade union publishes its salaries in its annual accounts. In a *Guardian* inquiry, in 1975, five unions refused point-blank to reveal the incomes of their general secretaries. The TGWU said Jack Jones' salary was only known to the union general council; the Civil and Public Services Association (CPSA) said 'it is against our policy to tell members how much officers are earning and I can't go further than that', and it was reported of David Basnett of the GMWU that 'he doesn't reveal his salary because he doesn't want to'. Indeed, the only major union which discusses its salaries in public is the Amalgamated Union of Engineering Workers (AUEW).

Yet in 1975, the guessed, estimated, leaked or reported salaries of some major union names were: Geoffrey Drain (NALGO) £11,500; Clive Jenkins (ASTMS) around £11,000; Sid Weighell (NUR) £8,500; Tom Jackson (UPW) £8,500; Frank Chapple (EEPTU) £8,000; Lord Allen (USDAW) £8,000; Joe Gormley and Lawrence Daly (NUM) £7,300; Hugh Scanlon (AUEW) £6,250; George Smith (UCATT) £6,000; Reg Bottini (NUUAW) £4,500. On top of this, most union leaders get expenses paid and have access to a union car. Most are chauffeur-driven although style varies. Len Murray is driven in a grand car, Jack Jones in a small blue van.

The top union leaders can supplement their union income by broadcasting and by doing other public jobs. The growth of government patronage for union leaders in recent years has been enormous. Between 1974 and 1975 alone, fourteen members of the TUC general council were given jobs by ministers. Bill Simpson, a former general secretary of the foundryworkers' section of the AUEW, was given the £16,550 full-time post as chairman of the Health and Safety Commission. Other union leaders, including Messrs Jones, Scanlon, Basnett, Jenkins, Smith, Lloyd, Stanley and Parry, got part-time jobs paying an average of £1,000 a year: although Tom Jackson set an example of unselfishness by refusing to take a salary when he was appointed a part-time director of British Petroleum.

Yet, union leaders earn their salaries. Most of them work long hours and happily surrender many of their evenings and weekends. An 80-hour working week is commonplace. Nearly all of them are dedicated. They almost all come from working-class backgrounds, so that the unions are now almost the only institutions in the country which are run for, and by, working-class men. This is a great strength.

Unions' office staff are not always so willing to put cause before cash. Roy Grantham's union, the Association of Professional, Executive, Clerical and Computer Staff (APEX), has begun to organise union staff, and their bargaining power is now emerging.

This has led to a handful of eye-catching rows in unions. In 1974, office staff at the AUEW headquarters came out on strike in protest at 'intolerable working conditions'. Poor Hugh Scanlon had to breach picket lines to enter his own office and had to suffer the indignity of calling in the police to protect him. The strike did not surprise those who knew the rigidity of life at the AUEW, with bells ringing at the start and the finish of the lunch-hour as though the office was a factory. Some of the striking staff described Scanlon as 'a nineteenth-century employer'.

In the summer of 1975, Clive Jenkins' staff all walked out on strike over the dismissal of a junior girl officer. But those who throw stones cannot expect to live in glasshouses.

The links with the Labour Party

We saw in Chapter 1 how the unions became involved in politics with some reluctance. As the Webbs observed: The trade unionists of Northumberland and Durham are predominantly Liberal. Those of Lancashire are largely Conservative. Those of Yorkshire and London are deeply impregnated with Socialism.

But in the twentieth century, the unions have become almost totally identified with the Labour Party. The unions run the Labour Party. The sixty-three affiliated unions provide around seventy-five per cent of the party's finance and more in election years when unions provide ninety-five per cent of the cash in special election appeals. At the Labour Party conference, they control five-sixths of the vote. On the ruling National Executive of the Labour Party they hold, by right, twelve of the twenty-nine seats and control elections to six other seats.

Unions raise money for the Labour Party through their political funds. Union members are expected to shell out extra money above their normal contributions to finance the fund. But should unions be able to force members to pay? In 1927, the Tories passed an act requiring that union members must specifically 'contract in', if they wanted to pay the levy. This

How unions finance Labour

Top dozen contributors to Labour Party funds, 1974

Transport workers (TGWU)	£150,000
Engineers (AUEW)	£108,000
Municipal workers (GMWU)	£ 97,500
Electricians (EETPU)	£ 52,500
Shopworkers (UDSAW)	£ 43,950
Miners (NUM)	£ 39,600
Builders (UCATT)	£ 27,600
Postmen (UPW)	£ 27,450
Railwaymen (NUR)	£ 24,600
Managerial staffs (ASTMS)	£ 22,650
Public employees (NUPE)	£ 22,500
Clerical workers (APEX)	£ 15,000

measure slashed the numbers paying the levy.

The unions had to wait until 1946, when the Attlee Government reversed the situation to the 1913 position. As a result, the number paying the levy rose sharply – in the TGWU, for example, from thirty-five per cent in 1946 to sixty-five per cent in 1947. Since then, there has been no more argument about the political fund, and rightly so.

The Tories are in no position to attack. Shareholders cannot opt out when their company gives money to Conservative funds. Both political parties are woefully short of money, and if coercion is needed to extract it, so be it.

The unions use their political funds in various ways. Some of the money is handed to the national Labour organisation or to local Labour parties. Some is used to sponsor candidates: in 1974 twenty-three unions helped out with candidates' expenses in the election campaigns.

Most unions have a panel of candidates whom they select as suitable. Unions usually nurse special constituencies, so that when the sitting MP retires, he is usually succeeded by another union nominee.

Trade union involvement in parliamentary politics has been a vital part of the development of British democracy in the twentieth century. Yet the public are curiously ambivalent about it. The opinion polls show that a clear majority of the public disapproves of the link between the Labour Party and the trade unions. However, few unions regard their sponsored MPs as an important means of exercising political influence. An interesting study by Irving Richter (*Political Power in Trade*

Unions, Allen & Unwin, 1973) showed that trade unions tended to ignore their MPs once elected. Trade unions sponsor MPs mainly to help the Labour Party rather than to exercise direct political influence. Trade unions exercise power not by lobbying MPs but by their economic threat to government policy.

7 The generals' centralism

In a leafy Westminster square, cheek-by-jowl with Conservative Central Office, stands Transport House, a tall red-brick building faced with dusty grey Greek pillars. Inside, the atmosphere is of some provincial town hall. The offices are spartan, often furnished only with filing cabinets and hard wooden chairs. The circular staircase windows are of green stained glass. It is normally known as the Labour Party's headquarters, but the Labour Party is only a tenant. The building is owned by what is universally known in Labour circles as the Tee and Gee, the mighty Transport and General Workers' Union.

The other general union, the General and Municipal Workers' Union, is smaller and less metropolitan. Few of the wealthy stockbrokers who live in Esher know that it operates from a country house on the northern outskirts of the town, called Ruxley Towers. It sounds like some haunt from a Bulldog Drummond story and indeed looks like one. The architecture is Victorian bizarre, with a central tower which is said to boast a ghost. If the ghost exists, it remains un-unionised. Ruxley Towers has its own pitch-and-putt course, an indoor swimming pool, several tennis courts and large gardens, and is screened from the main road by a long drive between comfortable mock-Georgian houses. It is not quite what one expects.

Both general unions were formed in the 1920s and both are run in a more centralised and undemocratic manner than most unions. Yet, both unions have traditionally been pillars of the TUC right wing. Let us look first at the TGWU.

Bevin's legacy

The TGWU is the creation of one man: Ernie Bevin. Bevin had won a brilliant reputation after the war, notably by his defence of dockers at a court of inquiry in 1919, and he was a towering figure in the Labour movement when he set himself to put together the TGWU in the winter of 1920. Bevin persuaded twenty unions, ranging from the Belfast Breadservers Union to the North of England Trimmers' and Teemers' Association, to merge in the new juggernaut, leaving their evocative titles in the dustbin of history.

The union has grown both by takeovers and by natural growth of membership. Some seventy unions have joined up with the TGWU, but there was a long gap between 1951 and 1961 when none joined. Since then changes in industry, rising unemployment and fast inflation have made life increasingly hard for the smaller unions. So another thirteen unions have joined in the last twelve years.

The union's constitution was tailor-made by Ernie Bevin to suit Ernie Bevin, and it provided for an unparalleled centralisation of power in the hands of the general secretary. The general secretary has to be elected by a branch ballot, but once elected, his power is almost unlimited. The other five hundred full time officials in the union are appointed by the general secretary (together with an executive sub-committee). None is elected. Theoretically, the union's executive (which is elected) can exercise some control over the general secretary: but since it only meets four times a year, in practice it does not. Anyone interested in the succession to the general secretary is likely to keep on the right side of the existing general secretary – who carries much influence in an election (Frank Cousins was the exception to this rule). In most unions, the annual conference exercises some restraint over policy, but the TGWU only holds a conference every two years and that is usually something of a formality. The TGWU is a highly undemocratic union in political terms. Yet the paradox is that in industrial terms the union is very decentralised so that the general secretary has little say in decisions on strikes and wage bargains.

The TGWU is divided by region and by trade. Every member is represented both by geographical units (like district and regional committees and regional members of the executive) and by trade groups (which also provide members of the executive).

The trade groups have almost total control over industrial decisions in their trade. Thus a decision about a dock strike will be taken by the dock group, a decision about a bus strike by the bus group. Normally, the trade group convenes a delegate conference to take major strike decisions. Before any strike can

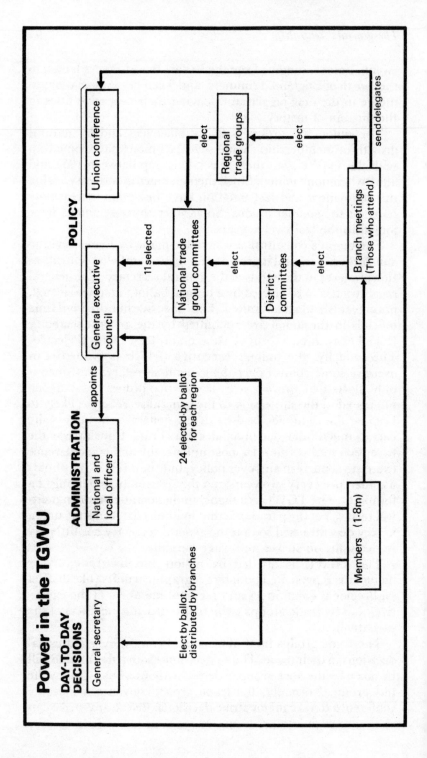

Power in the TGWU

DAY-TO-DAY DECISIONS

General secretary

Elect by ballot, distributed by branches

ADMINISTRATION

National and local officers

appoints

24 elected by ballot for each region

POLICY

Union conference

General executive council

National trade group committees

11 selected

Regional trade groups

elect

elect

elect

District committees

elect

Branch meetings (Those who attend)

elect

send delegates

Members (1·8m)

be official, it must be approved by the executive (in practice that means the general secretary) – but that does not mean that there cannot be an unofficial strike. For example, in 1972, Jack Jones urged dock delegates to accept the Jones-Aldington report on the container problem. But his view was rejected and the strike lasted another two weeks. It is seldom that the executive rejects a strike decision taken by a trade group: it is hardly practical politics. It did happen in 1958 when the executive rejected the decision to call the London bus strike but the strike went ahead and the executive was forced to endorse it. Significantly, the strike was a total flop.

In recent years, Jack Jones has attempted to accelerate the devolution of industrial decisions even further to the shop-steward level. Such decentralisation is partly deliberate policy, partly just a reflection of existing reality. In some sectors, notably the docks, the general secretary and the executive have very limited influence.

The chart opposite shows the details of the TGWU power structure. The oligarchic character of the union is perhaps natural enough given the low levels of membership participation. Turnover among the members is high – probably at least twenty-five per cent leave each year.

The communist influence in the union is variable. For many years after the war, members of the Communist Party were banned from holding power in the union. But this rule has now been abandoned. In 1975, roughly half-a-dozen of the thirty-nine members of the executive were communists. The communists capitalise on the apathy in the union, but their influence is limited by the dominance of the general secretary.

The union is, and always has been, a major force in Labour party politics and sponsors numerous Labour candidates. In the 1964-70 Wilson government, there were no fewer than nine TGWU ministers including Frank Cousins, George Brown, Anthony Greenwood, Reg Prentice, Peter Shore, John Silkin, Maurice Foley, Bob Mellish and Jeremy Bray. In 1975, there were twenty-three TGWU MPs in the House. But the variation in the politics of the TGWU MPs (including right-wingers like Reg Prentice) indicates how little influence the union exerts through its sponsored MPs. Instead, the union exerts its influence in more direct ways: principally through its block vote at the Labour Party conference.

Right, left, right

Until 1956, the TGWU was a right-wing union. Then it swung
sharply to the left. This was not due to any change of political
will among the union's members but to a personal accident.
The right-wing successor to Bevin, Arthur Deakin, died in May
1955. The following election was won by Jock Tiffin, who got
267,000 votes. Frank Cousins, once a miner and then national
secretary for the lorry-drivers' group, also stood but only collected 74,000 votes.

Cousins was a rebellious left-winger who was not popular
with the Deakin hierarchy. According to Cousins' biographer,
Geoffrey Goodman, 'Relations between the two were rarely
warmer than frigid'. Normally the structure of the TGWU
would have debarred a man like Cousins from getting to the
top. But he decided to apply for the number two job of assistant
general secretary. He was opposed by Harry Nicholas. The
union's inner cabinet, the financial and general purposes committee, voted four to three against Cousins, but the committee
chairman backed Cousins so the result was a tie. The issue then
went to the full executive. Cousins delivered a brilliant speech
which won him the job.

Hardly had Cousins taken this job, before Jock Tiffin fell ill.
He died within the year. Cousins was then appointed acting
general secretary and stood in the election in the spring of 1956.
Over forty-six per cent of union members voted (at least in
theory; see Chapter 16). Cousins steamrollered his unknown
opponent, Tom Healy, by 503,000 to 78,000 votes. As soon as
Cousins took over, the union was transformed. The pillar of the
right became the pillar of the left. Cousins backed unilateral
disarmament and helped drive the TUC and the Labour Party
to the left.

Cousins' fire was temporarily dampened in 1964 when Mr
Wilson persuaded him to take a seat in the cabinet. But not for
long. Cousins soon fell out with Wilson over Vietnam, incomes
policy and other issues. He resigned in 1966 and returned to the
TGWU to oppose Wilson from a more powerful position, helping to grind down the Wilson incomes policy with remorseless,
uncompromising speeches. In 1968, Cousins retired and was
succeeded by the then equally left-wing Jack Jones.

Jack Jones is an ordinary British name, and Jack Jones is,

above all else, concerned with ordinary British people; but
although he has a lot of power, Jack Jones is not a glamorous
man, As one union leader put it: 'Jones has a smile like the
sunlight glinting on the brass plate of a coffin'.

Jones was born in Liverpool in 1913. His grandfather was a
boilermaker, his father a docker. His life was political from the
start. As a boy of thirteen, he ran messages between different
offices of the union during the 1926 General Strike. By the time
he was fifteen, he had become secretary of the Garston branch
of the Labour Party, and at twenty-three, a member of the
Liverpool City Council.

It was a spectacular start, and it was critical to his later
success. To get to the top in the trade-union movement, it is
essential to begin early, because the ladder of power is a long
one. Few men who are not already branch officials in their early
twenties ever reach the summit of power.

At twenty-four, Jones moved on to wider frontiers. He went
to fight in the Spanish civil war in the Major Clem Attlee
Company of the International Brigade. In fierce fighting, Jones
was wounded in the shoulder. He later returned to take up the
full-time position of trade union organiser in Coventry. In the
sixteen years to 1955, Jones boosted the TGWU membership in
the city from three thousand to forty thousand.

Jones went on up the ladder of power. He had everything it
took to succeed. He was militant, but a good negotiator. Above
all, he was sincere and dedicated. By the early 1960s, he had
been chosen as crown prince to Frank Cousins, and in 1968 he
was elected as general secretary.

For the first four years of office, Jones continued the union's
opposition to the Wilson incomes policy and supported the
opposition to both Labour and Tory attempts to reform industrial relations. He favoured more nationalisation, more taxation of the rich, and was stridently opposed to entry into the
EEC. Thus he found himself regularly voting with Hugh Scanlon's AUEW and the two men were soon bracketed as the
'terrible twins'. It was a natural description, but there was
never any personal alliance. The two men never enjoyed any
social intimacy and came from quite different unions: Jones
from a union where the general secretary had almost unlimited
power, Scanlon from a union where he had almost none. Jones
often seemed to be a Marxist, but in fact was always a social

democrat. Scanlon, although never an intellectual, was always a Marxist. He left the Communist Party but continued to support an extreme left ideology and sometimes openly backed communists in elections; for example he campaigned for Jimmy Reid who stood as a communist cadidate for the AUEW in 1975.

The 1964-70 Labour government did not find Jones a cooperative man. Barbara Castle, who had been a great fan of Jones when she moved to become employment secretary (and apparently irritated civil servants with her constant references to 'Jack') soon tired of his opposition and inflexibility on incomes policy and industrial relations reform. The 1970 Heath government had little contact with Jones, but was unimpressed by what it knew of him. Inside the TUC, Jones used his votes to support the men and the causes of the left.

There was no stronger advocate of non-cooperation with the Tory Industrial Relations Act than Jones (although he was not prepared to take it to the same lengths as Scanlon's AUEW: in the late summer of 1972, he abandoned the policy of refusing to appear at the National Industrial Relations Court and, unlike the AUEW, paid the fines imposed).

It was not until late in 1972 that the first signs appeared that Jones' political position was beginning to change. In the pre-liminary incomes-policy talks with Heath and his ministers, Jones revealed a realism which took both ministers and fellow union leaders by surprise. At the same time, Jones suddenly took up the cause of better old-age pensions, which later became a crusade. He saw the chance to persuade Heath to boost pensions as part of an overall package, and his old unwavering defence of free collective bargaining began to flag. Jones' concern with pensioners was characteristic of the man: it was an issue that concerned the underprivileged but yet an issue which carried few ideological undertones – better pen-sions could be granted as easily by the Tories as by Labour (indeed, both parties accepted the Jones argument and ordered substantial boosts in pensions). At every TUC in recent years, Jones has addressed a beach rally of pensioners on the Sunday before congress: an emotional and a personal rite.

Jones never did a deal with Heath although his opposition to the Heath incomes policy was decidedly muted, and a mutual admiration was established between the two men which was never broken. Yet at the same time, Jones became increasingly involved in the formulation of Labour Party policy. He sat on the TUC-Labour Party liaison committee and worked together with Labour Party leaders on the formulation of the social contract.

When Labour came to power in 1974, Jones immediately assumed a position of great power: he was constantly consulted by cabinet ministers, especially Michael Foot, and he dominated the development of Labour's strategy. In 1975, he proposed the flat-rate pay limit and forced this through the TUC. At the 1975 congress in Blackpool, he delivered a memorable speech in which he roasted the left-wing opposition to this incomes policy.

The old Jones was an uncompromising, often arrogant, man. The new Jones was a more thoughtful and constructive man: a man who could listen as well as lecture. Jones' conversion meant that he was able to use his control of power in the union to reinforce the moderates at the TUC as he had earlier reinforced the militants, and with the same effect. In July 1975, he launched a ferocious attack on the *Tribune* group of left-wing MPs for opposing the government's incomes policy: a demonstration of how far he had moved across the political spectrum.

Jones has nursed his union's finances with some care. In 1972, the union's total assets stood at £22 million. He also has taken a ruthless attitude to the dead wood amongst the union's five hundred full-time officials. Some seventy officials have left or been sacked. The total staff has been reduced, although the union's membership and income continued to expand.

Jones has the biggest and most difficult job in British trade unions (something like being mayor of New York). At Transport House he has a central staff of seventy to back him up. But his life-style is unambitious. He lives in a simple flat in Denmark Hill in south-east London. He is married with two sons. His wife, Evelyn, is a magistrate, and once was a shop steward. She is more left wing than Jack (and an important influence on his politics).

Jones could step into the executive class any day he wanted. British Steel, for example, offered him a job as a labour director, at £16,000 a year. He turned it down, while Ron Smith, general secretary of the post office workers took it. Jones is a union man through and through. He once said: 'I am a trade unionist by birth and inclination. When I retire I'll go back to organising for the T & G. I don't want any cushy jobs.'

The GMWU: a giant awakens

The General and Municipal Workers' Union has until recently been a mirror image of the pre-1956 TGWU: staid, centralised, and conservative. But since 1972, when David Basnett was elected to replace Lord Cooper as general secretary, the union has acquired a more racy image.

Like the TGWU, the GMWU was founded and propelled by one charismatic figure: Will Thorne. In 1889 Thorne founded the gasworkers' union, which soon developed into a general union. Membership in 1910 was 30,000 but rocketed to 450,000 in 1920. Another union which developed at the same time was the Workers' Union, led by Tom Mann. Its membership topped 500,000 in 1920. But both unions went into sharp decline after 1920, and in 1924 they decided to merge, together with two other smaller unions. In February 1924, they all met in the Memorial Hall in Farringdon Street, London, to thrash out the details. There was a lot of argy-bargy about finance (a perennial sticking-point in union mergers), but the deal was finally agreed and the GMWU was formed, led by Will Thorne. Thorne stayed in charge until 1934, when he retired after forty-five years as a union general secretary – a record never equalled before or since.

Like the TGWU, the GMWU began as a right-wing union, but unlike the TGWU, it has stayed that way until now. The GMWU's traditional approach was summed up by an early president of the gasworkers, J.R. Clynes, who advocated 'moderation, avoidance of strikes where possible, the use of all possible means of conciliation, the establishment of good relations with employers and the virtues of political action'. The GMWU was not even an enthusiast for the 1926 General Strike. It backed the strike, but then condemned it afterwards. This has been partly because the union's constitution provides for centralised power, as in the TGWU.

In 1947, one delegate to the GMWU conference remarked that 'To my mind, the constitution of this union is undemocratic from beginning to end. The constitution is laid down on the assumption that the general worker is incapable of governing himself'. The oligarchic nature of the GMWU is emphasised by the union's family traditions. Lord Williamson, the third general secretary, was the nephew of the union's Liverpool secretary. Three generations of the Eccles family have held office in the GMWU in Lancashire, including Jack Eccles, who fought in the 1972 general secretary election and sits as one of the union's representatives on the TUC general council. Sir Fred Hayday, who was Lord Cooper's deputy for many years, was the son of a GMWU Midlands secretary. Lord Cooper, the fourth general secretary, was the nephew of Charles Dukes, the second general secretary. Even David Basnett, the fifth general secretary, is the son of a former regional secretary. It's not bad for a union that is only fifty years old.

Every general secretary since Thorne has been so proestablishment that he has been awarded a peerage (Lords Dukeston, Williamson and Cooper), and the union has consistently supported moderate Labour policies. It remained loyal to Mr Wilson throughout the 1960s. It was reluctant to deregister under the Industrial Relations Act. It supported the social contract in 1974-5, and it has been one of the few consistently pro-European unions in the TUC.

The union, the third biggest in Britain, has 880,000 members (1975) but dominates few industries, except gas. It recruits in two hundred and fifty separate industries, from laundries to glassworks, from churches to artists' studios. In many industries where it recruits substantial numbers it is overshadowed by other unions: in engineering by the AUEW, in public services by NUPE, in electricity by the EEPTU. So it is only a subsidiary force in industrial decisions.

For twenty years until 1972, the union ossified. It had few new ideas and few extra members. Then Lord Cooper retired and an election for a new general secretary was won by David Basnett.

David Basnett is a quiet, softly-spoken man with a dry sense of humour. He was an RAF pilot in the war. He flew Sunderlands with coastal command when he was twenty. Although he has to run a predominantly manual union, his first job was as a bank clerk. He has had no experience of manual work, unlike most union leaders – but no one holds this against him. He is an intellectual, unlike any of the previous GMWU leaders, and his politics are more radical although always coherent and middle-of-the-road. He is not hostile to incomes policy, but is a keen advocate of more extensive state involvement in industry. He is also an enthusiast for workers' participation: not just in industry, but within his own traditionally autocratic union.

The GMWU's power structure, like the TGWU's is centralised, but the general secretary has marginally less control. The union holds a conference every year, and the executive meets each month. All officers are appointed but have to submit to re-election after a two-year trial (although this is normally a formality). The general secretary is the only officer who is elected, but as in the TGWU, elections are by show-of-hands in branches. Votes are cast in blocks – so that a hundred member branch can cast a hundred votes for a candidate even though only ten people attend the branch meeting and vote for the candidate by a majority of one.

Until 1975, the executive was divided into two: the big general council which met every quarter and the executive, chosen by the council, which met each month. But the two bodies are to be merged into one, under a reform scheme masterminded by David Basnett. The new governing body will be called the executive council, and will be composed of twenty rank-and-file members (two from each of the ten regions) plus the ten regional secretaries. When it forms sub-committees, the composition will ensure that there is always a majority of rank-and-filers. Previously, the executive consisted of only five rank-and-filers and five regional secretaries. The new composition reflects Basnett's desire to give rank-and-filers more power in a traditionally bureaucratic union.

A peculiarity of the GMWU's power structure is the extensive power that rests with the regions: both with the full-time regional secretaries and with the regional councils. This often gives rise to uncomfortable friction between the GMWU head office and what are known in the union as the 'regional barons' – especially in the north-east where the union has always been very strong. Each region is governed by a council, elected by the branches. This meets infrequently, so many of its powers are often conferred on the regional secretary. This council in turn elects a regional committee made up of officials and rank-and-filers. The committee has the power to call official strikes in the region if less than three hundred workers are involved. It can also fine and punish unofficial strikers in strikes of which it disapproves. The committee also decides how to spend the union's local political funds.

The GMWU does not yet have the formal system of trade groups as in the TGWU, but since 1969 it has begun to develop a series of industrial conferences where rank-and-file delegates in each industry can meet and decide the union's strategy. The development of these conferences should represent a significant devolution of power within the union and form an important element in David Basnett's new strategy. The GMWU has, in some senses, shifted to the left since Basnett took over, but this is only a reflection of the more active role the union is now playing. The only danger in the Basnett approach is that the devolution of power within the union may only be to the activist level rather than to the level of the members. In many unions, such trends have led to an unrepresentative shift leftwards. In the GMWU it played an important role in the 1973 gas strike (the first the union ever called). The strike was called by a delegate conference, although if the officers alone had been in charge it might never have begun. The eventual offer that ended the strike was accepted by a vote of 19,000 to 11,000 in a secret ballot, although a re-called delegate conference opposed acceptance of the offer.

There is, as yet, no sign that Basnett intends to replace the system of appointment of officers by more democratic elections. This is perhaps not surprising, because the union has gained from the present system. Elections tend to make it hard for younger men to make the top: long-serving union officials usually come out best. But an appointment system allows the quick promotion of young officers. The GMWU has several such men: like John Edmonds (gas officer) who was educated at a public school (Christ's Hospital) and Oriel College, Oxford. Edmonds was only twenty-nine when appointed to the senior job as national officer in charge of the gas industry. David Warburton, the national officer in charge of the chemical industry, is another young and energetic union officer. The GMWU also has an energetic research department, staffed by budding young Labour politicians like Giles Radice (now Labour MP for Chester-le-Street), a Jenkinsite who ran the department for several years before Basnett was elected. Since 1972, the GMWU has been one of the few unions to employ a professional business economist to scrutinise company accounts.

The GMWU is professional in many ways. It runs its

finances better than most unions. Under Lord Cooper's reign, it managed a smart financial coup when it moved from its old base in Thorne House, Bloomsbury, to Esher.

The union sold Thorne House for a cool £600,000 and bought Ruxley Towers for just £80,000 – or rather £50,000 since it was soon able to sell off £30,000 worth of housing land. It was an impressive piece of property dealing, and it was little wonder that under Lord Cooper the union's total funds doubled from £5 million to £10 million.

The GMWU is also professional about education. It has its own training school at Woodstock in Surrey. The GMWU claims that Woodstock is the best trade-union education centre in Europe. It is entirely financed by the GMWU and is part of a large education programme costing over £100,000 a year. Woodstock has a full-time staff, who run regular courses for shop stewards and other union officials. They are taught everything, from work study to the use of slide rules. It is not surprising if GMWU shop stewards tend to be more progressive than other union officials.

Woodstock looks like some new university, with lecture theatres, a cinema and plush accommodation. Employers are always keen to give their shop stewards time off to attend courses there. Indeed, quite often the employers themselves enrol for courses. When bosses sit in the same classroom as shop stewards and drink beer with them afterwards, remarkable things happen.

Not long after the GMWU's disastrous 1970 strike at Pilkingtons' glassworks, one of the Pilkington brothers spent three days at Woodstock with GMWU shop stewards from Pilkingtons. Relations were greatly improved, and there has been little trouble since. The union is now planning to open a second training school in Cheshire.

8   The unstoppable miners

Stanley Baldwin used to say that there were three interests in Britain that no government could afford to annoy, the Vatican, the Irish and the miners' union. But the power of the miners, which had become a legend by the 1920s, appeared to have been cracked for ever in 1926. In the spring of that year, the miners went on strike to oppose wage cuts. The TUC called a general strike in their support, but this was called off after nine days. The miners' strike lasted until December, when the union's leaders had to settle on ignominious terms – considerably worse than the terms they could have had at the start of the strike. The country suffered severely during the 1926 miners' strike. Industrial production slumped by fifteen per cent, the steel industry came to a standstill, transport was crippled (trains ran on coal), and unemployment soared by half-a-million in the second half of the year. The strike, however, was beaten by massive imports of coal, mainly from Poland and the United States and, towards the end, by widespread blacklegging as impoverished miners drifted back to work. After the 1926 defeat, the union called no national strike for nearly fifty years.

As Britain switched to other fuels in the 1950s and 1960s, the industrial power of the miners seemed to have declined even further. Transport was no longer dependent on coal: the railways carried less and less freight and, anyway, were no longer directly powered by coal. Power stations began to switch to oil and nuclear power. The miners also feared for their jobs – as it was, 420,000 jobs disappeared between 1958 and 1972 out of a labour force of 700,000. It was hardly a position of strength. Or so it seemed.

Industrial relations were never good even in the 1950s. Between 1944 and 1964, there were 28,168 separate strikes in the pits – more than half the total number of strikes in all industries in the same period – an average of 1,409 a year. But these were all local strikes and because wages were bargained pit by pit, there was no danger of a national strike.

Yet both union leaders and the National Coal Board realised that this toll of strikes should be reduced. They thought the best way to achieve this was to standardise pay throughout the country. The union backed standardisation because it wanted to boost wages in the lowest-paid areas like Scotland and Wales. So, in 1966, the two sides agreed to the so-called 'power-loading agreement' plus a standard 'day-wage'. The effect on strikes was dramatic. In 1966, only 118,000 days were lost in strikes – the lowest figure ever recorded since strike statistics were first collected in 1893. In 1967, only 105,000 were lost. In 1968, only 57,000 were lost. The number of strikes also declined dramatically. The great problem of industrial relations in the coal industry had, it seemed, been solved. Lord Robens, the NCB chairman, was hailed as the man who had humanely run down the industry, had established excellent relations with the National Union of Mineworkers (even though the union's general secretary was a communist) and had cut strikes by a record margin.

Yet these years of peace shrouded growing resentment at the demotion of the role of the miner – so long a heroic figure of the working-class. In 1960, underground miners earned ten per cent more than the national average in manufacturing industry. By 1971, they were earning three per cent below the average. The decline was sharpest between 1967 and 1971. Even in 1967, miners were still earning seven per cent above the average. In some areas of the Midlands, some miners had actually suffered a cut in money wages thanks to redistribution under the terms of the power-loading agreement. So by the 1970s the old militancy had begun to return, encouraged by the new faces in the leadership.

In July 1970, the NUM conference voted to back a thirty-three per cent wage demand. When the NCB made an offer way below this, the union called a national ballot. Over 55 per cent of miners voted for a strike, but the union's rule book then said that a 60 per cent majority vote was needed to call a strike. But a wave of unofficial strikes broke out: 36 per cent of the miners, mainly in Yorkshire, Wales and Scotland, walked out. Eventually, they returned to work – but it was a warning of what was to come in the next year. In July 1971, the NUM conference again insisted on voting a specific wage claim – in direct contrast to the traditional conference policy of calling for a substantial wage rise, but leaving the bargaining to the negotiators. The conference, which met in the ballroom of the Douglas Hotel in Aberdeen, this time demanded a forty-seven per cent rise. More important still, the conference voted to change the rules of the union so that a strike could be called on a 55 per cent majority rather than the old 60 per cent majority.

When the miners' leaders met the NCB team in November, they were offered a 7½ per cent wage rise. They turned it down and again called a ballot of all their members. This time, the pro-strike vote was 58.8% – only fractionally higher than in 1970, but under the new rule sufficient to call a strike.

Although the overall swing to the militants was small, there was a wide geographical variation. The traditionally militant areas had become more moderate, while the more moderate areas had become militant. This was the result of income redistribution carried out under the power-loading agreement.

Before 1966, miners in areas where the pits were rich in coal (and thus very profitable) were paid more than those in the fringe areas, where pits were usually poorer. The new agreement put all miners on the same pay. So miners in Scotland and South Wales did very well, those in areas like Nottingham and Kent did badly. Between 1970 and 1971, the strike vote dropped in Scotland and South Wales but rose in Nottingham and Kent.

Even after this vote, few people believed that the miners would actually strike. For a start, their bargaining position seemed appallingly weak. Power-station coal stocks were at a record level of over fourteen million tons. This would have been enough for eight weeks' normal winter consumption, and no one thought the miners could strike for that long. All that seemed necessary was for the NCB to make a marginal improvement in the offer a few days before the strike was due to start. This was just what happened.

The strike was scheduled to start on 9 January 1972. On 3 January Joe Gormley of the NUM and Derek Ezra of the Coal Board found themselves at the same lunch. Afterwards the two men adjourned to another room and agreed to meet again the next day. Ezra and his colleagues went to the union's headquarters on Wednesday, 5 January, with a final offer. If the miners improved their productivity, the NCB was prepared to offer them a deal which would have been worth nearly twelve per cent. Ezra seems to have been told privately by Gormley that such an offer would be accepted by the union. If so, Gormley had badly misjudged the mood of his own executive. The executive voted overwhelmingly to reject the new offer.

So the first national coal strike in forty-six years began in January 1972. At first it had the impact of a wet sponge. Life went on as normal. Industry was almost unaffected. Power stations continued at full output. The strike soon ceased to be front-page news. The miners themselves did not expect to win. The mood was well captured by Eric Jacobs, the *Sunday Times* labour correspondent, who wrote on the weekend the strike began:

> I want them to win. But I doubt if they will. It is a failure of leadership to have chosen this moment, when coal stocks have rarely been higher, when the Government is fighting everybody's battle by resisting inflationary wage claims, and when the union has refused in advance to coordinate its claims with those of other public employees. Already the bitter atmosphere of 1926 hangs over the coalfields.

So it might have been, but for one factor: picketing. Everyone expected the miners to picket the pits (although this was hardly necessary), but no one ever dreamt that they would picket power stations, coal depots, steelworks and ports. The idea only seems to have occurred to the miners themselves after the strike started.

There is certainly little doubt that the militancy of the miners hardened as the strike went on (as is usual in most strikes). On the third day of the strike, Gormley told the press:

> The men are being a damn sight more militant than we would want them to be and they are ignoring advice on safety manning. As national officials, we regret this, and we shall once again tell them that it is in their own interests to provide the essential services.

It was not till the strike was in its second week that the miners organised pickets for depots and power stations in London. Even then, it hardly seemed to matter, because the power stations had such large stocks of coal inside their gates. What everyone had forgotten was that power stations need other things besides coal. They need oil and hydrogen, for example. The miners at the gates were turning away all lorries. At the same time, public opinion remained firmly sympathetic to the miners' cause. Polls taken during the strike showed that the public agreed that the miners deserved to be treated as a special case.

By the second week of February, the miners had the government on the run. A state of emergency was declared. Blackouts began. The lights went off in houses. Traffic ran into chaos as traffic lights went out. Industry began laying off men, as machines had to stop. The miners now knew they were winning. When the NCB came back with an offer worth seventeen per cent, the miners laughed in their face. They were not prepared to compromise. They were not even prepared to talk until the NCB conceded the full claim. Their intransigence was well calculated. Within days, the Government indicated that surrender was at hand and appointed a court of inquiry, chaired by Lord Wilberforce. The court concluded, in the space of four days, that most of the miners' demands were justified. They awarded wage rises of around twenty per cent. But even now, the miners did not accept. The strike went on. So the miners were called to Downing Street, and there they extracted eleven more major concessions (including an extra week's holiday): the equivalent of another four per cent. Then they held a ballot, and over ninety-six per cent of miners voted in favour of acceptance. They had won a famous victory.

How they overthrew Heath

The militants in the NUM hoped to capitalise on their 1972 victory in the following year. The 1972 conference again backed a big wage claim and was supported by the executive, who called another strike ballot in early 1973. The claim was in strict defiance of the new Heath incomes policy, but the ballot produced a sharp reverse for the militants. Over sixty-three per cent voted against strike action, and the miners' leaders were forced to settle under the government's stage-two formula. The mood of peace was short-lived. The 1973 conference, undeterred by the reverse in the ballot, demanded another big rise of thirty-five per cent.

Meanwhile, the Heath government was working out stage three of its pay control policy. Ministers calculated that the miners might pose a challenge to the policy, so they carefully designed stage three to provide for an extra large wage rise for the miners. The NCB helped advise the Department of Employment how to do this: the policy included an additional rise for all those who worked 'unsocial hours'. The DE calculated that few others besides the miners would be able to benefit from this clause.

The NCB made an offer to the NUM as soon as stage three was published. It offered the absolute maximum permitted – up to 16½ per cent (including a productivity deal). This proved to be a grave mistake, because it left no room for the NUM to bargain: the union either had to meekly accept or call strike action. When the miners' leaders walked out of the NCB headquarters in Grosvenor Place, they told waiting reporters that they had rejected the offer – and so, almost unconsciously, they had committed the union to strike.

Joe Gormley, the NUM president, wished to avoid a strike, but Lawrence Daly, the general secretary, and Mick McGahey, the communist vice-president, were both thirsting for a fight. The twenty-seven man NUM executive was divided. The last round of elections had brought gains for the militant left, who could command a majority on the exeuctive if any of the floating voters backed them. Mick McGahey had defeated a moderate for the vice-presidency, and militant young men like Arthur Scargill and Peter Heathfield had won seats on the executive. They too were thirsting for battle.

In this situation, the moderates were scared of being seen to be less tough than the militants – and so they did not dare to oppose them directly. Instead they preferred to try to outwit them by pretending to be even more militant than the militants. This strategy by the NUM moderates must be reckoned to be the second bad mistake: it played completely into the militants' hands from the start.

The NUM executive met on 25 October 1973 to discuss whether to begin industrial action. The majority of the six communists on the executive, and their allies, had decided to back an overtime ban. They hoped that this would run for a month and would be followed by a strike ballot which would go in favour of a strike because the men would by then feel more frustrated.

The moderates decided that they could not successfully

oppose an overtime ban, so they agreed on a seemingly clever strategy. They decided to back a total overtime ban instead of the partial overtime ban as operated in the autumn of 1971. The difference was crucial: a complete ban meant that no safety and maintenance work could be done· at the weekends.

It would have to be done on Mondays, so that an extra day's production would be lost each week.

The moderates hoped that such a ban would provoke a strike ballot decision at an earlier stage. Joe Gormley expected that a complete ban would bring many pits to a complete halt and so force a 'go/no-go' decision on the strike. He thought that an early strike ballot was more likely to go against a strike.

Several militants also·backed the complete ban (although Mick McGahey opposed it), and the decision was supported by a miners' delegate conference the following day. The ban proved much less effective than the miners expected: mainly because the Government immediately introduced restrictions on the use of power and (after Christmas) ordered industry to work only three days each week.

Some of the NUM moderates decided in mid-December to try to press for a strike ballot. They reckoned that a ballot at that time would oppose strike action and so force a settlement within stage three. But only five men – Tommy Bartle, Les Story, Maurice Rowe, Roy Ottey and Les Atkinson – voted for a ballot. Joe Gormley, by then, also favoured a ballot but he did not say so in public.

The Government now failed to play a trump card. The NCB's offer was worth sixteen and a half per cent in total, but only seven per cent in terms of cash down: the rest was fringe benefits plus a productivity deal. The Government could have amended stage three to include the following clause: 'Any group of workers entitled to any benefit under this code may receive that benefit in cash provided the total cost per man employed is no higher.'

The Government refused to consider any such concession because it would have meant a partial victory for the miners in forcing a change in the law. But it would have meant that the NCB could have offered thirteen per cent in straight cash. The moderates are convinced that this would have produced a majority in any ballot in favour of accepting and against strik-ing. Such a move would also have given the floaters on the

NUM executive an excuse to support an early ballot.

By January 1974 the situation had become critical. The three-day week had begun, and there was a brief but serious threat of general strike action, which was neatly defused by Len Murray of the TUC. Murray finessed union militants, who wanted to call a special congress of the TUC, by suggesting a conference of union presidents and general secretaries to discuss the crisis. This made sure that the conference (a) had no constitutional power and (b) was made up of the mild-mannered men at the top rather than the more militant delegations that would attend a full congress.

Soon after, Murray told the Government that the TUC would make sure no other union used any special deal for the miners as a lever for demolishing stage three. This offer was fraught with problems – (How could the TUC enforce it? Would the TUC congress back Murray?) – and the Government rejected it. In retrospect, it was clear that this was the fourth bad mistake. If this offer had been accepted, the miners' strike could have been avoided and the dispute settled for less than the thirty per cent which was to be the eventual price for peace. It was the first time in three-and-a-half years of Tory government that the TUC had promised anything helpful on tackling wage inflation: and it was a chance that could have been grasped.

The TUC, for its part, was running scared at the prospect of a snap election. The TUC reckoned that an election on the 'Tories versus the unions' issue could only end in victory for the Tories. That was why it was prepared to make such a big concession. The TUC might eventually have reneged on its promise, as it did on the similar promises it gave to the first Wilson government – but this would only have added weight to the Tories' claim that a statutory incomes policy was necessary.

Once the Tories had rejected this offer, they had one chance left: that the miners' inevitable strike ballot would not produce a majority for a strike. Joe Gormley told friends just after Christmas that he was still certain that a ballot would not produce a pro-strike majority. However, it was Gormley himself who made sure that this prediction was wrong. On 21 January 1974, he declared that he was in favour of a strike, and together with Lawrence Daly and Mick McGahey, he asked the executive three days later for the go-ahead for the ballot. The executive voted sixteen to ten in favour of a ballot.

Why Joe Gormley backed the strike remained unclear: probably he still did not want a strike, but thought a ballot would reject the idea. Yet because he, the union's leading moderate, seemed to support the strike, it was inevitable that there would be a majority for strike action. The ballot hinged on an appeal to miners' loyalty to their union and its leaders in a battle with a Tory government. That was why eighty-one per cent of miners backed a strike.

Ted Heath reluctantly called an election, although making it clear that there would be a surrender to the miners (under the guise of a pay board inquiry into miners' relative pay).

The Tories lost the election, although, after having been far behind in the opinion polls only a month before, they came within an ace of winning. They got a higher share of the popular vote than Labour and would probably have had an overall majority but for the effect of the opinion polls during the election (which indicated a clear Tory victory), which may have induced some Tory-inclined voters to vote Liberal. Another key factor was the row over the arithmetic on miners' pay.

The pay board inquiry into the miners' case during the election discovered that the relationship of miners' earnings to average earnings had been distorted in official statistics because of the calculation of holiday pay: a distortion which operated to the miners' disadvantage. This was leaked on the last Friday before the election, and on Saturday several papers ran it as their lead story – suggesting that an error of arithmetic had caused the strike and the election. This was soon denied, but the story cast doubt on the Tories' case. The leak has often been attributed to the deputy chairman of the pay board, Derek Robinson (a Labour supporter and former aide to Barbara Castle), who gave the story to industrial correspondents on the Friday evening. This was quite unfair. Robinson did brief correspondents but did not put any political interpretation to them. The political slant was given by the NUM and by Harold Wilson in a speech the same evening. It seems that Wilson was tipped off by an NUM official.

Unfortunately for the Tories, no one in the government knew what was happening. Ministers were all out campaigning. Willie Whitelaw, the employment secretary, was asked after a meeting to comment, but could not do so because he knew nothing about it. Officials at 10 Downing Street only learnt the news when they saw the story coming over the news-tapes. It was not till Saturday morning that Heath could be briefed and comment. By then, it was too late.

Are the miners invincible?

The new Labour government made every effort in its first year to ensure peace in the pits. It allowed the NCB and NUM to settle for over thirty per cent and the following year agreed to an even bigger rise of nearly thirty-five per cent (including thresholds and extra holidays). But before long, some government will ask itself if it can risk another confrontation with the miners.

A future government's best hope of winning any battle with the NUM leadership is to win support among the rank-and-file miners. because no all-out strike can be called by the NUM without a majority in a pithead vote. But if it comes to a strike, a government can only win (a) if it has stockpiled sufficient coal, oil and other power supplies, (b) if it is prepared to risk a strike of at least six months and major, 1926-style, losses of production in the rest of industry, (c) if it is able to import coal, which means having the authority and support to break picket-lines, and (d) if it is fighting a strike which is in clear defiance of popular opinion (perhaps expressed in a referendum), so that some moderate unions – like the power workers – will be prepared to handle imported coal. In 1974, none of these conditions held. Even if the Tories had tried to import coal, Frank Chapple would have advised his members who man the power stations not to handle it (even though he was personally opposed to the miners' strike).

Power inside the NUM

The NUM was only formed in 1944. Its forerunner was the Miners' Federation, which had been formed in 1888. In the federation, each area of the union maintained considerable independence. Each ran its own strike fund (until 1972, when the Industrial Relations Act's provisions made it more attractive to hive off the strike funds). The federation consisted of forty member unions. In 1944, they were recomposed into twenty sections of which fourteen are geographical regions, and six are occupational sections for groups like the colliery over-men. They vary in size from the 63,000 strong Yorkshire region to the 1,700 strong Cumberland area.

Each section sends between one and three men to the national executive, normally including the area secretary. Most of the members of the NUM executive are full-time officials. Elections take place every two years, but election practice varies between sections: some merely appoint their representatives by vote of the section's council. Most elections take place by branch ballot in which a tiny fraction of miners vote (unlike the pithead ballots where turnout is very high). Thus the executive, which is the most powerful decision-taking body in the union, is not chosen in a notably democratic way. The delegates to the annual NUM conference are chosen by a similar process.

However, the NUM also has some exceptional democratic features. Joe Gormley once told me, perhaps a little optimisti-cally, 'We are a real picture of what a democratic union should be'. These features include:

1   The rule that no national strike can be called without a fifty-five per cent majority in a pithead ballot (although an overtime ban can be called without any ballot).

2   Pithead ballots ensure a high turnout and some secrecy. Miners vote in special booths near the pithead which they have to pass on their way to work: so turnout is often between eighty and ninety per cent in strike ballots, and around sixty per cent for election of the two leading national officials. Secrecy is not strict: branch officials can often see how miners vote and many of them are able to count the votes before they are sent to the independent Electoral Reform Society in London (which is why ballot results are often leaked in advance in the press): but, on balance, the system is pretty fair.

3   Pithead ballots are used for the election of the NUM's top two officials: the president and the general secretary (although the vice-president is elected by the annual congress).

4   The NUM headquarters has to keep every branch well informed on all union business. For example, the minutes of every executive meeting in London are sent to each branch in the country for inspection.

The ballots of the 1970s

Principal pithead policy votes

Issue	Militants = % for	Moderates = % against
1970, strike	55	45
1971, strike	59	41
1973, strike	37	63
1974, strike	81	19
	= % against	= % for
1974, productivity	61	39
1975, pay limit	39	61

The branches of the NUM are based on the place of work rather than a geographical area as in many unions. Each pit has its own branch. So branch officials act as shop stewards. This means that there is close personal contact between these officials and the men. One branch president I met (at Baddesley in Warwickshire) knew the name of every one of his nine hundred members. It also means that the average attendance at branch meetings is higher than in many unions (although the meetings are often held at weekends, away from the pit, usually in a pub or working-men's club).

The union's president since 1971 has been Joe Gormley. He is a miner first, trade-union leader second, and politician third. Unlike most union men who get to the top, Gormley only became active in the union relatively late in life. His father was a miner, who came from Ireland to work in a Lancashire pit. Gormley followed his father into the pits at the age of fourteen, and worked there for thirty years. He became involved in Labour politics well before he became a union activist. Gormley hardly ever worked the day shift. For thirteen years in a row, he only worked the afternoon or night shift. So it was natural that he should argue that the night-shift workers should not have to work for long periods without a turn at the day shift. He led a successful two-day strike on this issue in 1949, and that propelled him into the local group of union activists.

From then on, he began attending his branch meetings regularly. Within four months, he was elected president of the branch, defeating a communist who had been in the job for many years. It was the first of many battles that Gormley was to fight against the communists.

In 1958 he was elected to the national executive of the union. A few years later he fought the election for the secretaryship of the north-west area, and won. But after his victory the local communists accused him of rigging the ballot.

Gormley was enraged by these allegations – they came soon after the communists' ballot-rigging in the electricians' union had been exposed. He reacted by resigning his post, and demanding a new election. He was then re-elected with an even bigger majority, crushing the communist opposition.

After eleven years on the national executive, Gormley decided in 1969 to stand for general secretary. He was opposed by Lawrence Daly. Gormley was expected to win easily, since Daly was an unknown figure. But Gormley was a member of the Labour Party's national executive, and the Labour government's reputation had just sunk to a new low. Although Gormley had argued strongly against the government's policies, he was tarred with their brush. Daly was not part of the establishment, and was backing a much more militant approach. He also advocated a tactic of guerrilla strikes, while Gormley thought cooperation was the best strategy to save jobs.

Daly won by a narrow margin. His victory represented a sharp swing to the left after a period of moderate leadership under the former general secretary, Will Paynter, and the president, Sir Sidney Ford. Paynter was a member of the Communist Party, but was not a militant. His membership of the party was a historical accident. He was, says one NUM man, 'a Welsh communist', as if that explained everything.

But in 1971, the union president, Sir Sidney Ford, had to retire because of illness, and Gormley joined battle to succeed him. Once again his opponent was a Scottish militant – Mick McGahey, a leading communist. This time, Gormley organised a better campaign, and he beat McGahey by a comfortable majority.

Gormley is a right-winger, but not always an effective one. Too often, he has been unwilling to provide the leadership the moderates in the NUM need. He has not been a good judge of the mood of his executive or his members: in both 1972 and 1974 he made crucial errors of judgment. He also tends to be

over-subtle. In March 1973 for example, he argued at the TUC
in favour of a general strike against the Heath stage-two policy
as the only realistic alternative to cooperation with the government. He obviously assumed that the delegates would
choose cooperation but, to his chagrin, his bluff was called. The
TUC voted in favour of a one-day general strike.

Yet Gormley is a reassuring personality. He lacks panache,
but can be refreshingly blunt. He lives in suburban Sunbury-
on-Thames and has two grown-up children. His son went into
mining (although Gormley advised him not to do so) but as yet
has shown little interest in union politics.

Since 1971, Gormley and Daly have struggled to grasp the
reins of power. The union's constitution divides the leadership
between these two offices. The president has a few extra powers: for example, he chairs all union meetings and, unlike the
general secretary, has a vote at committee meetings. Since the
union was founded in 1944, there have been four general secretaries and three presidents. In only one case was a general
secretary clearly more powerful than the president.

In 1972 Daly was a commanding figure in the union. He is a
more impressive orator than Gormley (he also has a reputation
as a singer, and once recorded a selection of Robert Burns' love
songs for television) and has a better intellect. But a prolonged
illness later kept him on the sidelines of the union. Daly is a
hard-line left-winger although he left the Communist Party in
the 1950s, but he is prepared to talk seriously about incomes
policy. He has always declared himself in favour of incomes
policy – provided it includes full-scale socialism. In 1974, he
proposed the support for the social contract at the TUC
(although he was less enthusiastic for the £6 pay rise limit in
1975).

But Daly was eclipsed after 1974 by other, newer, left-wing
faces. First, by Mick McGahey, the communist vice-president,
who won the election for vice-president in 1972. McGahey was
catapulted into the public eye in 1974 when he suggested that if
troops were brought in to deal with the strike, they might be
persuaded to mutiny. McGahey is a severe, drably-dressed,
puritanical Scottish communist. He has almost no sense of
humour and his political devotion is total: he is a member of the
Communist Party's political committee. The story is told that
when his elderly mother died, McGahey and his brother

marched behind the coffin over which were draped the words
'Mary McGahey: murdered by capitalism'.

But McGahey, in turn, was overshadowed by a new group of
left-wingers who did not belong to the Communist Party, but
endorsed policies which were just as Marxist. They included
men like Yorkshire's Arthur Scargill and Derbyshire's Peter
Heathfield. Scargill was only elected in 1972, but soon became
a national figure because of his uncompromising support for
massive wage rises. He made himself extremely popular in his
native Yorkshire, but he angered the older traditional NUM
leaders. Few who were at the NUM's 1975 conference at Scar-
borough will forget the verbal lashing that Lawrence Daly
dished out to Scargill, after Scargill had attacked the NUM's
leadership of the 1960s. Scargill's arguments about wage
demands are simple: in a capitalist society, everyone is entitled
to ask for all they can get and the miners deserve more than
anyone. He will not even start to consider the arguments about
inflation (or helping the Labour Party) which less simplistic
militants take seriously. But some NUM observers think Scargill will turn more right-wing if he is ever elected to a full-time
national office.

Life in the pit

Underneath the economic and political arguments about the
miners runs another seam. Every leader-writer and politician –
indeed every member of the white-collar classes – feels sympathy for the miners' job. Many feel that the job is so awful that
the miners are entitled to any rate of pay they care to name –
although few of them pause to consider whether many other
manual jobs are not equally unpleasant. So just how hard is the
miners' lot? George Orwell's vivid description sums up how life
used to be:

> It is even humiliating to watch coal miners working. It raises
> in you a momentary doubt about your own status as an
> 'intellectual' and a superior person generally. For it is only
> because miners sweat their guts out that superior persons
> can remain superior. You and I and the editor of the Times
> Lit. Supp. and the Nancy poets and the Archbishop of
> Canterbury . . . all of us really owe the comparative decency
> of our lives to poor drudges underground, blackened to the

eyes, with their throats full of coal dust, driving their shovels
forward with arms and belly muscles of steel.

> George Orwell: *The Road to Wigan Pier* (1937)

Orwell described how miners had to walk and crawl several
miles, often bent double, just to get to the coal face, and then
had the incredible physical effort of continually shovelling coal
on to a conveyor belt. Today, travelling to the face is less
painful: a miniature railway, known as the man-rider, takes the
miners most of the way, and it is possible to walk upright in
most of the tunnels. At the face itself, the coal is cut and loaded
onto a conveyor by machine. Only a minority of the men
underground work at the face itself. The two main jobs at the
face are moving the hydraulic pit props forward as the face
advances, and drilling the tunnels that lead to and from the
face. Most of the men underground are working on supply,
safety, transport and other such jobs. These are not substantially more unpleasant than factory work.

Working at the face, however, is still pretty fair hell. The
atmosphere is dusty, and most men wear masks to stop inhala-
tion of the dust. Others chew tobacco as they work, to spit it out
with the dust. The conditions are incredibly cramped. Even at
the best of faces, one can only move between the props by
bending double. I found it physically exhausting just to walk
the length of a face, perhaps only two hundred yards. At the
faces which are neither very deep nor far from the shaft, the
temperature is no problem. But at the deeper faces, it can be
extremely hot. The miners work stripped to the waist, with
sweat pouring down.

To the visitor, the most wretched aspect of the job is its
claustrophobia. The miner is confined to this darkness for eight
hours a day, usually with only a plastic carton of water and a
packet of sandwiches to refresh him. Cigarettes and alcohol are
strictly forbidden. Officially, miners are only allowed twenty
minutes' break, known as snap-time, during their eight-hour
shift: but this rule is widely abused (it is hardly conceivable that
it would not be).

Yet for all this, every pit exudes an atmosphere of solidarity
and friendliness that almost seems to override the conditions.
Unlike a car factory, workers in a mine usually work in groups.

The challenge and the danger of the job seem to bring miners together. They have a pride in their work, their pit and their industry. They like to know the pit's profit figures and the weekly production total.

Most miners are miners because their fathers were miners. Few of them have thought of doing another job – although at many pits in Kent and the Midlands there is no lack of alternative jobs. Curiously, many miners say they do not believe they would be much good at any other job. I have met a miner who had qualifications in chartered accountancy, yet decided to stay in mining.

Mining is not as dangerous as it used to be. It is only marginally more dangerous than working on the railways or on the farm, in terms of deaths at work, and considerably less dangerous than deep-sea fishing. Yet disaster is part of the way of life of a pit. At every mine, a room is set aside for use in directing operations in an emergency. There are still rows of Davy lamps and budgerigars in cages, to warn of gas.

Even though deaths are now less frequent, the incidence of diseases like pneumoconiosis is still appallingly high. But many miners who do move to factory jobs do so for better pay rather than for the working conditions. Often they hang onto their pit tackle in the hope of returning to the pits one day. That is the best measure of their attachment to an occupation which so horrifies the comfortable middle class.

9 Civil war at the top

In this chapter, we look at the politics and character of two other major industrial unions: the militant Amalgamated Union of Engineering Workers and the ultra right-wing Electrical, Electronic Telecommunication and Plumbing Union. In these two unions, the political struggle between left and right has been far sharper than in most unions and has led to much in-fighting, bitterness and ballot-rigging.

The AUEW was known in the nineteenth century as the new model union, because of its effective organisation and centralised administration. It traces its history back to the Friendly Society of Journeymen, Steam Engine Makers and Millwrights, formed in 1826. Since then it has grown by three major mergers: in 1851, when the FSJSEMM merged with several unions to form the Amalgamated Society of Engineers; in 1920 when the ASE merged with nine more engineering unions to form the Amalgamated Engineering Union; and in 1967-70 when the AEU merged with the foundryworkers, construction workers and the draughtsmen's union to form the present Amalgamated Union of Engineering Workers.

The union was originally a snooty craft union: until 1912, it would not admit unskilled workers. It admitted them between 1912 and 1917, then once again became an exclusive craft union until 1927. An indication of its traditional conservatism was that it did not admit women members until 1943.

How the left took over the AUEW

Unlike the big general unions described in Chapter 7, the AUEW is a highly democratic union in the sense that most posts are filled by election not appointment. It has an elaborate constitution, based on that of the United States, with careful provision for an elected parliament, executive and judiciary. But as we shall see below, this does not mean that the political views of AUEW members are reflected in the union's government.

Until 1968, the AUEW was right-of-centre union. In that year, Bill Carron retired as president. His chosen successor was another right-winger, John Boyd, a highly conservative tuba-playing member of the Salvation Army. But Boyd was defeated by a new man from Manchester called Hugh Scanlon, a milit-ant ex-communist. Scanlon's election marked the triumph of the left – although by itself it did not transform the union in the way that Cousins' victory in 1956 transformed the TGWU, because the AUEW's constitution does not give so much power to the president. But the left also won key elections for the executive and for the all-important national committee. They capitalised on a general resentment against Carron's leader-ship and against the Labour incomes policy which Scanlon resolutely opposed. The battle between left and right had been going on for years, but the right had been on top until the 1960s.

Under the new leadership, the AUEW swung dramatically to the left. Between 1969 and 1973, it supported seven one-day political strikes. It opposed every form of incomes policy, and was the most strident opponent of the Tory Industrial Rela-tions Act: after 1972, it was the only TUC union that refused even to appear before the industrial court and it refused to pay any of the fines imposed by the court. When fines of £50,000 and £75,000 were imposed on the union, court sequestrators had to take money directly from the union's bank account. In May 1974, when faced with further sequestration, the union called a national engineering strike. This only lasted a day until an anonymous industrialist agreed to pay the money for the union.

Yet after 1974, the right wing in the union began to reassert itself, and between 1974-5 its candidates began to win back many of the posts they had lost in the 1960s – partly because union members had become disillusioned by the left-wing lead-ership and partly because the introduction of postal ballots raised the turnout and thus hindered left-wing candidates. In 1975 John Boyd, who was beaten by Scanlon in 1968 and in 1970, triumphed over left-winger Bob Wright, to win the gen-eral secretaryship. At the same time, right-wing candidates began to win elections for the national committee and local officerships.

But to understand how the battle was fought, we must understand the complicated structure of the AUEW. The chart

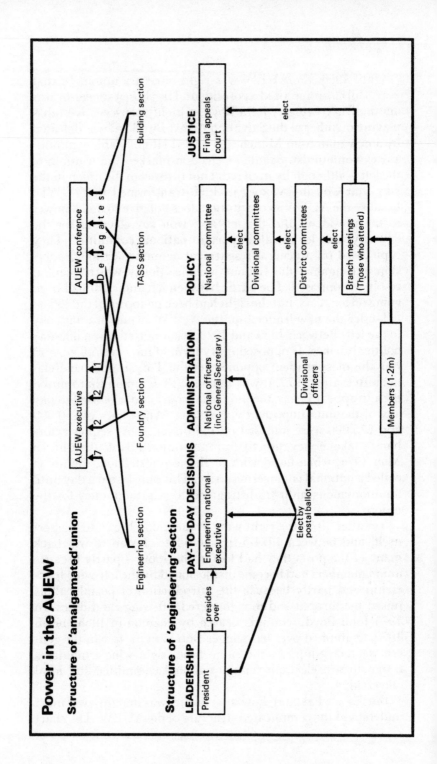

Power in the AUEW

Structure of 'amalgamated' union

Engineering section

AUEW conference

Delegates

Building section

TASS section

Foundry section

AUEW executive
1
2
2
7

JUSTICE
Final appeals court

elect

POLICY
National committee
elect
Divisional committees
elect
District committees
elect
Branch meetings
(Those who attend)

Members (1-2m)

Structure of 'engineering' section

LEADERSHIP
President

presides over

DAY-TO-DAY DECISIONS
Engineering national executive

ADMINISTRATION
National officers
(inc. General Secretary)

Divisional officers

Elect by postal ballot

opposite shows the four component sections of the post- 1970 AUEW (the four sections have never been properly amalgamated). The only section that really matters is the engineering section to which 1.2 million of the total AUEW's 1.4 million members belong.

The AUEW constitution is closely modelled on the American theory of the balance of powers. The national committee, with its members elected from the rank-and-file, is meant to be the union's parliament. The president and the executive, re-elected by nation-wide poll, represent the administrative arm of the union. Finally, the union has its own version of the Supreme Court, known as the Final Appeals Court. This court enforces the rules as laid down in the union's rule book.

Let us look at each in turn. The national committee normally meets once a year for a fortnight in a seaside resort to determine the union's policy for the following year. It is made up of fifty-two delegates, two from each of the union's twenty-six regions. All are rank-and-filers, but they are elected in a most undemocratic fashion. Each delegate is chosen by his divisional committee, a committee which in turn is elected by the smaller district committees, which in turn are elected by badly-attended branch meetings. This wedding-cake tier structure successively distils and exaggerates the effect of participation. Given that when one group elects representatives by a small voting turnout, the results tend to be distorted, it is not hard to see how successive repetition of this effect, tier-by-tier, will accentuate the distortion. That is why eighteen of the fifty-two delegates elected in 1976 were members of the communist party.

On the Sunday before the committee meets, the two rival political factions meet at separate pubs to plan their tactics for the fortnight. The first battle is the elections to the standing-orders committee. Each faction fights hard to win control of this committee, because it determines the course of business and chooses which motions are debated. The results of these elections provide a good guide as to which faction will dominate the committee over the fortnight.

The fifty-two men of the committee sit round long trestle tables watched by the executive members who sit on a platform overlooking the whole proceedings. The debates have a curious formality. Before they begin, the president conducts a roll-call

to check that every member is present. Any unfortunate committee member who oversleeps has to explain if he turns up
late.

The policy adopted by the committee has to be enforced by
the executive throughout the following year. If the executive
wishes to change its policy, it has to re-call the national committee. Until the late 1960s, the right-wing faction had a slight
predominance on the committee, and could usually fend off the
left-wing motions. Then a few key divisions changed hands,
and the left wing took control.

No other union is so hamstrung by the decisions of its annual
conference. Although the national committee is greatly
influenced by the union's president, it commits him and the
executive to a fixed line of policy for the following year.

If the union wishes to change its policy even on such a
detailed matter as a national wage claim, it has to re-call the
committee. A re-call is a long, slow and cumbersome process.

In most unions, the officers are either appointed by the
executive or elected for life. The engineering union is one of the
few unions that requires all its officers to be regularly re-
elected. Even its general secretary and president have to submit
themselves to the electorate. All officers have to be re-elected
after three years, and subsequently after every five years of
office.

The union's executive is made up of full-time officers. It is
therefore a more effective restraint on the power of the president and general secretary than the executives of most unions,
which are made up of relatively ill-informed part-timers who
meekly submit to their leaders' advice. The executive meets
every Tuesday at the union's Peckham headquarters.

The union has taken a great step forward by introducing a
postal ballot for its officer elections. Every member now
receives an individual ballot paper through the post. This
means that the number of people who vote in any election has
jumped dramatically. Turnout in elections now varies between
thirty per cent and fifty per cent. The turnout is usually higher
for local elections, where more members know the candidates.

The introduction of the postal ballot was pressed by the
union's right-wing faction, which believed that it would benefit
from higher participation. For just this reason, the left wing
vehemently opposed it. The national committee approved the

introduction of the postal ballot by a vote of only twenty-six to twenty-five in 1971. The left wing, however, continued to take every opportunity to reverse this decision. It attempted to kill it in 1972, and only lost by twenty-seven to twenty-five. It could hardly argue against the principle of the postal ballot, so it concentrated its fire on the practical difficulties. It claimed that the postal ballot would be far too expensive, and produced greatly exaggerated estimates of the cost.

When these arguments failed, the left wing took up the battle at branch level. Many branches refused to supply the names and addresses of their members to enable the ballots to be posted. By early 1973, over eighty branches were still refusing point-blank to operate the ballot. The executive, which by then was in the hands of the left wing, refused to discipline these erring branches.

However, in the first few rounds of elections that followed the introduction of the postal ballot, the left wing managed to maintain its hold. In the spring of 1973, the one official communist member of the executive staved off a challenge from an elderly right-winger, albeit by a narrow margin. This dashed the right-wing's hope that the postal ballot would quickly upset the left-wing bloc.

Then in 1974-5, the postal ballot at last produced the swing to the right that the right wing had expected. John Boyd swept into power as the new general secretary against left-winger Bob Wright by a majority of 164,000 to 96,000 in a poll of over thirty per cent (compared with the turnout of eleven per cent in the non-postal election of 1968 in which Hugh Scanlon beat John Boyd). There was a clear correlation between other right-wing victories and high turnout. Thus communists were defeated in Barrow (turnout 55 per cent), Ashton-under-Lyne (47 per cent), Cardiff (38 per cent), Glasgow (37 per cent) and Oldham (37 per cent), but in the ballot for national organisers, left-wingers won three (average turnout under 30 per cent).

This turnround severely threatened the left-wing leaders' control of the union. At the national committee that summer they returned to the argument about costs, claiming that the new higher rates of postage meant that the ballot was too expensive and should be scrapped. But they were just outvoted by twenty-seven to twenty-five. The left did not give in so easily. A local member of the Communist Party in Merthyr wrote to the executive to complain that one of the two delegates from South Wales (both of whom had voted in favour of the postal ballot) was ineligible because, although he had been branch president for eight years, he had not been formally re-elected in 1975. This was quite true, so the executive expelled him and asked South Wales to send a substitute. But the left wing soon found a flaw in the substitute; he had only been an adult member of the union for six years, whereas the union rules require every delegate to have been a member for at least seven years. So the executive of the union meeting on 13 May agreed to expel the substitute as well. No mention was made of any other complaint. That decision meant that there was still a twenty-six to twenty-five margin in favour of the postal ballot. But the executive met again three days later, when John Boyd, then executive member for Scotland, was absent. He little realised the plans that were afoot. The left-wingers had discovered by now that the second of the South Wales delegates had been elected at a meeting of nineteen people (a typical level of turnout) at which the credentials of two people were in doubt (although this was quite irrelevant since sixteen voted for him). The executive voted three to three on a motion to expel the delegate, so the casting vote rested with the president, Hugh Scanlon. He voted in favour of expelling the delegate. With the two delegates now out of the way, a new vote was taken of the whole national committee which produced a tied vote, twenty-five to twenty-five. So once again Scanlon had a casting vote. He cast it against postal ballots.

Whereupon the right-wingers took the dispute to court. On 11 June, the high court ruled that not only was the executive wrong to expel both the Welsh delegates, but also that Scanlon had misread the union's own rules, which did not allow him a casting vote on the national committee. The court therefore banned any more elections unless they were held by postal ballot.

The row was typical of the shenanigans that are a commonplace in the union. Both factions are so desperate for power that each will use any trick to win – although the left wing tends to be rather more unscrupulous.

The third body in the union's constitution is the Final Appeals Court. The court consists of eleven men, elected by branch ballot from eleven regions. Like the national committee, the court is entirely composed of rank-and-filers. It deals mainly with appeals against executive decisions, which may come from members or union officers. However, the court is overtly political. It is divided between the two factions of left and right, like all the other bodies of the union. Thus, for example, in October 1973, the court split six to five on a disputed election result involving a communist and a moderate. The moderate court members voted for the moderate, the communists for the communist. Given the court's totally political approach, it cannot play an important role as the independent judiciary that the union's constitution hankers after. That is why so many of the union's internal rows end up in the civil courts.

Because the court is elected by branch ballot, it is as undemocratic as the national committee and just as open to ballot-fiddling. In 1973, for example, a ballot in a key election to the Scottish seat was forged so as to allow the election of a communist candidate, which gave the left a one-vote majority on the court.

Communist supporters at one branch in East Kilbride forged sufficient signatures to give the communists a majority. But, unfortunately for the communists, they were discovered by several legitimate members of the branch who had been unable to find the meeting on the night the vote was alleged to have been held. They complained to the union headquarters in London, who duly dispatched an investigator. He confirmed that the ballot had been rigged. But the union executive only voted by four to three to annul the result (the left wing would not accept the evidence) and then voted four to three to take no disciplinary action whatever. There the matter might have rested – but the story was then published in the *Economist* and later by the television programme 'This Week'. This prompted parliamentary questions and eventually a police investigation. As a result of the investigation, two men were convicted and jailed on fraud charges.

The union still retains the centralised administration which earned it the nickname of the new model in the nineteenth century. Some fifty-five per cent of the union's staff work at the head office in Peckham (compared with the TGWU, in which only ten per cent work at head office, and the GMWU where twenty-two per cent work at head office).

The union's headquarters has been in Peckham since 1900. It consists of the original redbrick Victorian mansion, with the union's name emblazoned on the front, linked to a newer and duller modern office block. The office is run by the general secretary. It boasts a large ICL computer, which stores and processes everything from postal ballots to wage agreements. Once the engineers' was one of the few unions that owned a computer, but now the electricians, the TGWU, the journalists, the builders, the railwaymen and NALGO all own computers or regularly buy computer time.

The engineers' computer is under-used, and unlike most computers is left idle at night. Their computer chiefs have tried to press the TUC to set up a central computer service for all trade unions, but without success.

Hugh Scanlon has his office at Peckham, but is seldom to be found there. He is usually kept busy by the ceaseless round of conferences, committees, meetings, strikes and foreign trips. However, he is normally in the office for each Tuesday's executive meeting.

Scanlon was born in Australia, although he came to Britain at the age of two. When he left school, he started work in Manchester as an instrument maker. He was reared in the traditional militant Merseyside engineering industry. He became an official of the union, and in 1936 joined the Communist Party. He was not one of the many passive communists who joined the party in this period, but a dedicated activist and convinced Marxist. In 1941 he addressed the anti-war communist 'People's Convention'. In 1945 he was adopted as a communist candidate for Stretford, but was never elected.

After the war, he continued his rise in the union and became a divisional organiser. In 1954 he made his first bid for a seat on the executive, but was defeated. In the following year he left the Communist Party. He did not try again until 1961, when he ran again against a right-winger. After the election, there were allegations of Communist Party interference, and the result was declared null and void. Two years later, Scanlon finally triumphed.

As a member of the executive, Scanlon soon built up his reputation as a militant. It was on an avowedly militant platform that he stood for the presidency of the union in 1967 against John Boyd. Scanlon was elected, and although another of his opponents, Reg Birch, was a communist, the official communist organ, *Morning Star*, supported Scanlon. Scanlon won the second ballot by a few thousand votes. Yet only 11 per cent of the union members voted in the election, 5.7 per cent for Scanlon.

Since then, Scanlon has established himself as a national figure and the personification of hard-line trade unionism. He is a more political and less practical man than Jack Jones. His Marxism is more ruthless and less democratic than Jones'. In September 1968, for example, he addressed a fringe group of militants known as the 'Engineering Voice Assembly' in London and urged a national engineering strike that autumn with the following dictatorial words: 'We must face facts. If we balloted the whole membership, the decision to strike would be defeated. The membership want leadership: they have leadership. It is up to all militants to explain to the membership what the leadership is doing.' Such rule by decree has characterised his presidential years. Yet few men who are such keen golfers as Scanlon (handicap eight) turn out to be revolutionaries.

Scanlon's life style is somewhat more expansive than one might expect. He does, for instance, have two houses (one rented on a low rent from the union) – even though, some years before, he lost a house which almost literally fell over a cliff because of soil subsidence. The union provides a variety of perks, including a car and cheap housing. But he shares little of the flamboyance of militant comrades like Clive Jenkins. His rhetoric is intense but the arguments are drab and repetitive. He does, however, get on well with engineering employers; he has a reputation as a man who keeps his promises.

The crumbling merger

In recent years, the AUEW's power has been on the wane. Its cash flow has been in terrible shape (even though it has invested in valuable property assets). It lost over £1½ million in 1971 and £1.7 million in 1972. It broke even in the next two years but in early 1975 was back in deficit. Between 1969 and 1973, membership fell steeply. In many industries, AUEW men left the union to join the TGWU. The AUEW, failed to win support for any national strike action over engineering wages, mainly because the devolution of wage-bargaining had robbed the union's national negotiations of all but symbolic significance. In 1972, a guerrilla-style sit-in campaign was totally defeated by the employers, and in 1974 a national overtime ban was abandoned because of lack of support. Even in the one-day political strikes, most AUEW members worked normally.

At the same time, the four-way merger began to crumble. Successive attempts to agree a common rule book were voted down by the engineering section's national committee because the rules gave too much representation to the other three sections. The 1975 proposals suggested that the engineering section, with eighty-five per cent of all AUEW members, would only get fifty-eight per cent of the seats on the executive (seven out of twelve) and only sixty per cent of the delegates to the national conference (182 out of 300). The right wing in the engineering section was especially concerned because two of the other three sections (the white-collar section, the Technical and Supervisory Staff (TASS), and the construction section) were communist dominated. The merger is unlikely to collapse altogether, but the prospects of a truly integrated union are now remote.

How the right overthrew the communists in the EEPTU

In the AUEW, the left-wing faction threw out the right-wing faction in the 1960s. But in the electricians' union (now called the EEPTU) the right wing threw out the left wing and has since dominated the union so that it has become easily the most right-wing in the TUC. (An excellent and detailed account of this affair can be found in *The Road from Wigan Pier: a biography of Les Cannon* by Olga Cannon and J.R.L. Anderson, Gollancz 1975.)

The union (originally called the ETU) was founded in 1889 and until the second war was in the middle-left of the political spectrum. It is a craft union, but one in which participation tends to be low because of the dispersed nature of electrical work.

The communists began their assault on the union in the early 1940s and produced such a wave of resentment in the union that in 1943 the leadership called a special conference to discuss the problem.

In 1948, communist Frank Haxell fought moderate Jock

Byrne for the general secretaryship of the union. On the first ballot, Byrne led Haxell by 27,000 votes to 25,000, and was expected to win easily on the second ballot. But Haxell got over 33,000 votes on the next ballot while Byrne could only muster a little under 29,000.

The ballot had been fiddled in at least ten branches (although not by Haxell himself). Woodrow Wyatt, who led the campaign to expose the corruption in the union, found that one branch in Blackpool 'voted' on the first ballot: Byrne 5, Haxell 695; and on the second ballot: Byrne 5, Haxell 695. The branch had only 559 paid-up members.

Haxell's victory marked the beginning of the communist takeover of the ETU, although domination of the union was not complete until the mid-1950s. In 1956, the communists held the following positions in the union: president, general secretary, assistant general secretary, six out of the eleven-man executive, four out of five national officers, and twenty area officials out of thirty-nine. This list does not include 'fellow-travellers' and other near-communists. It was a startling achievement, since only some 700 out of a total union membership of 220,000 were members of the Communist Party.

The communists might have easily maintained their domination for many years, had it not been for a member called Les Cannon who quit the party and exposed its misdeeds. At the age of twenty-five, he had been elected to the ETU's national executive: the youngest member of the executive ever. He would not have climbed the ladder of power so quickly had he not joined the Communist Party at the age of nineteen. He seems to have joined the communists for the same reason that so many on the left did in the 1930s: a feeling that only total revolution could solve the appalling problems that then faced Britain. It may also have been due to opportunism: a realisation that membership would help his progress within the union.

In 1954 he left the executive to take a job as an assistant education officer at the union's training college at Esher. Already friction was developing between him and the communists. There was a row over his salary. He only got £672 a year, although he had been promised more when he took the job. Two years later, Cannon quit the Communist Party. According to his biographers, this was not because of the Soviet invasion of Hungary, but because of a long period of reappraisal. Cannon's decision precipitated the showdown between him and the communist clique. The first move was made by Haxell and his men: Cannon was given the sack on the spurious grounds that the union could no longer afford to run the Esher college, and the college was closed. It reopened within a year, but Cannon remained excommunicated.

This move stung Cannon into action. He decided to try and get his own back on the executive by throwing all his energy into fighting division nine in the south of England. He would easily have beaten the sitting communist member, but the ballot was rigged. This was done by declaring invalid the returns from a series of branches that had backed Cannon, on the pretext of a technical breach of the rules. From then on, Cannon embarked on a desperate campaign to fight the communists. At his own expense, he circularised the union's 675 branches, but to little avail.

The next crunch came after another round of elections in London. Cannon was attending a count at a branch, and noticed a Communist Party member walk in with a large holdall stuffed with ballot forms. Not unnaturally, he put in a complaint and asked for an investigation. The union leadership did not investigate Cannon's complaint, but accused him of trying to discredit the union. Cannon was fined and disqualified from holding office for five years.

Cannon had been elected as a delegate to the TUC just before his disqualification, but never received his credentials. He was able to show that the decision to withdraw his credentials had been taken before he was expelled. He then held a press conference just before the congress began, outlining what had happened. The reaction from the TUC was characteristically wet. It took no action at all, although Walter Padley of the shopworkers brought up the issue in debate. Subsequently only Padley and Vic Feather (who was later to be TUC general secretary) took up Cannon's cause.

By now, a group was forming around Cannon to fight the communists. The leading figures besides Cannon were Frank Chapple, Mark Young and Jock Byrne.

The TUC slowly became involved, but it was not till May 1960 that it issued an ultimatum to the ETU: either there must be a judicial inquiry, or the ETU must bring a libel action. If the ETU did neither, it would be booted out of the TUC.

However, by this time the law had overtaken the ETU. A case was pending in the courts, brought by Chapple and Byrne.

Byrne had once again fought Haxell for the position of general secretary. He had lost by 19,611 votes to 18,577. The returns from 109 branches had been disqualified because they were said to have been posted too late.

The Cannon team was convinced the disqualifications were a fraud and began to collect the evidence that was to convict the communists. This involved some incredible detective work. Cannon managed to get hold of the ballots that were disqualified for 'late posting'. He travelled round and asked the branches involved when they thought they had posted them. They gave a variety of dates, all well before the deadline. Cannon then studied the postmarks on the ballots, which were a series of dates after the deadline. He suddenly spotted the telltale mistake: all the dates were in geographical order. So he deduced what had happened: a man had been sent out with the ballots to re-post them after the deadline, and had travelled around the country doing so. Cannon was able to work out the likely route he must have taken.

The trial eventually opened in April 1961. The judge found in favour of the plaintiffs and declared that Byrne had been elected in the 1960 election; and recommended that there should be stringent safeguards on the next elections.

Byrne took office and promptly appointed Chapple and Cannon as his assistants. But many of the old communist clique remained in office, headed by the union's president, Frank Foulkes.

It was at this point that the TUC, belatedly, took action. The TUC demanded a fresh election for the presidency and also demanded that all those ETU members found guilty should be barred from holding office for five years. The communists, who still had a majority on the ETU executive, refused: and so the TUC expelled the ETU. The communists' final demise was now close at hand. In the next round of elections for the executive, they were slaughtered. Six out of the eight communists lost their seats.

Meanwhile, Cannon dropped out of the limelight. He went back to work at the union's Esher college, and at the same time began to read for the Bar. But his interest in the union did not dwindle. In 1963, after the communist attempts to appeal against the court verdict failed, Frank Foulkes was expelled from the presidency. Cannon decided to stand for the position of president himself. Curiously, many of his colleagues urged him not to do so. Some distrusted Cannon for his arrogance and intellectualism. Others said that he would not get on well with Frank Chapple, who had now been elected as assistant general secretary.

Cannon won by a huge majority. This marked the final humiliation of the communists by the moderates. He and Chapple then proceeded to reform the union from top to bottom. They reformed the ballot procedure. The job of running the union's elections was given to the independent Electoral Reform Society. A direct postal ballot was introduced, so that all the union's members could receive their ballots directly. A computer was installed with every member's address on tape, so that ballots could be organised efficiently. The control of the appeals committee (which hears members' appeals against executive decisions) was put in the hands of rank-and-filers. Previously, the communist leaders had been able to control the committee which investigated appeals against their own decisions. A full-scale reform of the unions' structure was also carried out. The old geographical branches were replaced by industrial branches. This meant that each branch was made up of union members in a similar industry, rather than members who lived in the same locality. Cannon also set up national industrial conferences. The eleven executive positions were made full-time instead of part-time, and the term of office was extended from two to five years. Over-frequent elections can mean that executive members spend more time electioneering than doing their executive jobs.

Cannon also had the tricky problem of what to do about the communists. Should they be banned from holding office? It was decided to ballot the members on this issue. The vote was: Yes 42,187, No 13,932. That was the end of the road for the communists in the ETU. Under Cannon's leadership, the union's recruitment soared after years of stagnation, and in 1967 the union merged with the plumber's union. Earlier, Cannon had got the union's name changed to the Electrical, Electronic and Telecommunication Union, to give it a modern flavour. After the merger with the plumbers, the union's name became Electrical, Electronics, Telecommunication and Plumbing Union:

such a long-winded name that it is seldom used in print.

Cannon himself was not elected to the TUC general council until 1965, and then only with some difficulty. Most of the big unions opposed him.

For the next five years, Cannon fought in the TUC for moderation. He argued passionately for incomes policy against the left-wingers who surrounded him. He also took a surprisingly middle-of-the-road view of the industrial relations law. When the Tories published their plans for the Industrial Relations Act in 1970, Cannon took a pragmatic view. He did not believe that such legislation was necessarily harmful to trade unionism, and he criticised the TUC for its dogmatic refusal to discuss the details with the government.

But tragically, at the age of fifty, Cannon died of cancer. His death left a gap in the leadership of moderate trade unionists that has never been filled since. No one has emerged with the same combination of sanity and intellect. Had Cannon lived he would almost certainly have become a trade-union cabinet minister in a future Labour government, and the first successful one since Ernie Bevin.

The EEPTU has remained firmly anti-Marxist since Cannon's death. Frank Chapple was elected general secretary in 1966, after Jock Byrne resigned because of ill health (Byrne died in 1970, the same year as Cannon). After Cannon's death, Chapple was elected president in 1972.

Chapple, who before 1942 was a full-time organiser for the Young Communists League, became the most right-wing member of the TUC general council. He has led the EEPTU in a series of bitter attacks on the TUC. In two successive TUC conferences, Chapple and his men walked out in disgust. Indeed, by a strange irony, the EEPTU came close to being expelled from the TUC once again. The union strongly disagreed with the TUC's non-cooperation policy towards the Industrial Relations Act. In particular, it wanted to register. The TUC made it clear that anyone who disobeyed the TUC instructions would be expelled. At the 1972 Brighton conference, thirty-five small unions were suspended pending total expulsion. The EEPTU might easily have been among them, had not Chapple and the EEPTU executive decided to delay the decision to register. Earlier, Chapple had promised to ballot his membership on the issue, and nobody doubted that

that would produce a decision to register.

Chapple is moderate about everything except the wages of his own members, when he is as militant as the next man. He has none of the polish of Cannon. He is a tough and blunt man, who seldom minces his words. He is still unabashedly working-class, and his main hobby is racing pigeons. He believes that unions should keep out of politics, and is adamant that unions have no right to challenge the law or interfere with the democratically elected government of the day.

Who jilted who?

The electricians' union was only founded in the first place because the old Amalgamated Society of Engineers refused to admit electricians to its membership, and ever since there has been a curious love-hate relationship between the two unions. In 1920, nine craft unions merged with the engineers. The ETU would have been among them, but a ballot of its members showed a majority against.

The idea of a merger was revived in 1970. The logic of a merger was industrial : there was a large amount of duplication between the two unions in many industries, and the same job could be done for a lower cost per member by a merged union. The same was true of the EEPTU and the GMWU: and talks about a merger were also started with the GMWU.

Although there was industrial logic in a link-up between the ETU and the engineers, there was little political logic. The engineers were the most left-wing of unions while the ETU was one of the most right-wing. One theory was that Frank Chapple hoped that in a merged union the balance would be tipped to the right, and he (or another right-wing EEPTU man) might be elected leader. This seemed a bit fanciful. The talks dragged on and off for years, but neither merger now looks likely to happen.

10   Four industrial giants

This chapter analyses the other powerful unions in the TUC, in railways, steel, shipping and building. First, the railways. The National Union of Railwaymen is the biggest railway union and has much in common with the NUM. Both unions operate in heavy and, until recently, declining nationalised industries. Their headquarters are almost opposite each other in London's Euston Road, and they have often worked together ever since the brief Triple Alliance when the two unions allied with the transport workers. But there are two other important unions on the railways, unlike the mines. They are the Associated Society of Locomotive Engineers and Firemen (ASLEF) and the Transport Salaried Staffs Association (TSSA).

Railwaymen have traditionally been as militant as the miners – notably in the period between 1908 and 1926 when their power was at its height. But there has only been one prolonged railway strike since the war, in 1955, although only ASLEF took part. However, there have been innumerable disputes, work-to-rules and go-slows. ASLEF, for example, ordered varying forms of strike action in 1965, 1967, 1968, 1971, 1972, 1973 and 1974.

The NUR, founded in 1913, represents all kinds of railwaymen, from porters to drivers, while ASLEF represents drivers. The NUR is mainly interested in getting general wage rises and helping the lowest-paid, while ASLEF is concerned with raising the wages of the drivers. This means that ASLEF tends to stick out for high differentials.

ASLEF is only one-eighth the size of the NUR, but it has considerable power, because if all its members strike, the whole train system comes to a halt. This was demonstrated in the one-day ASLEF strikes in 1972-4, when the union repeatedly stopped the whole rail system, even though the NUR was working normally.

ASLEF is a typical craft union. Its membership has declined fast, and this has made its attitude more conservative and restrictive. Its militancy has paid off in that drivers' earnings have risen faster than average industrial earnings, but differentials have not been widened. Between 1961 and 1974, for example, drivers' pay rose by only 176 per cent, while average railway earning rose by 210 per cent (in a period when average industrial earnings rose by 160 per cent). However, the death of the steam-engine has made train-driving a much easier job.

Today, the leadership of the NUR is politically moderate. Sir Sidney Greene, the NUR general secretary up till 1975, was one of the few modern trade-union leaders who was actually more moderate than his predecessors. He was unexpectedly propelled into the top job in 1957, when the general secretary, Jim Campbell, and his probable militant successor, Tommy Hollowood, were both killed in a car crash in Russia.

Greene is not a flamboyant man. He did not abandon his family life for the union, like his predecessors. He values his privacy, and keeps his telephone number ex-directory. As Anthony Sampson put it, 'Sidney Greene . . . seems the quintessence of the modern moderate – clerical grey, quiet voice, garden in Middlesex' (*Anatomy of Britain Today*, Hodder, 1965).

Greene was succeeded in 1974 by the equally moderate Sidney Weighell (pronounced 'wheel', appropriately enough). Weighell comes from a line of rail-union men. His grandfather was one of the founder members of the NUR, and his father was an unpaid NUR official. When he was twenty, Weighell had ambitions in soccer: he played inside-left for Sunderland although he never made the first team. Two years after he went into football, he returned to the union, his family love, and worked his way up through the union. He had started as a train-driver, but moved up through the union hierarchy to become assistant general secretary before he got to the top in 1974.

His union career was marred by an acute personal tragedy in 1956, when his wife and young daughter were both killed in a car crash. Weighell was left with a two-year-old son. But he later remarried and now lives at Bishops Stortford. He travels to work every day by train: second-class and paying the fare himself. He is an amiable man, whose passion for railways quite eclipses his interest in politics. He is more approachable than Greene, but as yet lacks the grip on the union that Greene achieved. In 1975, his first year of office, he nearly found himself leading a national railway strike – much against his own will. His executive, egged on by its Marxist president, Dave Bowman, insisted on pressing its full thirty-five per cent claim. Fortunately for Weighell, British Rail decided to give in.

The NUR is one of the few unions that believes that not all its members are entitled to stand for office. Anyone can stand for the executive, but to be elected a full-time officer, a candidate must pass special exams. Only the ISTC (Iron and Steel Trades Confederation) and UCATT do the same. The exam papers cover general knowledge, arithmetic, English, accountancy, politics and trade-union affairs. The papers are set by a special sub-committee set up by the executive. The rule reflects the professional approach of the NUR.

The twenty-four man NUR executive is made up of four representatives from the six areas. Each area elects one man to represent each of the four groupings of railwaymen (drivers/freight men/workshop men/others). It sits round an oval table in one of the most elegant trade-union rooms in the country.

The executive has not become much more militant in recent years, although there were six communists on the twenty-four man executive in 1974. The NUR's election system makes it tough for the communists to make much headway. Every member of the executive is elected for three years, and is not allowed to stand for re-election. This means that any individual's term of power is limited, and that officials like the general secretary have correspondingly greater power over the executive.

The contrast with ASLEF is notable. ASLEF also has three-year terms, but executive members are allowed to stand for re-election, and normally do so. Although the ASLEF executive is made up of part-timers, most of them spend more time working for the union than for the railways. Thus, most of the men on the ASLEF executive are professional unionists, with greater power over the general secretary. ASLEF only has nine men on its executive.

The NUR has an imposing headquarters in the Euston Road, just down the street from the miners. ASLEF is tucked away in an Edwardian mansion in Hampstead and does not even have a nameplate outside: it was stolen many years ago. When ASLEF first acquired the building in 1921, there was a local outcry: the middle-class residents of Hampstead did not approve of trade unionism on their doorstep. The building used to belong to the Beecham family (of Beecham's powder fame). It was built by Sir Joseph Beecham in 1903 at a cost of £40,000, although ASLEF bought it for just £10,000. Inside, the building is full of elaborate decoration: mahogany carvings, splendid ceilings, and a great carved oak staircase with a large turquoise bauble at the foot (the 'Beecham pill').

At one end of the building there is an old ballroom, where King Edward VII was once entertained with music. Now, this fine room only echoes to the sound of wage demands. The offices of the ASLEF officials are lined with prints of steam locomotives, and in the executive meeting room there is a gleaming model locomotive, carefully preserved in a glass case. The hearts of all ASLEF men belong to the days of steam.

Ray Buckton, the ASLEF general secretary, has an office with a bay window fronting onto a grassy garden, full of mementoes from railwaymen all over the world: a reminder of the international loyalty of railwaymen, unmatched in any other industry. Abroad, as in Britain, most train-drivers have their own exclusive union.

Ray Buckton is one of the most charming and friendly men in the trade-union movement. But his politics are confusing. He appears on *Tribune* platforms as a dedicated socialist. But he has to represent a highly-paid group of men: and the battle to maintain differentials on the railways is the very reason why ASLEF exists as a separate union from the NUR.

Buckton is too nice a man to be a natural militant, but he has to play the part because of the militancy that dominates his executive. His parents were both Tories, and Buckton himself was briefly a Tory. He was an activist in the Young Imperial League, but soon changed to socialism. He began life as a landscape gardener at Nunappleton Hall in Yorkshire, but in 1940 he moved to become an engine-cleaner at York. He quickly became involved in the labour movement, first as a union branch secretary, and then as a York city councillor. He was short-listed for several parliamentary seats, but withdrew when he decided to make his career in the union.

In 1956, he was elected to the ASLEF executive, and in 1960 he became a full-time officer. He was posted to Dublin as the union's Irish officer (a branch of the union which was later disbanded). In July 1963 he became assistant general secretary, and when the then general secretary, Albert Griffiths, died. In 1970, Buckton was elected to the job by a crushing margin.

Since then, he has had a torrid time, in a series of strikes. He has had to suffer the full force of public hostility, ranging from threatening phone calls to excreta in envelopes. For some of the time, he has had a Special Branch bodyguard.

ASLEF's membership has declined fast, due to the rundown of the railways and to the elimination of firemen when the steam engine passed into history. It reached its peak membership of 77,152 in 1948, although it enjoyed a brief revival when many drivers deserted the NUR to join ASLEF after the seventeen-day strike in 1955. The strike had been staged by ASLEF and opposed by the NUR. As a result, ASLEF's membership rose by 5,000 to touch 74,000. But, in almost every year since, ASLEF's membership has dropped. In 1975, it stood at just 28,899, and was still falling.

The decline in membership has contributed to ASLEF militancy: the union has felt a greater urge to assert its individuality. On many occasions, the NUR has suggested that it should take over ASLEF. Indeed, this was backed by the TUC in 1966. But ASLEF has resisted stoutly. If the merger had taken place, it would almost certainly have improved the railways' strike record: nearly all the full stoppages on the railways in the 1960s were caused by ASLEF action.

ASLEF fought a long drawn out battle between 1972 and 1974 to increase drivers' pay, relative to other railwaymen. The other two unions, British Rail, and the government firmly opposed the ASLEF claim. In the winter of 1973-4, the ASLEF action reached its peak. There was no regular weekly train service and no Sunday service for over two months. Then, in February 1974, ASLEF postponed action for the course of the election campaign to help the Labour party.

In the same period, the militant influence on the ASLEF executive increased: after the 1973 autumn elections, the Marxist left took a five to four majority, and the one communist, Bill Ronksley, was elected president of the union. The ASLEF campaign proved a total success. In the summer of 1974 an inquiry awarded nearly all that the union had demanded.

The third railway union, the Transport and Salaried Staffs' Association, is more moderate than the other two. It represents the railway clerks and a hotchpotch of other white-collar workers, ranging from Thomas Cook staff to Waterway Board clerks. But railway clerks account for some 52,000 of the union's 72,000 members.

The union was founded in 1897, but nearly collapsed soon after. Its first full-time general secretary, John Challenger, faced a barrage of criticism, and became so depressed that he committed suicide in a Paris hotel in 1905. But the union managed to stay alive, although it hardly ever organised a strike, except in 1926. Usually the union's members work normally and allow the other two unions to strike, knowing that they will share the proceeds if the strike is successful. This moderation is partly due to the fact that the union's members are more moderate, and partly because they have little industrial power, compared to the other two unions. In 1972, TSSA, for the first time, did join in a campaign of industrial action: banning overtime and working to rule. In practice, the TSSA action was meaningless, since few of its members worked overtime anyway, and the rules could not be stretched to cause chaos, as elsewhere on the railways. But it reflected the increasing nationwide militancy among previously moderate unionists.

When the ballot was held in 1973, under the Industrial Relations Act, members in all three unions voted to reject the wage offer. ASLEF members voted to do so by a twenty-three to one margin, NUR members voted to do so by a seven to one margin, while TSSA members voted to do so by only two to one: a surprisingly accurate reflection of the individual union leaders' militancy.

The TSSA is now led by David Mackenzie, who was elected in 1973 to succeed Percy Coldrick. Mackenzie narrowly beat Tom Jenkins (Clive's brother) for the job. But no major change of direction can be expected under his leadership.

Nerves of steel

In the steel industry, like the railways, there is a major industrial union and a small craft union, but there are also competing white-collar unions. The big industrial union is the Iron and Steel Trades Confederation (110,000 members) and the craft union, the National Union of Blastfurnacemen (11,000 members). These two have clashed just like the NUR and ASLEF.

The NUB has called two strikes – in 1971 and 1975 – in the hope of improving differentials, but both were defeated when the NUB came under heavy pressure from the ISTC and other TUC unions.

The ISTC is an intriguing union because it is so opposed to strikes. It has never called a national steel strike (apart from the 1926 general strike) which would be highly damaging, because it could permanently wreck many furnaces and bring much of industry to a halt. It is prepared to discipline leaders of any unofficial strikes, and has often sacked officials who have called strikes without approval from the national executive. The union has managed to preserve this authority because it is highly undemocratic. It has never held a conference of its members (unlike any other union in Britain), although the first one ever is planned for 1976. The general secretary is not elected but appointed by the executive council.

The last general secretary, Sir Dai Davies, kept well out of the public eye and refused to talk to journalists. The new secretary, Bill Sirs, is just as moderate but is concerned to modernise the union and to be more open. However, he is determined to maintain the union's relatively strike-free record.

The NUB is led by Hector Smith, but the union has had a battle to survive. Both the ISTC and the TGWU have tried to take it over and the union's membership has anyway been on the decline.

The union that rules the waves

The National Union of Seamen is an eccentric union – mainly because most of its members are normally out of the country.

The NUS (not to be confused with the National Union of Students) organises merchant seamen, and finds it difficult to call a strike by the nature of its industry. It has about 50,000 members but has never been a home for militants.

The union has only organised two major strikes: in 1911 and in 1966. The 1911 strike qualifies as the world's first multi-national strike. Seamen from five countries took part. The strike was based on demands about manning, accommodation and hours of work. But the main motives were wages and the refusal of the International Shipping Federation to even discuss the claims with the International Committee of Seafarers'

Unions which they claimed did not represent the seamen. The strike lasted two months, and ended in partial victory for the NUS and the other unions.

The NUS has twice led a right-wing palace revolt against the TUC: the first occasion was in 1926, when the NUS executive was the only union executive which did not support the general strike. Indeed, the union, under the leadership of Havelock Wilson, who had led the union since its foundation, actually voted to lend £10,000 to a breakaway right-wing miners' union set up in Nottinghamshire to oppose the official strike – the Miners' Industrial (Non-political) Union. The money was never, in fact, lent, but the TUC did not get the assurances they wanted from the NUS, and in 1928 the TUC annual congress voted unanimously to expel the NUS. TUC unions began to recruit seamen in competition with the NUS. However, the quarrel did not last long. In 1929, the NUS stopped backing the breakaway miners' union, and the union was readmitted to the TUC. The second occasion was in 1972, when the NUS were booted out of the TUC for cooperating with the Tory Industrial Relations Act.

The strike in 1966 in support of a wage claim was therefore out of character with the union's record of moderation. The strike dealt a damaging blow to the economy. It weakened the balance of payments, and Harold Wilson claimed it was partly responsible for the draconian measures of freeze and squeeze which his government had to take later that year.

The dramatic feature of the strike was Wilson's allegation that the strike was organised by a 'small group of politically motivated men'. This allegation was probably based on some private discussions with the NUS general secretary, Bill Hogarth, who may have told Wilson that he was being out-voted by communists and other left-wingers on the executive. The Wilson claim was airily dismissed by many as 'reds under the bed' rhetoric, but it was not an inaccurate description.

Up till then, the NUS electoral system was rather loose. It was naturally difficult to keep an accurate record of members, and to set up permanent branches for men who were always on the move. Such branches as there were, were based at ports, but there was no register of members at each branch.

As in the EEPTU, the mobility of members made it easier for militants to get control. There is little doubt that communists travelled from branch to branch of the NUS, voting at each, to ensure the election of left-wing candidates to the executive.

The communists were not defeated until the round of elections in 1972, when a series of reforms in the union's rules made the going harder for the communists. These reforms were linked to the union's decision to register under the Industrial Relations Act, with the object of getting an approved closed shop (under the Act, only registered unions could apply for a closed shop). This was in direct defiance of TUC policy, and led to the suspension of the NUS at the 1972 Trades Union Congress. The burly NUS leaders stormed out of the TUC with gestures of disgust.

Before the union could register, it had to submit its rules to the Registrar for approval. The Registrar asked for some changes, and the union's leadership took this opportunity to reform the rules entirely. In Folkestone, in May 1972, Bill Hogarth put a long list of rule changes to the NUS conference. Some of these reforms were merely administrative: reducing the number of branches, raising contributions, and deciding to hold conferences biennially. The two important reforms were:

1   Introduction of strike ballots. In future, a ballot must be held before a national strike is called. A simple majority will be needed to call a strike. If this provision had been in force in 1966, there might not have been a strike. Previously, there was a provision in the rules for the calling of a ballot, which needed a two-thirds majority to endorse a strike, but the executive was not compelled to hold a ballot (and did not in 1966).

2   Registration of all members. In order to vote in elections, each union member must register at a branch and cannot transfer to another branch without thirteen weeks' notice. If a member votes on any motion, he cannot vote on a similar motion at another branch within thirty days.

As Bill Hogarth put it: 'This is really to avoid a member jumping back and forward, up and down and around the country attending different branch meetings and dealing with the same subject matters.'

The rules were all passed, and significantly the leading militants on the NUS executive, like the 1966 strike leader, Joe Kenny, were defeated in the elections in the same year. Left-wingers in the union were also defeated in their attempts to get the union to merge with the TGWU, which has long wanted to

take the NUS over. A merger would give the TGWU real
industrial power in sea transport, which it has always lacked
except in the docks.

However, the union's move to the right was partially
reversed in January 1974, when a militant new general secretary, James Slater, was elected in a very low poll. By a strange
irony, the new voting system helped the left wing because so few
seamen registered that the turnout was only two per cent. Mr
Slater was among the group of militants in favour of the 1966
strike, some of whom were branded by Mr Wilson as 'politically motivated men'. The next round of executive elections
also brought a sharp swing to the left.

The builders' new union

The Union of Construction, Allied Trades and Technicians,
the main builders' union, is a recent amalgamation. It sprang
from the old Amalgamated Society of Woodworkers which, like
the engineers in the AUEW, still remains the dominant section
of the new union. UCATT formally came into existence in
1972, with a membership of 280,000 and a headquarters just off
Clapham Common. The woodworkers took over three ailing
unions in succession at the turn of the 1960s: the Association of
Building Technicians, the Amalgamated Union of Building
Trade Workers, and the Amalgamated Society of Painters.

Nearly all of these unions had hit rough times, and their
finances were near to bankruptcy. But the kindly woodworkers
agreed to rescue these lame ducks to form the new builders'
union. It was an odd animal from the start, and some doubted
whether it would survive.

But in 1972, its first year of operation, it mounted a major
national strike which helped to create the union's identity.
After ten weeks, the employers caved in and conceded a large
wage award, which raised basic wage rates by thirty per cent
and minimum earnings by sixty per cent over two years.

Building is such a decentralised industry that the union finds
it hard either to recruit members or to have real control over
actual earnings. Industrial relations are chaotic. This is mainly
because work is done on a casual basis. Men are only employed
for short periods on one building site, and then move on to
another. At the same time, the industry is fragmented into
70,000 different firms. Few jobs last long, and secure jobs are

extremely rare. On top of this, the industry is highly cyclical. Between 1966 and 1971, some 300,000 building jobs disappeared, while between 1971 and mid-1973 another 150,000 appeared. It is a hard, tough industry and it breeds hard, tough individualists.

It is also an industry where the worker is king. As George Smith, the Scottish leader of UCATT, put it: 'I have sacked more employers than have sacked me'. When times are good, the building worker can simply quit one site and join another if he dislikes the conditions or the boss.

Naturally in these tough conditions there is much hostility to the bosses. The union militants tend to interpret this bloody-mindedness as a sign of political radicalism.

What really angers the unions is that some 400,000 building workers belong to 'the lump'. All these men are self-employed, and usually operate in gangs. A typical lump gang will include plasterers, bricklayers, plumbers and other trades – so that an employer can get a job done by hiring one gang. Traditionally, men were attracted to the lump because it was an easy way to avoid paying income tax and national insurance contributions. Employers paid in cash and no one asked any questions. Various government attempts were made to crack down on this. These cut down some of the abuse, but few people in the industry believe that tax evasion has yet been ended.

Because the lump wages are determined by on-site bargaining, they can be extremely high in times of labour shortage: in 1973 some bricklayers in south-east England were earning weekly wages equivalent to £7,000 a year. The lump produces a number of damaging effects. First, no one is trained by the lump, because its gangs only recruit men who have already got skills. This helps to produce an artificial shortage of skilled men. This is worsened by the fact that the building unions, like so many unions, insist on absurdly long apprentice periods for those who do train – up to four years for a job which can easily be learnt in six months. Second, the lump helps to create a local labour monopoly on individual sites. This helps to force wages up in a more inflationary way than national agreements negotiated by the unions. Moreover, the lump gang can not only bid wages up before it starts work, but can, and frequently does, bid them up during the job by threatening to quit *en bloc*. Third, the lump style means that nobody takes responsibility for safety or insurance. Legislation on redundancy pay, industrial relations and contracts of employment is completely ignored. This helps to brutalise life on building sites. It is little wonder that many workers die and many are maimed every year because of the inadequate safety precautions, or that there is so much thieving and violence. The violent picketing during the 1972 building strike was the reflection of the industry's atmosphere.

UCATT has been under strong pressure from its militants to mount a tough campaign against the lump. The building militants have their own organisation called the Building Workers' Charter Group. This is made up of an odd assortment of left-wing activists, and its main aim is to pressure UCATT into more militant action.

Because of the nature of the industry, there is a very low level of participation in the union, which makes it easy for the militants to exercise a strong power.

George Smith, the UCATT leader, is a typical trade union official. He was born near Dundee, and began work as an apprentice carpenter. His father was an activist in the old Independent Labour Party, and he inherited the radical tradition. He soon became a union activist and also joined the Communist Party. He climbed up through the woodworkers' union and was elected assistant general secretary in 1949 as a communist. He left the communists in 1954, because he did not feel that communist dogma 'had much to do with the realities of trade unionism'.

Now, as general secretary, Smith appears a quiet but obviously frustrated man; frustrated by the stupidities of his fellow unionists, frustrated by the mindless militants below him, and frustrated by what he regards as rather crusty and stupid employers. He only seems really able to relax when he disappears into the dark room to practise his amateur photography.

11 Spanner in the works

Trade unions are frequently blamed for perpetrating a wide variety of restrictive practices, and sadly this allegation is often justified, although there is no reason to suppose that by so doing they are not representing their members' wishes. This normally springs from a historic fear of unemployment: the unions reckon that by stringing out work, they can keep more members employed. Unfortunately, today, many restrictive practices – for example, in shipbuilding – actually damage job prospects by lowering the industry's competitiveness.

Some unions have taken a progressive attitude to inefficiency. Perhaps the most notable example is in the electricity industry, where in 1967 Les Cannon's electricians pioneered a successful productivity deal which cut the labour force by over fifty thousand in the next seven years, while output per man rose sharply. Many of the top-rank union leaders are sympathetic to such progress, but lower down in the union hierarchy there is often intense suspicion of new technology and new working practices. Thus, for example, none of the unions involved at British Leyland can admit that the company is over-manned even though its output per man is only half the level of most of its European rivals.

This chapter is principally devoted to an analysis of restrictive practices in the printing industry. Printing is not typical, but it does exemplify the most restrictive union attitude to industrial progress.

The printing unions are the oldest in Britain: some can trace their history back two hundred years. As a result, they have established an unrivalled power and control of pay and conditions in the industry. In Fleet Street, above all, the printing unions have achieved phenomenal levels of pay. In mid-1975, for example, many compositors (the men who set type) were earning £10,000 a year (roughly four times the average industrial pay) and many of the most unskilled workers (like the men who stick on the labels in dispatch departments) were earning as much as £5,000 a year.

The main printing unions are:

● ·SOGAT – The Society of Graphical and Allied Trades. It has 183,000 members, many of whom are in the newspaper industry. Its members, who work in printing, are mainly unskilled men doing simple jobs in places like publishing (dispatch) rooms.

● NGA – The National Graphical Association. This was formed by a series of mergers in the mid-1960s, which took in the old Typographical Association, the Association of Correctors of the Press, the National Union of Press Telegraphists, the Associated Society of Lithographic Printers, and several others. It has 103,000 members: nearly all of them doing fairly skilled jobs. Unlike SOGAT and NATSOPA, it is a craft union.

● NATSOPA – The National Society of Operative Printers, Graphical and Media Personnel. It has 51,000 members, mostly in London. They do similar work to the SOGAT men, except that NATSOPA's membership is confined to the printing industry. The divisions between SOGAT and NATSOPA arise from a series of historical and geographical accidents. In many cases, towns are divided up between the unions according to agreed 'spheres of influence'.

● NUJ – National Union of Journalists. It has 27,000 members most of whom (though not all) are journalists. It would resent being classed as a printing union, but in recent years it has increasingly tended to behave as if it were one.

● SLADE – Society of Lithographic Artists, Designers, Engravers and Process Workers. It has 17,000 members, and is a craft union. Its members work on the production of plates, which are used for printing photographs, cartoons and drawings. They include camera operators, designers, engravers, etchers and photo developers.

● Institute of Journalists. It has 2,500 members. This is a right-wing rival to the NUJ. It is not affiliated to the TUC.

Politically, the non-craft unions are the most left-wing. NATSOPA and SOGAT are among the most militant unions in the TUC. The craft unions are more right-wing. The NGA registered under the Industrial Relations Act and was expelled from the TUC. The NGA also holds ballots before authorising strike action. In 1973, for example, its members voted by two to one not to take part in the TUC May Day protest strike.

Everyone in the printing unions agrees that the present gallimaufry of unions is undesirable. Every union leader says he is in favour of creating one printing union, but their words have not been translated into action. The NGA merger is the one major step towards unity that has been taken in the last decade, although SOGAT has absorbed several small unions.

Before 1966, SOGAT was known as the National Union of Printing, Bookbinding and Paperworkers. A plan was drawn up to merge the NUPBPW with NATSOPA to form a new union to be called SOGAT. The plan was agreed by both unions in 1965, and came into operation in 1966. The SOGAT executive consisted of the twenty-four-man executive of the NUPBPW plus the nineteen-man NATSOPA executive. Each of the two original unions remained in existence, but were known as SOGAT – Division 1 (NATSOPA), and SOGAT – Division A (NUPBPW).

The aim was to harmonise the two old unions' rules and create a completely new union by 1968. But the scheme collapsed in ruins in November 1968, when delegates to a conference at Brighton refused to agree the necessary new rules.

There have always been bitter personal rivalries between and within the printing unions. On several occasions in the past, NATSOPA's headquarters have been physically attacked by discontented members. In 1898 malcontents ripped out the gas fittings in the union's waiting-room and destroyed and stole union property. In the same year, the general secretary was assaulted by a member, and the executive advised 'extreme measures' to be taken to ensure his safety. Today, perhaps mindful of the past, the entrance to the union building is sealed off by electronically operated doors.

In 1964, NATSOPA and the NGA also had talks about merging, but it came to nothing. NATSOPA's former leader, Lord Briginshaw, was determined to achieve one printing union before he retired, but he failed. Briginshaw ran NATSOPA from 1951-75 and pursued a policy of what he called 'controlled militancy'. That means that the union was militant, but was run from the top. Briginshaw could personally halt any national newspaper whenever he liked. It was little wonder that managers cringed before him.

The general secretary of NATSOPA has to be re-elected

every three years: which means that he is always under pressure to keep delivering the goods (i.e. wage rises). But Briginshaw was never opposed after he took over: a measure of the personal dominance he achieved in the union.

The printing unions have more control over day-to-day management than unions in any other industry. Indeed, on the shop floor, management is completely under their control. The 1966 Economist Intelligence Unit report found that 'FOCs (fathers of the chapel, the printers' shop stewards) carry far more power over the employees than do management'. The father of the chapel is the effective department manager and can control up to nine hundred employees.

This extraordinary form of workers' participation is the anchor of the panoply of restrictive practices that characterises the industry. Since the men elect their immediate bosses – the fathers of the chapel – their bosses are naturally mainly concerned with reducing the workload and increasing wages. The real job of management, maximising output per man, is simply not performed. Thus, in Fleet Street, at least, productivity has stagnated although the industry has tremendous technological potential for productivity growth.

The real measure of restrictive practices in the industry is the extent to which machines are overmanned. The Royal Commission on the Press concluded after a detailed investigation:

> In the national newspapers, manpower is being squandered. If conditions there were to form a pattern for industries which have no shelter from foreign competition, it would be disastrous to the economy of the nation. In some newspapers, it would not be unreasonable to look for a reduction of about one third in the wages bill.

The *Daily Mirror* told the commission that about forty per cent of the labour it employed was unnecessary. The commission asked a management consultant firm, Personnel Administration Ltd, to report on the manning situation. The PA report showed that there was about fifty-three per cent overmanning in the production and distribution departments. It also found that overmanning was greater in those jobs which involved least skill. This meant that SOGAT and NATSOPA were the main offenders. The PA report reckoned that overmanning accounted for about eight per cent of the total budget of an average London newspaper office.

The 1966 Economist Intelligence Unit report, three years later – the most exhaustive study of the national newspaper industry ever carried out – reached similar conclusions. Overall, it reckoned that there was overmanning to the tune of thirty-four per cent, with the worst excesses in the production department. It estimated that overmanning cost Fleet Street about £4.9 million each year. But it emphasised that these estimates were very conservative: 'We believe we have underestimated the true potential' for manpower savings, its authors claimed.

Both the Royal Commission and the EIU suggested ways in which this overmanning might be reduced, but their recommendations were ignored. Nothing more was done until 1970. Then after a strike in Fleet Street in June, a 'steering committee' was set up to discuss how productivity might be improved. But it led nowhere.

The real scope for manning improvements is greater than either the Royal Commission or the EIU indicated. Both reports were concerned with working practices related to existing production techniques. They did not consider what could be done if newspapers were given a free hand to introduce modern-day printing technology: such as computerised typesetting, photocomposition, and automated binding and packing machinery. One newspaper told me that, with a free hand, Fleet Street management could reduce its labour force by a total of at least fifty per cent.

The unions have pursued a consistent policy of refusing to accept manning reductions, opposing nearly every form of technological advance and insisting at the same time that printers be paid higher wages and work shorter hours than any other section of the industrial manual labour force in the country.

It is quite understandable for unions to be deeply concerned with their members' job security and to oppose redundancies. They would not be acting for their members if they did not. But the printing unions go much further than this. Not only do they refuse to accept redundancies, but they will not even allow the labour force to decline by natural wastage.

There is a long tradition in printing of son following father into the trade. This leads to the belief that a printing worker has permanent property rights on a job, which can be handed down from generation to generation. So there is strong opposition to the disappearance of jobs, even if no one is made redundant.

The unions also have a strong interest in job preservation to maintain their own strength, which is directly dependent on their membership. This is a strong factor in the bitter demarcation disputes that occur from time to time. The unions do not want to lose membership by allowing men from a different union to do a job which their own members could do.

The first and most important restrictive practice perpetrated by the printing unions is control on entry into the industry. It is the unions who tell management how many new men they can recruit, and it is the unions who determine how long apprenticeships need to be. As the EIU report discovered, 'The industry is almost unique in the degree to which control of labour is in the hands of the unions'.

The unions insist on preserving various jobs for their own members and maintaining absurdly long apprenticeships. Most printers have to serve six years as an apprentice, and then twelve years in the provinces before they can work in Fleet Street. In fact, most printing skills can be taught within six months.

SLADE has one restrictive practice that is unique even by the standards of printing unions. Whenever a vacancy crops up for a job that can be filled by a SLADE member, the union refuses to let more than one man apply for the job. The union issues a white card to the chosen applicant, who can then go to management and apply for the job. Occasionally, the union issues a second white card if the management decides the first applicant is incompetent, but this is rare.

The NUJ also adopts a restrictive attitude to recruitment. It will not allow any Fleet Street paper to recruit journalists who have not served a three-year apprenticeship on a provincial paper. The NUJ maintains that this makes sure that all Fleet Street journalists have a proper training.

This restrictive practice is based on the understandable principle of Buggins' turn, but it has certainly deprived Fleet Street of a number of able journalists.

The next group of restrictive practices is designed to limit the amount of work done by each man. This arose from the (then) admirable practice of work sharing which was begun in the

1930s to avert redundancy. Unfortunately, since the war, these restrictive practices have tended to grow rather than shrink. Here are a few examples:

● In the composing room, no piece worker will begin work until enough copy has arrived to provide every worker with twelve lines' worth of setting. This means that twenty or thirty workers will not handle any copy until the last man gets his. This introduces long and unnecessary delay.

● Workers known as 'case hands' and 'stone hands' will not swop duties (although the work is similar) even though case hands tend to be under-occupied when the stone hands are very busy.

● Machine running speeds tend to be lower than the 'negotiated' running speeds. Negotiated speeds are nearly always well below the designed running speeds.

The final group of restrictive practices is merely designed to create excuses for additional payment. Here are some examples:

● Fat money. This is the term for money paid to setters when 'plates' have been set at another print works, and then brought in. The theory is that fat money is compensation to the setters for work, and thus money, they might have been able to earn themselves. But in effect it is a payment for doing precisely nothing. The amount paid out can be large. The EIU found that one paper paid £15,000 in fat money in 1965.

● Ghost money. This is paid when fewer casual men are employed than agreed by the union. The theory is that when there are fewer casual workers, the permanent workers have to do more.

● Historical extras. Special payments to encourage fast work for a particular reason are seldom discontinued when that reason vanishes. For example, an extra payment used to be made for a fast handling of the Saturday sports news for the *Evening News*, in order to get the presses clear for printing the *Sunday Dispatch* (which used the same process). The *Sunday Dispatch* is no longer in existence, but the extra payment is still made.

The level of earnings by Fleet Street printers is far in excess of what they deserve, whether measured by supply and demand, the skill required, the conditions of work, or even what public opinion considers to be fair. The EIU reckoned that 'The general level of pay is out of all proportion to the effort expended and the skill employed compared with most other industries.'

The EIU team were told by SOGAT men that some of the work was dangerous, but the EIU noticed that these same men performed what they claimed to be dangerous jobs when they had had too much to drink. Indeed, the EIU rather surprisingly found that 'drunkenness was such as would never be tolerated in other industries'.

The origin of restrictive practices cannot be blamed entirely on the unions: both the EIU and the Royal Commission found management was pretty lousy. Most Fleet Street managers go home before printing starts in the evening, and so manage to stay well out of touch.

Weak-kneed management has developed as a result of the industry's structure, and is more evident in Fleet Street than in the provinces. This is because national newspapers are often financed by wealthy peers, whose goal is political prestige rather than profit maximisation. They have been willing to continue to run newspapers, even on the basis of making a permanent loss.

The unions may have acted as a deterrent to the introduction of new national newspapers, and have certainly acted as a deterrent to the introduction of new provincial papers.

The Thomson organisation, for example, ran into tremendous labour problems when it tried to introduce major new provincial dailies in Reading and Hemel Hempstead. The unions would not agree to the manning of the web-offset presses which were critical to the profitable operation of the new papers.

Web offset presses first appeared in Britain around 1962. These presses are based on the dual principles of lithographic (i.e. photographic) reproduction plus indirect printing using a blanket roller which transfers the print from the plate roller to the paper. They have the particular advantage that they can produce excellent colour printing and can operate at high speed. They are more practical for provincial papers than national papers, for various technical reasons.

The presses were first introduced on provincial weeklies. There were few problems here, because the weeklies employed no NATSOPA men on the presses. The first problems began to arise when the larger weeklies and the provincial dailies tried to switch to web-offset printing.

NATSOPA saw the move to web-offset printing as a new opportunity to get their members into a new type of job. It claimed that since the process was quite new, the traditional who-does-what rules no longer applied. At the same time the craft unions like the NGA saw that their own members could be replaced by unskilled NATSOPA men. This clash between NATSOPA and NGA wreaked havoc with the attempt to introduce web-offset printing.

Both unions had a reasonable case, but neither was willing to accept compromise. Each feared that any agreement in the provinces would be the model for Fleet Street if it ever introduced web-offset printing, and should one union give in to the other, it would lose a lot of members.

There was a series of battles up and down the country. When the *Daily Mirror* tried to set up a web-offset plant in Belfast, it had so much trouble with the unions that one machine for double-width printing was never used.

The two biggest battles were with the International Publishing Corporation at Southwark and with Thomson Newspapers at Hemel Hempstead. In both cases it was not until the company decided to abandon the project that the unions made any serious attempt to cooperate.

IPC decided to set up a new printing works in 1964 in London rather than the provinces, because it felt it had a duty to expand employment for the traditional printing labour force in London. It was a decision it was soon to regret.

In January 1964, the management wrote to the unions and promised to pay higher than average wages in the new plant, as well as providing exceptionally good fringe benefits (longer holidays, better pensions, etc.) on the condition that the unions would cooperate to ensure that productivity was maximised (although IPC's proposed manning was higher than that on equivalent presses in Europe and the United States). The unions agreed.

Then, after IPC had gone ahead with the investment, the NGA suddenly announced that there should be three-and-a-half machine minders per press instead of two provisionally agreed. At the same time the familiar NGA versus NATSOPA clash reared its ugly head.

The dispute dragged on for months. Then the TUC was called in to investigate. NATSOPA asked the TUC to listen to its case, and naturally the TUC agreed to do so. When the NGA heard this, it refused to attend any TUC hearings on the ground that NATSOPA had nothing to do with the issue. The TUC inquiry never took place.

On 29 April 1966, IPC decided to close the works. A week later, they were re-opened after a new formula was agreed, subject to an investigation by a court of inquiry under Lord Cameron.

The Court criticised both sides and suggested a compromise formula. An interim agreement was reached, but it was far from adequate for IPC. The new plant steadily lost money, and by 1973 losses were running at £750,000 a year. It was finally closed in 1974.

Few other unions have developed such power or such a framework of restrictive practices as the printing unions. But the general approach to technological change is characteristic of the trade-union movement. Its hallmark is suspicious conservatism.

When confronted with innovation, the usual response is 'There must be something in it for management, therefore it must be against our interests as workers'. So the union either opposes the change, or demands pay rises to compensate for any benefit that management may gain.

The printing unions have no scruples about the use of industrial power: they will threaten strikes whenever they find that the newspaper is particularly vulnerable. For example, in November 1973, Fleet Street process workers refused to print pictures of Princess Anne's wedding unless they were paid extra money.

Some of the printing unions seem aware of what they have to hide. Two unions, SOGAT and SLADE, refused to cooperate with the Royal Commission. The commission was forced to conclude: 'The real reason why each of them refused to cooperate was fear of what might be revealed.'

Throughout the 1960s and early 1970s, the printing unions supported overmanning and remained implacable in their hostility to innovation. But provincial papers did manage to start introducing new technology, and in 1975 several major national newspapers, led by the *Financial Times*, declared that they intended to switch to computer typesetting. The state of the recession was so severe that the unions did not declare their outright opposition: especially since they realised that several newspapers were on the brink of closure. At the *Observer*, unions agreed to a twenty-five per cent cut in manning to stop the paper closing although no new technology was planned. This could mark a new era in union attitudes – but it will be a miracle if national papers succeed in introducing new technology and achieve low manning levels (which is the object of the new technology) without continuous union opposition, especially when the recession ends.

12   The white-collar revolution

'I am a round peg in a round velvet-lined hole. I am doing exactly what I want to do.' So says Clive Jenkins, the most imaginative, witty, brilliant, well-paid, opinionated trade-union leader of post-war Britain. Jenkins is the leader of ASTMS, the Association of Scientific, Technical and Managerial Staffs, Europe's fastest growing union. The union is Jenkins' personal creation and he runs it as his fiefdom.

Jenkins himself is now authentically middle class, but he began life as authentically working class. He was born the second son of a railway clerk in Port Talbot, in the South Wales steel belt. He left school at the age of thirteen (for which his parents were fined £5), and began training as a metallurgist.

As a metallurgist, he joined the Association of Scientific Workers. At the age of eighteen, he was elected a branch secretary. Soon afterwards he met Harry Knight, the general secretary of a rival union, ASSET (the Association of Supervisory Staffs, Executives and Technicians). Knight spotted Jenkins' talent and promptly offered him a job as a full-time officer of ASSET (even though Jenkins was not then a member of the union). So, in 1947, aged twenty, Jenkins became a full-time union man. Soon afterwards he became the union's organiser at London Airport, and organised his first big dispute when the old British South American Airline threatened large redundancies after two aircraft disasters over the Atlantic.

From then on, Jenkins scorched through the union hierarchy. At the age of thirty-four, he was appointed general secretary and became the youngest man ever to be general secretary of a British union. At that time, the union's membership was 18,000, and its annual income was £60,000. By 1975, there were 315,000 members and its annual income topped £3 million.

The union's explosive growth began in 1968, when Jenkins engineered the merger of ASSET with his old union, the Scientific Workers, to form ASTMS, with a membership of 75,000. This figure was quadrupled in the next five years, partly by a takeover campaign of smaller unions like the National Union of Insurance Staffs and the Medical Practitioners' Union and partly by continually searching out new areas for unionisation. The greatest influence in ASTMS' outstanding growth has been Clive Jenkins himself. He has been responsible for most of the ideas for the union's expansion, and he constantly keeps the union before the public eye.

He has tried to get his three assistant general secretaries and his national officers to do more of the pioneering work in new fields. But Jenkins still takes over when any of his juniors runs into problems. Today ASTMS organises the British Museum, the London Zoo, doctors, publishers, insurance clerks, foremen, dons, chemists, technicians, and many, many others. Its members earn between £20 a week and £15,000 a year.

The union's officers are the youngest of any British union, and many of them are graduates. They are also the best-paid union officers in Britain. Jenkins' own salary was around £11,000 a year in 1975. Characteristically, he works on a contract with the union.

Jenkins once had ambitions to become a Labour MP. In 1964, he got his union executive to approve his application for the Labour nomination at Shoreditch (few other unions would allow a man to be both an MP and a general secretary). Shortly before he appeared before the selection committee, a letter was circulated to the committee which attacked Jenkins in savage terms. It accused him (untruthfully, but not unconvincingly) of entertaining Trotskyists on board his yacht. Jenkins was not selected.

He later sued a right-wing official of another union for publication of this libel who then settled by paying a sum of money into court before the action was heard.

He used to be a communist. He joined the party in 1947 in protest at Bevin's foreign policy, but left in 1952 because, he says, 'it was too authoritarian'. He does not sound ashamed of having been a member, but speaks of it as of a diverting interlude which was rather fun. He is still a Marxist sympathiser in theory, but his life style is hardly Marxist, and he will only admit to being an admirer of Marx's philosophical forerunner, Hegel. However, he can lend himself to the most sycophantic defence of communism: notably on the occasion of the visit to Britain of Soviet union leaders in 1975.

Potential middle-class recruits may dislike Jenkins, but he is the kind of tough, clever man that everyone likes to have around to deal with a boss. Jenkins has the ability to keep spotting new areas for unionisation, and to keep his face regularly before the public. He is one of the union world's leading TV performers. As he puts it: 'I have always been fascinated by the media . . . I am interested in floating off ideas into the public consciousness.' (Jenkins, incidentally always appears hypnotised by his own vocabulary.)

The ASTMS headquarters is a modern block just off Camden High Street. Even the entrance, with its cactus garden, has the Jenkins stamp. Nature seems to have invaded the building. Ivy crawls up the staircase, and Jenkins insists on fresh bowls of flowers in every office. His own room is as expansive as his vocabulary, complete with fitted carpets, a row of telephones, colour TV and a red leather armchair. On his desk lies a sensuous nude statuette given to him by a friendly lady potter.

On his way to fame, Jenkins managed to make himself reasonably rich, unlike any other trade-union leader. He lives in a sixteenth-century house in Essex with two children and Moira, his wife. He runs a cabin cruiser, on the Regent's canal alongside his regency house in London. Altogether, he owns property once estimated to be worth around £100,000.

His life style is exuberant and expensive. At the same time as he denounces the capitalist system in flesh-creeping terms, he personally exploits it to the full.

Jenkins is popularly believed to be a militant left-winger. In his speeches, he certainly plays up to this image. He has, for example, been one of the loudest voices to attack every form of incomes policy. In January 1973, he cheerfully told a radio interviewer that his union was adopting every means available to destroy the Government's wage freeze: 'We are indulging in our normal Vietcong guerrilla activity. Our responsibility is to be bright, sharp and alert'. And within the TUC, Jenkins always casts his votes with the far left.

The paradox is that he is one of the most pragmatic men in trade unionism. His union only calls some 40 strikes a year, usually on specific economic issues. Jenkins has always believed in the need for an Industrial Relations Act (though rather different to the Tory version), and he also believes in the radical redeployment of labour.

The real Jenkins character is revealed by other people's attitudes towards him. He is disapproved of by nearly every other trade-union leader, except a few personal friends like Ray Buckton, David Basnett and Geoffrey Drain. Other trade unionists feel he is too slick and too clever. They envy his stinging phrases, his elegant wit and his regular TV appearances. They are jealous of his union's phenomenal expansion. And, often as not, they find that he is trying to recruit members in industries they consider their own.

As a result, Jenkins was not elected to the TUC general council until 1974. In 1968, when the TUC created a new seat for the Professional, Scientific and Technical Sector, Clive Jenkins lost to George Doughty of the draughtsmen by the crushing majority of six and a half million. For years, ASTMS was the biggest union unrepresented on the general council. In 1967, at the annual conference of the Confederation of Shipbuilding and Engineering Unions, Jenkins led his delegation out of the meeting when the chairman refused 'a point of order' and told him to 'hop it'. That was typical of the prevailing attitude of union bigwigs to the upstart Jenkins.

On the other hand, employers who deal with Jenkins respect him. They admire his intelligence and the speed with which he will make a deal. They prefer dealing with a union that is competent and never luddite. They know that Jenkins will stick to a deal.

Jenkins has also spotted that, for white-collar workers, security of employment can be more important than income. In the late 1960s and early 1970s, there was a spate of big company mergers. Many of these led to widespread redundancies, in which white-collar workers suffered even more than manual workers. One of the most obvious economies in any merger is to remove the duplication of head-office staff.

Jenkins capitalised on this trend in a series of advertising campaigns. In November 1968, for example, he ran a full-page advertisement in *The Times* which read: 'A man gets the push because his face doesn't fit. It could only happen at one level in British industry – at the top'. The way to avoid this, the advertisement went on, was to join ASTMS.

Another campaign was run in 1971-2 on a larger scale. It took a series of newspaper advertisements and hoardings alongside commuter railway stations in the south-east,

designed to catch the eye of those millions of overworked,
underpaid clerks who commute to their offices each day. The
slogan was unmistakably middle-class in its appeal: 'My
tragedy was that I picked up a pen instead of a shovel'. This
campaign was part of Jenkins' attempt to take over the City of
London. He aims to unionise insurance workers, shipping
office clerks, brokers' clerks and even the merchant banks staff.
So far, most of the City has been able to ward off the Jenkins
challenge, but there have been significant breaches in the
dykes. Jenkins began his attack on the insurance companies.
He saw fertile ground here in what he described as the 'sky-
scrapers about to be depopulated by the twin pestilences of the
computer and the consultant'.

A typical example of Jenkins' practical and sensible
approach was his early conversion to flexible working hours,
pioneered in West Germany in the late 1960s. The theory was
simple: workers should not have to work a fixed day, but should
be able to vary their hours of work. In the past, this would have
been dismissed as impractical on the grounds that if everyone
came and went at different times, the efficiency of the business
would be impaired. But the Germans devised a scheme to beat
these objections: every worker would have to work the 'core
time' in the middle of the day, say between eleven o'clock and
four o'clock. Outside these hours, they could work as they chose
provided they clocked up a total of forty hours a week, or 160
hours a month. This system proved a great success.

By 1972, the idea was spreading quickly through western
Europe. It was obviously more suitable to offices, than to
factories (where workers are more interdependent and so usually all have to turn up at the same time).

In Germany, the system had not been enthusiastically supported by the unions, for rather absurd reasons. The chief
objection was that it allowed workers to do more than an
eight-hour day, which contravened the long union campaign
for short hours. The advocates of flexible hours expected
British unions to be equally blinkered, and many reacted sus-
piciously and argued that they provided more benefits for
managers than workers.

But Jenkins recognised a popular reform of working conditions, which could improve the quality of life for his members.
He gave full support to flexible hours and used his power to

persuade employers to adopt them.

Another example of Jenkins' pragmatic attitude was his policy towards the Industrial Relations Act. Jenkins was naturally an opponent of the Act, but a reasoned oppponent. He had always supported the idea of extending the influence of law to industrial relations: and had long argued for legislation to protect workers from unfair sacking.

Jenkins was reluctant for his union to deregister, as the TUC campaign against the Act demanded. He knew that it would cost ASTMS a lot of money (because of lost tax privileges), but he was also worried that deregistration would critically weaken ASTMS in its struggle against staff associations and mini-unions, with which it had to compete in many offices.

The ASTMS conference, however, voted to deregister, but in order to change its rules (which said the union should be registered), a two-thirds majority was needed. By a narrow margin, a blocking third triumphed. This, it seemed, was a convenient position for ASTMS: it had shown it had tried to carry out TUC policy, but had failed to do so, apparently because of a technical hitch. However, the TUC did not buy this, and it listed ASTMS for suspension along with other erring unions. On the eve of the 1972 Brighton TUC conference, Jenkins dramatically announced that he had written to the Registrar asking for.ASTMS to be deregistered. The TUC reluctantly judged this as sufficient reason to give ASTMS a stay of execution.

It was a revealing episode of Jenkinsology. It showed how reluctant Jenkins was to deregister, and the extent of his personal power. Few other general secretaries would have been able to take such a major policy decision without consultation.

Most unions not only refused to register under the Act, but also refused to take any advantage of those parts of the Act designed to help unions. They would not appear in the National Industrial Relations Court, they would not talk to the Commission on Industrial Relations, and they would not make any use of the new law on unfair sackings.

Jenkins adopted a completely different approach. He did appear in the NIRC, and used it and the CIR to advantage. For example, he had a recognition dispute with Horizon Holidays. It was taken to court and then referred to the CIR. The CIR backed Jenkins, and the Act's machinery enabled Jenkins' union to win more ground.

Jenkins also made a lot of use of the unfair sacking law. He was the first union leader to take up members' cases and argue them before industrial tribunals. Nothing could better show the style of Jenkins' leadership: militant rhetoric combined with pragmatic action.

Jenkins accepts the need for redeployment of labour: he accepts that economic progress will require vast changes in the employment structure. But his views on incomes policy are neanderthal. He has stridently opposed every attempt at incomes policy. His claims to be able to wreck any incomes policy seem to have helped recruitment to the union (though he has, in fact, been much less successful at breaking incomes policies than some other union leaders).

Jenkins wrote of the 1961-2 pay pause:

> The active, the clever and the frustrated who had been 'paused' looked around for a vehicle to carry their resentments; they found it, often to their surprise, in the unions that had been set up and were standing bonily waiting for this fleshing-out to happen.
>
> *Tiger in a white collar*, Penguin, 1965

He has also been one of the few British union leaders to go European. In 1971, the whole ASTMS executive travelled to France to discuss the consequence of British entry into Europe. Although the union decided to oppose British entry, Jenkins has made sure that the union has stayed closely in touch. ASTMS has employed an observer in Brussels to file regular reports on European affairs.

Jenkins is also fond of saying that he would like to go and unionise the French and Italian middle classes, and it is quite possible that he might do so, one day.

Jenkins' whole approach to union strategy is summarised in a remark he made in early 1973: 'I don't care whether there are Heinz's 57 varieties of Government. Our job is to look after our members.'

The TASS challenge

The main rival union to ASTMS is the 120,000 strong Technical and Supervisory Staff, one of the AUEW's four regiments. Unlike ASTMS, TASS membership is entirely confined to the engineering industry, in which both unions now have almost the same number of members. There is not much love lost between them. TASS regards ASTMS as over-concerned with publicity and under-concerned with providing services for its members. It does not believe a general white-collar union like ASTMS can match its quality of specialist services.

The annual subscription to TASS is higher than to ASTMS, but TASS does provide more special features, such as a technical service. In 1973, it had around eighty technical booklets in print, available to members at cheap prices. These included such spellbinders as *Axial Vibrations of Motorship Crankshafts, User's Guide to Slurry Pumps* and *Cavitation with Centrifugal Pumps*. The union also supplies a special service for any invention made by their members: ensuring that the inventor, rather than his employer, gets the profits from it.

The TASS headquarters is a pale yellow Georgian house, next to a theatre, overlooking the delightful green at Richmond in Surrey (previously it has been, in turn, a riding-school, a manor, an air-raid shelter, a refugee home and an employment exchange). Inside it boasts a large computer, which is used to provide a variety of information for union members. Each union member's personal and financial profile is on tape, and each union member fills in a form with details of working conditions in his company (everything from wages to the ventilation system). This information is then used by other TASS members who want to change jobs, and need background on a company they consider joining. TASS (previously known as DATA, the Draughtsmen's and Allied Technicians' Association) has always been one of the most militant unions, and is still the most militant white-collar union. Most of its members are draughtsmen.

The union is famous for its pioneering of plant-by-plant guerrilla action, leading to big national settlements. The aim is to win concessions at key plants, and then force other employers to follow suit. As a former TASS leader George Doughty put it: 'We like to concentrate the action. If you spread the butter too thin, well, it isn't very nutritious'.

A measure of the union's militancy was proved in the DATA evidence to the Donovan Commission. Between 1951 and 1964, there were official DATA strikes at 238 firms, involving 15,157 members and a strike payout of nearly £1 million. In this period, DATA spent a higher fraction of its income on strike pay than any other union in the country.

Another measure of the union's militancy was provided in 1973 when over eighty-five per cent of TASS members struck on May Day during the TUC protest day. This was a much higher response than in most unions. A survey carried out in 1968 showed that draughtsmen were more militant than most technicians. For example, sixty-two per cent of draughtsmen who were union members said that they had been involved in wage claims, where they would have been prepared to go on strike. Equivalent figures for laboratory staff, quality controllers and planning engineers were thirty-two per cent, thirty-nine per cent and thirty per cent respectively (*Reluctant Militants*, by B.C. Roberts and R. Loveridge, Heinemann Educational, 1972).

The militant George Doughty retired as general secretary of the union at the end of 1973, and was succeeded by the equally militant and communist Ken Gill.

All go with NALGO

While Clive Jenkins has captured all the headlines, other white-collar unions have also been growing quickly. The most prominent is the National and Local Government Officers Association (NALGO for short). In 1973, its membership passed the 500,000 mark, and will probably top 600,000 within a few years. Unlike ASTMS, NALGO has grown not because of personal flair and publicity, but merely because it has been able to tap the fast-growing public service white-collar labour force, from local councils, where it began, to nationalised industries and the universities (where it clashes with Clive Jenkins). The reorganisation of local government in the early 1970s produced a wave of apprehension and uncertainty among local government employees, which encouraged many of them to seek the protection that NALGO could offer.

NALGO's role as a trade union, bargaining for its members' pay, is a recent development. It was originally founded as a professional association, designed to advance standards of education and administration in local government.

In 1910, the NALGO general secretary, Len Hill, remarked that 'anything savouring of trade unionism is nausea to the local government officer'.

It was not until 1921 that it decided to call itself a trade union, and even then the title had no significance. NALGO did not belong to the TUC, it did not organise strikes, and it did not even take part in wage-bargaining. Any thought of behaving as a trade union disappeared with the General Strike. NALGO members felt no sympathy for the strike, and almost certainly a majority of them were Tories (as they are today).

NALGO's early achievements were considerable. It successfully fought to improve standards in local government. It struggled to stamp out jobbery, corruption and nepotism, and introduced such radical innovations as examinations. NALGO's first great battle was to establish pensions for local government officers.

But until the second war, NALGO remained a social, educational and welfare society. It continued to expand its social facilities. It could offer free beds in a convalescent home, cheap dental and optical treatment, widows' pensions, grants for hospital costs, life and endowment insurance and easy mortgages.

Holiday centres up and down the country were bought for exclusive NALGO use. In 1933, a NALGO motoring club was set up and in 1934 a plan was agreed to give cut-price boarding school education for members' children. The 1930s were a time when most unions were in decline, but NALGO flourished as never before.

After the war, things began to change. In 1943, a National Whitley Council was set up to bargain local government pay. NALGO got eight out of the fifteen seats for employees, and for the first time had the job of bargaining pay and conditions for its members. This was the start of NALGO's move into trade unionism.

As NALGO began to behave more and more like other trade unions (although it did not call strikes), it was argued that it should join the TUC. The idea had been raised back in 1921, but had been dismissed on the grounds that NALGO could have nothing to do with the TUC, because of its close attachment to the Labour Party. The debate inside NALGO raged until 1964, when a referendum of NALGO members produced a majority in favour of joining.

NALGO still remains a relatively moderate union by TUC standards. It might have broken with the TUC over the registration issue, had local councils not told NALGO that they would continue to deal with it exactly as before, whether or not it registered. This meant that NALGO had little to lose by deregistering.

However, by 1973, the moderation of the general secretary, Walter Anderson, formerly working as a solicitor, was noticeably out of tune with the new militancy, both on his executive and at the union's annual conference. Anderson argued for some months, on the TUC general council, that the unions should cooperate with the institutions of the government's pay and prices policy, such as the pay board. Then one Saturday in late spring, Anderson found his policy repudiated by a meeting of the NALGO executive. This was his breaking point, and he decided to resign and take an early retirement. Another moderate bit the dust.

NALGO's present general secretary is Geoffrey Drain. Drain is ostensibly more political than Anderson: he stood as a Labour candidate in 1950 and was a Labour councillor for Hampstead for many years. He is more ready to talk of NALGO organising strikes – although the union has never had a national strike since it was founded (and no strike of any kind before 1965). He also wants to politicise NALGO, although not to the extent of affiliating NALGO to the Labour Party.

Drain, although more left-wing than Anderson, is still a right-winger in trade-union terms. He is a close friend of Clive Jenkins (and still a member of ASTMS), but more distinctly middle-class, and had a university education. He belongs to Labour's social-democratic wing: he was one of the leading members of the Labour Committee for Europe, which represented the Labour pro-marketeers, and has little sympathy for extensive nationalisation.

Drain looks, talks and gesticulates exactly like former Tory minister Robert Carr: the similarity is almost uncanny. Like Carr, Drain seems to be an apostle of fairness, and it is no surprise to learn that Drain enjoys days in summer umpiring cricket matches. Indeed, Drain is often to be seen in the pavilion at Lords on a free afternoon. Maybe Drain followed a career in NALGO because it was the nearest union headquarters to cricket's headquarters. In the winter, he may be seen at White Hart Lane urging on Spurs. He is also a keen bridge player and bird watcher. Drain is nothing if not an enthusiast.

One of his problems as NALGO's general secretary is to bridge the gulf between the militancy of his activists and the conservatism of his members. The new left-wing militancy among the NALGO activists does not seem to reflect any widespread militancy amongst the rank-and-file. The NALGO activists are not prepared to acknowledge that the rank-and-file moderation is genuine; they talk as though members are merely 'unenlightened' or 'not very advanced in their thinking'. The fact that the majority of NALGO members probably vote Tory does not seem to bother them.

On every major issue which has faced NALGO in recent years, the response from members, as measured by the postbag, has been overwhelmingly conservative. When Anderson decided to quit, he was deluged with telegrams and letters of support from NALGO members. But attempts to move NALGO even further to the left have so far failed. The unofficial 'NALGO action group' (NAG for short), consisting of youthful leftists, tried to mobilise support for more militant politics. Although they have managed to get two NAG men on to the executive in the London area, their support seems to be waning. At the 1973 NALGO conference their performance was jeered. Optimistic right-wingers said they had been permanently discredited.

13 The weaker brethren

This chapter looks at some of the larger, but industrially weak unions. Their weakness is based on the fact that their industry is not a vital service (postmen, civil servants), or that the industry is not fully unionised (farmworkers, shopworkers), or that there is no closed shop.

The postmen's union (the Union of Post Office Workers) only discovered its weakness after the 1971 postal strike. Before 1971, the union had never held an all-out strike (except in 1926). Its predecessor, the Postmen's Union, called a strike of London postmen in 1890 after the Post Office insisted that all union meetings should be reported by official shorthand writers, but it was a fiasco and 450 postmen got the sack.

The UPW was formed in 1920 by a ten-way merger of miscellaneous Post Office unions, although it has never covered all Post Office employees. The Post Office engineers have their own union and several groups of workers still belong to civil service unions. Most, but not all, telephonists belong to the UPW.

This means that the UPW is not even master in its own house. With no closed shop and no industrial power, it is hardly surprising that the UPW has not been a strike-happy union. It has called the odd one-day strike and work-to-rule, but until 1971 firmly avoided all-out strikes. However, by the end of 1970, the UPW saw strike action as the only way to keep postmen's wages up with the average.

Tom Jackson, the union's general secretary, agreed that the union should take strike action in 1971, but he believed that an all-out strike would be a disaster. He favoured a guerrilla campaign – pulling out sorters unexpectedly in key offices like Mount Pleasant to produce maximum chaos at the cheapest price. But his executive was thirsting for stronger action. Its members were sure that an all-out strike would cripple the country in a few days, and they did not believe Jackson when he warned them that it could last up to three weeks.

In fact, the strike lasted seven weeks. During this time, the public found no difficulty in managing without letters. The telephones worked normally and dozens of private postal services sprang up to handle essential mail. The union was forced to an abject surrender. It had originally been offered an eight per cent rise, and finally achieved a nine per cent rise.

Tom Jackson and his postmen were bitterly disappointed, but they were most angry about hypocritical sympathy from other unions. Other militant union leaders declared that the postmen were the vanguard of the movement, but did not provide the cash the union needed. By objective standards, other unions were generous: the TGWU gave the postmen an interest-free loan of £100,000. But the postmen had hoped for more. They still believe that, if other unions had been a little more helpful, they could have won.

The impact of this defeat was startling. According to the conventional wisdom of industrial relations, a defeated union tends to become more embittered and militant. But the post-men's strike showed quite the reverse. The union veered sharply to the right. It realised that in the free-for-all world of collective bargaining, it was the weakest who suffered most. They also realised that leaders of the left-wing unions did not match their rhetoric with cash and support. Tom Jackson became more sympathetic to the need for an incomes policy and his public speeches grew steadily more moderate.

Jackson has a bristling handlebar moustache, but he is one of the younger trade union leaders – he was only forty-three when elected general secretary in 1967. He was born in the slums of Leeds, and his father died when he was only four years old. He left school at the age of fourteen and started work as a telegraph boy. It was a tough and grim childhood, but he only began to warm to radical politics during the war. He served in the navy in Ceylon, and was attracted to the revolutionary nationalist movement which was then developing on the island. He involved himself with the Trotskyist Sri Lanka Freedom Party.

When he returned home after the war, he was more angry about the poverty which still remained in Britain – of which he had seen so much as a child. In 1946, he joined the Communist Party. The Party members told him that he should try and get into a trade union, where the real power lay. So Jackson joined the UPW and became a branch activist. However, his disillusion with the Communist Party was swift. He left eighteen months after he joined.

He thought about a career in politics, but he felt that trade-union politics produced more power and more satisfaction. In a trade union, he felt he could achieve more improvements for his men than any backbench MP could ever hope to do. Jackson went quickly up the ladder of power in the UPW. In 1967 the then general secretary, Ron Smith, left unexpectedly to take a lucrative post as industrial-relations director of the British Steel Corporation. The assistant general secretary also left unexpectedly, and Jackson found himself the front-runner for the leadership. Jackson was elected by a vast majority, taking two-thirds of the votes, although three candidates stood against him.

He is a popular and friendly man, who has become one of the most robust moderates in trade unionism. He works intensely hard, with an average week of eighty hours. He lives in Brighton, and commutes between there and the union's Clapham office, but every week he spends several nights in the small flat which abuts the main office. At home, he enjoys impressing dinner guests with his own cooking.

His command within the union is complete. His executive is made up of twelve full-time officers and nineteen lay members who are elected by the annual conference each year. Since 1971, it has been rather too docile even for Tom Jackson. He complains that the executive does not pass on many of the grumbles of the members. This lack of communication can lead to trouble flaring up at the annual conference. The conference is bigger and more powerful than in most unions. Nearly every branch sends delegates, so that over 1,500 people attend. Besides electing the lay executive members each year, it also elects the full-time officers, although they do not have to submit to re-election once elected.

Down on the farm

One of the weakest unions in Britain is the farmworkers union: the National Union of Agricultural and Allied Workers. It is one of the few unions which has got smaller and less militant over the years. Since the war, it has organised no major strike, and its membership has dropped from 162,000 in 1947 to 90,000 in 1973. In the same period, total employment in farming has dropped by nearly forty per cent, but the proportion of workers who are unionised has also been almost static at twenty-five per cent. And although farming has been very profitable since the war, with an average annual growth in productivity of six per cent, farmworkers are still badly paid.

The weakness and apparent moderation of the farmworkers is a reflection of the change in British agriculture over the last century. In the nineteenth century, there were successive waves of strikes and lock-outs on farms all over Britain. The initial bitterness was a consequence of the enclosures movement, which deprived peasants of their land and drove them into the service of farmers. They lost their independence, and often suffered a cut in their standard of living.

There were frequent outbursts of rural riots: haystacks were set on fire and farm buildings and equipment destroyed. It was this rural violence that led to the savage sentences imposed on the Tolpuddle martyrs. These outbreaks took place well before trade unionism established itself on the farms. But in the second half of the nineteenth century there were regular strikes and lock-outs, organised in local areas by local unions.

Agricultural trade unionism began on a local basis. Although a national union was founded in 1872, strikes were mainly confined to regions. There was plenty of trouble at this time. The Lincoln Labour League, for example, fought thirteen separate battles with farmers in 1873 alone. In the year before, over 10,000 men were involved in a five-month lock-out in East Anglia (which has always been the strongest area for unionism on the farms: even today, some ninety per cent of East Anglian farmworkers belong to the union.)

Militancy on the farms persisted till the 1930s. The union's biggest strike ever was held in 1923 in Norfolk to fight wage cuts. Over 10,000 workers took part, and won a partial victory. Since then, militancy has steadily waned. The key reason has been the swift decline in the agricultural labour force. This has had two effects. First, because farmworkers knew that they might lose their job, they did not dare to strike. Second, the decline in the numbers employed per farm made union organisation much harder.

Today, when most farms only employ two or three men, it is almost impossible for the union to organise a strike. Three-quarters of farmworkers do not even belong to the union. (Yet even so, British farmworkers are more unionised than their colleagues in the United States or Europe.) At the 1972 union conference, the delegates urged the union to consider strike action. But the union's county committees advised that this would be quite impossible.

One reason why many farmworkers do not belong to the union is that it is one of the few remaining big unions which does not determine its members' wages by collective bargaining. Wages, in practice, are determined by individual farmers according to local supply and demand. However, every year the Agricultural Wages Board raises the minimum wage. The union has seats on the board, but the wage award is made by five independent members of the board. This means that the union can have a strong influence on the award by its arguments, but it does not bargain for it. In recent years, the minimum wage has risen substantially: up eighty per cent between 1970 and 1975. But even so, in the summer of 1975 it was only £30.50.

The union's social role is perhaps more important than its economic role. Its main function is that of a friendly society, providing a wide variety of benefits, insurance and help. As the union's general secretary, Reg Bottini, told me, 'one of our main functions is to act as a wet nurse'.

Farmworkers are not the most literate and educated men, as a result of their isolation. Thus they appreciate an organisation which will help them deal with the problems of twentieth-century life. The union is prepared to help with any problem, however small. Here, for example, are some of the cases the union dealt with in 1972, as noted in the union's annual report:

● [A company] Ltd were demanding £40 from our member to settle the bill for a hair piece which was £192. However, he had already paid the full bill, and on representation he received an apology for error.
● Following representation by union officer to local authority, members' children are now picked up and set down by school bus nearer home.
● Member's lettuces were ruined by spray drift applied by farmer. On officer's representation, compensation was received from insurance company.
● On officers's representation, an account for £1.10 sent to

the member in error by a television rental company was cancelled.

● Member tripped in pothole injuring her leg. After union's negotiations with insurance company, a full county council compensation was recovered.

● On union's representation, member's wife received needlework cabinet which was ordered in August and had not arrived.

● Union obtained compensation for damage done to member's garden by farmer's sheep.

(Source: *NUAAW Annual Report*, 1972)

These may seem trivial examples, but in today's complex world, people need more and more help with the maze of officialdom they have to confront. The unions have a vital role – to use their countervailing power against the stupidities and complexities of both private and public bureaucracy. They could develop such 'consumerism' a lot further. Unfortunately, few unions provide the same quality of service that the farmworkers get. The union also spends much of its time defending members from eviction from their tied cottages. In 1972, the union defended their members in 448 court cases.

Reg Bottini, the union leader, is a quiet man with a plaintive voice. He runs the union from a smart office in the Grays Inn Road in London. The site of the union's building used to belong to the National Union of Railwaymen. This reflects an old link between the two unions. In the days when a farmworker faced the sack if he became a union activist, the local railway porter would often be appointed branch secretary of the farmworkers' union.

Bottini does not look like a farmworker – and indeed he only became one by accident. He used to work as a clerk in a counting-house. But he was a pacifist when the second world war began (as he remains today). He was accepted as a conscientious objector and was set to work on land drainage in Huntingdonshire. During the war, he became a union activist, and in 1945 rose to the headquarters bureaucracy.

He was elected general secretary in 1969 as the centre candidate, against opposition from left and right. His private life is as unostentatious as his public life – he likes to spend his weekends gardening at his home in Oxted, on the edge of the Surrey stockbroker belt.

A nation of shopworkers

The biggest of the weak unions in the TUC is the 325,000-member Union of Shop, Distributive and Allied Workers founded in 1947. USDAW is a semi-general union, although its net is not cast so wide as that of the TGWU or the GMWU. Its main membership is in shops, but it also covers a range of light industry, from corsets to sweets, from slaughterhouses to tin box factories, from glue-making to perambulator-making.

The majority of USDAW members are women. In most of its industries, only a minority of workers belong to USDAW. As a result, USDAW is often not powerful enough to bargain wages. It is in a similar situation to the farm union: wages are effectively determined by supply and demand, but wage councils (appointed by the government) set a floor by prescribing a minimum wage each year. Any employer who pays less than the minimum wage can be taken to court.

USDAW is a moderate union, both politically and industrially. This is not surprising in view of the nature of its membership. It nearly decided to register under the Industrial Relations Act, but pulled back when it faced expulsion from the TUC.

The union's general secretary is Lord Allen (born in 1919). He is a short man with black-rimmed spectacles, who commands great respect within the union. At the USDAW conference, his command is complete, and his speeches alternately passionate and workmanlike. He has been a member of the TUC general council since 1951 and is one of the inner cabinet. He is such a charming and reasonable man that unionists and employers find it hard to disagree with him. His politics are moderate, but he has seldom challenged the left wing in public.

USDAW is one of the few major unions whose headquarters is not in London. It is based near Manchester airport in a modern building tacked on to a country mansion. Allen spends his days commuting between Manchester and London. He is one of the trade-union movement's committee men. He is a Crown Commissioner and also serves on such bodies as the British Productivity Council, the Central Training Council, the Manchester Business School Council, the National Economic Development Council, and a host of trade-union committees. He is a cricket fan and (like so many trade union men) a keen gardener – but his exacting schedule leaves little time for such pastimes. He was created a life peer in 1974.

Aggro in Whitehall

While unions like USDAW and the farmworkers have shown little tendency to get more militant in recent years, other weak unions have got so angry that their bitterness has overflowed into strikes. These have usually been predictable flops.

In the spring of 1973, the biggest union in the civil service, the Civil and Public Servants' Association, launched guerrilla strikes in protest at the Government's wage freeze – which had hit civil servants harder than most because they had been expecting a bumper rise that January (following the biennial review of the Pay Research Unit which sees whether civil servants' pay is up to the level of other similar jobs in business).

In February there was a one-day strike, followed by selective strikes by customs men (to the great delight of all travellers). The union spent £300,000 to finance these strikes, and then had to admit total defeat. This was the first ever major strike action in the Civil Service (although it had been seriously threatened in 1968).

Bill Kendall, the CSPA general secretary, justified the strike by saying that it showed that the union had some bargaining power and did not always have to accept what the Government offered. Unfortunately for Kendall, it is not at all clear that this *is* what the strike showed. Most people reckoned that it showed precisely the reverse. It confirmed the generally held view that if the entire Civil Service carelessly walked under a bus one fine day, the country would carry on much as before.

A more serious threat, however, was made at the CSPA's annual conference that very year. The conference told its members not to pay out increased pensions and social benefits in the autumn of 1973, unless their pay demand was met (the CPSA includes the workers in the Department of Health and Social Security who pay out these benefits).

This vote produced a storm of recrimination and angry speeches. Bill Kendall moved adroitly to 'refer the motion to the branches', which produced a majority the other way, and the action was never taken. But the first vote at the conference and the spring strikes revealed a new pitch of militancy in the union.

In the 1950s and early 1960s, the CPSA was dominated by moderates who had been elected in a post-war backlash against communist influence in the union. By the turn of the 1960s, this generation was showing some wear and more leftists were elected to the union's national executive. In 1968, Bill Kendall, a militant socialist, replaced W.A. Lines, a moderate, as general secretary. Kendall insisted that the union should draw up a strike strategy for the first time in its history – because he wanted to give some teeth to his bargaining power.

Kendall seems to be a relaxed member of the professional class: he looks and talks more like a doctor or a lawyer than a union leader. But his career is remarkably similar to that of the leaders of most manual unions. He left school at the age of thirteen, and started a clerical job. Later he joined the RAF and had, on his own admission, an undistinguished record. After the war he wanted to be a teacher, but joined the Civil Service as a stopgap job, then got drawn into trade-union affairs, and by 1952 was an officer of the union. He has remained in the union bureaucracy ever since.

His union is the biggest in the Civil Service and the most militant. The table below explains how other unions fit in. Only the CSU took any part in the 1973 strike action, and that was only in support of the one-day strike. It did not back the guerrilla campaign. But the Society of Civil Servants has followed the CPSA in swinging left since 1968.

Union	*Who belongs*
Civil Service Union (44,000)	The lowest paid: messengers, cleaners, etc.
Civil and Public Servants Association (215,000)	Clerical level: clerks, typists, computer girls, people behind counters.
Society of Civil Servants (92,000)	Executive officer level (small-decision takers)
Institute of Professional Civil Servants (100,000)	Assorted professionals like scientists, architects and accountants.
* First Division Association (5,000)	The top people, including permanent secretaries

* Non TUC affiliated. There are also some smaller unions covering particular departments like the Inland Revenue Staff Federation.

Before 1926 the CPSA was affiliated to the Labour Party, but this was banned by the Trades Disputes Act of 1927 as part of the Tory Party's revenge on the unions after the General Strike. When the CPSA was allowed to reaffiliate again in 1946, it did not do so because it would have had to set up a political fund. Two ballots of the members produced strong majorities against affiliation, and it is now unlikely ever to happen.

In the classroom

The National Union of Teachers is in many ways a similar union to the CPSA. It is theoretically not party-political, and until recently it sponsored parliamentary candidates in all three parties. It only joined the TUC in 1970, and is a moderate union with little bargaining power. Yet the NUT, like the CPSA, has moved sharply to the left in recent years and supports Labour Party policy on all the major educational issues. It is, for example, in favour of the abolition of all public schools and grammar schools. Its move to the left was partly a consequence of its strike campaign in the winter of 1969-1970. The NUT did not, like so many moderate unions, strike for the first time in this period. The first NUT strike had been called as long ago as 1907, when it spent £34,000 on strike pay in a campaign against the West Ham Council. It also held several long and bitter strikes in the 1920s, one of which lasted eleven months.

After the war, the idea of striking began to seem old-fashioned, so the NUT actually decided to do away with its strike fund. But in the 1960s it came to believe that militancy paid off. Its members grew resentful at the large wage increases which manual workers were getting. They felt that their profession deserved a high differential. In the autumn of 1969, the NUT put in a claim for a £135 rise on the basic salary scale. The Burnham Committee, which decides teachers' pay, made an offer of £50, which was promptly rejected. The union then called a series of local strikes throughout the winter to support its claim.

The effective bargaining power of the teachers in economic terms is actually negative, because a teachers' strike saves local councils a good deal of money and it is one of the few industries where the consumers (i.e. the children) actually prefer an interruption of service.

The teachers' only leverage in 1969-70 was political. Since

1970 was an election year, this power was obviously significant for the Labour government, and almost certainly influenced the decision to cave in in the following March and give the teachers a rise of £120 – almost all they had demanded.

The NUT also embarked on a massive publicity campaign, believing (probably wrongly) that influencing public opinion would be its strongest card. Still, the strike campaign evidently paid off, and helped convince many doubtful moderate teachers that militancy was a good tactic. This led to a swing to the left, and a majority at the union's conference supported joining the TUC although the majority of union members were probably opposed (and indeed may still be so).

Many of the older generation of teachers resented the decision to join the TUC, because it associated them with the manual workers. In the past, many people went into the teaching profession because it enabled them to get a better education and move upward in the social hierarchy. They therefore felt conscious of their professional status and responsibilities. But today many young teachers do not feel this form of professional pride, and for many it is 'just another job'. This means that they are not prepared to accept financial sacrifice, and are prepared to strike to get a good rate for the job. Those with university education are likely to be philosophically more disposed towards left-wing ideas, and more easily attuned to militancy.

The executive of the NUT is, however, unrepresentative of its members in political terms. Although it is openly admitted that probably more teachers vote Tory than Labour, every member of the executive is Labour except the half-dozen who are members of the Communist Party (including the 1973 President, Max Morris). Few teachers are active in the union. Only a small minority take part and turnouts in elections are around the ten per cent mark.

The general secretary of the teachers' union is Fred Jarvis, an intelligent Fabian, who was elected against a strong left-wing challenge. Jarvis' teachers tend to find themselves fighting on several fronts at the same time. They are usually busy sniping both at the government and at their main rival union, the Association of Schoolmasters, led by Terry Casey. The schoolmasters are a much smaller union, and most of their members are graduate teachers at the upper end of the salary scale. Many NUT members are women primary-school teachers, without a university education.

The schoolmasters like to throw chalk dust into the eyes of the NUT whenever they get a chance. In the pay-claim season, the schoolmasters stick up for the interests of the career teacher (i.e. the teacher who stays in teaching for a long time) while the NUT sticks up for the poorer, and newer, teachers at the bottom end of the pay ladder. The interests of the two tend to conflict.

The schoolmasters do not belong to the TUC and are more right-wing than the NUT. They like to think that they represent the old-style professional tradition that the NUT once embodied. The NUT tries to wave its cane at the schoolmasters, but it cannot eliminate them since there is no closed shop in schools, and many teachers, particularly the older ones, are glad to find an alternative to the strident politics of the NUT.

14   The reluctant TUC

Cartoonist David Low always portrayed the Trades Union Congress as a carthorse: strong, but slow to move. This is an apposite symbol. The TUC has almost always been more conservative than the rest of the Labour movement. It has traditionally been led by a general secretary chosen from its own bureaucrats, and the members of its ruling general council are so elected that it takes years to alter the council's political composition. Its inertia and its conservatism have, in many ways, been moderating qualities. It has prevented the growth of extremism within unions and helped to concentrate the power and activity of unions on practical issues. In 1926, the TUC called a general strike, but its inherent caution forced it to call off the strike in nine days and abandon the militant miners. Equally in 1974, the TUC leadership tried hard to persuade the miners to call off the strike which defeated Mr Heath's Tory government.

Yet the TUC's inertia has also prevented it taking a more positive role: notably on incomes policy. It has always been scared of instructing its member unions, so its power has rarely been put to constructive use. Even so, in the 1970s the TUC – with only thirty full-time professional staff – has become the most influential political lobby in Britain.

The TUC was founded in 1868, when thirty-four men met in the Mechanics' Institute in Manchester in June. According to a contemporary report in the *Manchester Guardian*, the proceedings opened with 'a rather long discussion on standing orders' and then the congress adjourned for lunch. The TUC began the way it meant to continue. Since 1868, the congress has never been used as a vehicle for revolutionary change. The vocabulary of the conference corridor is of 'compositing resolutions' and moving of the reference back, rather than of Marxism or syndicalism.

The early years

No one was quite clear in 1868 what they were founding at the Mechanics' Institute. Nor has anyone been quite clear ever since. The foundation and growth of the TUC just happened. In the words of Professor Ben Roberts: 'The growth in status of the Trades Union Congress and its Parliamentary Committee had been achieved in a typically British way. It was not planned; it conformed to no explicit theory; it simply acquired its functions as it went along.'

Initially, the TUC had only two arms: the annual congress and the parliamentary committee (set up in 1871). The job of the parliamentary committee was to lobby MPs for legislation in the interests of the working class. It concentrated on getting Parliament to liberalise restrictive anti-union laws. It quickly achieved this aim. By 1875, Disraeli had put through the key bills on trade union law, which entirely satisfied the committee.

From then on, the committee devoted its time to supporting measures for social reform. According to one estimate, the TUC parliamentary committee played some role in the passage of one hundred and twenty-three Acts of Parliament passed between 1868 and 1901. The TUC embodied the liberal progressive attitude in these years. It did not embrace the new socialism. Instead it stuck to the aims which had been voiced by the TUC's first president, W.H. Wood, in 1868. He said that the TUC ought to be pursuing 'the rectification of existing grievances and preparing the way for the amelioration of the social condition of the working-class community'.

The first leaders of the TUC were the secretaries of the parliamentary committee. For twelve of the first eighteen years of the parliamentary committee's life, the secretary was Henry Broadhurst. Broadhurst was one of the first Lib-Lab MPs, returned at the 1880 election. He was no radical. He had a great admiration for Gladstone, and was regarded by many union leaders as far too conservative. In 1885, Broadhurst was actually given a post in the Liberal Government.

The new radical union men made a big impression at the 1889 conference in Dundee, but the mood still remained moderate. The successor to Broadhurst was Charles Fenwick, a Gladstonian liberal who strongly opposed state intervention. At this congress, a motion calling for the nationalisation of the means of production was easily defeated. The trade-union movement remained more liberal than socialist.

Moves were made to turn the TUC into a federation, which could finance strikes. But these were diverted into the formation in 1899 of the General Federation of Trade Unions. Its main object was to set up a mutual strike insurance fund; so that if one union had a long dispute, it could be financed by others.

The General Federation was a flop from the start. Only a quarter of the TUC union membership enrolled, mainly weak unions which had the most to gain from such a fund. As a result, the federation has never played more than a marginal part in British trade-union history. Its main role has tended to be dissuading its member unions from striking – as might be expected from a strike-insurance agency. For a while, the General Federation took over the job of representing the TUC abroad, but the TUC resumed this after the first world war. The General Federation still exists, but is never heard of.

The decision in 1899 to summon a conference of unions and socialist groups to discuss Labour representation in Parliament marked the beginning of a new era of political trade unionism. But the TUC kept its distance from the Labour Representation Committee and then the Labour Party. Today, no trade unionist is allowed to sit on both the TUC general council and the Labour Party national executive. Although the unions have direct links with the Labour Party, the TUC remains independent of the party. This independence was most marked in recent years towards the end of the 1964-70 Labour government, when Harold Wilson was attempting to separate the government from over-close association with the unions. The unions equally drew away from a government which intended to introduce what they saw as restrictive union legislation. But after Labour's defeat in 1970, both sides tried to repair the links. A TUC-Labour Party liaison committee was formed to achieve better relations.

This committee was attended by representatives of the TUC general council, Labour's national executive and the Parliamentary Labour Party. In July 1972, it reached agreement on the legislation to repeal the Tories' Industrial Relations Act, and in February 1973 it reached agreement on the outline of the social contract. This committee continued to meet at monthly intervals after Labour's 1974 victory: it provided a convenient forum for ministers and union leaders to meet, although few decisions were taken by the committee thereafter.

At the turn of the last century, the TUC parliamentary committee began to acquire new functions. It started to intervene to sort out inter-union disputes. This has remained a key part of the TUC's work ever since. At the 1939 Bridlington congress clear rules were laid down about inter-union competition to guide the TUC's decisions. Today around eighty union disputes are taken to the TUC each year. Many are settled informally, but around thirty are settled after formal hearings and rulings by the TUC disputes committee.

The TUC did not exert much influence until the war. Then two things happened: (1) its membership doubled between 1913 and 1918, and (2) it began to be consulted by the government, because its help was critical to the war effort. As a result of these changes, the TUC's constitution was rewritten after the war. The old parliamentary committee was replaced by a general council which became the TUC's cabinet. Since then, the formal structure of the TUC has changed little.

How Congress works

The policy-making body in the TUC is the annual congress. This meets every year in the first week of September, usually at Brighton or Blackpool. Each union can send one delegate per five thousand members, although the bigger unions seldom send their full quota.

Normally, around one thousand delegates attend. The vast majority are male: there have never been more than eighty-four women at the TUC. This reflects the male dominance of the union movement. A woman has never led a major British union, and in 1975 there were thirty-two male officers for every woman – although over thirty per cent of trade-union members are women. The biggest unions are the worst offenders. The TGWU has 498 male officials but only two women officials. The AUEW has only one female official out of 195. Several unions do help the advance of women by providing special seats on their executive for women only – including the TUC which provides two such seats. But this only serves to emphasise the under-representation of women.

None of the delegates at a TUC annual congress can cast an

individual vote. All votes are cast in blocks according to each union's paid-up membership. This may often exceed actual membership, because unions do not have to prove the size of their membership. Provided they pay the appropriate dues to the TUC, their figures are not questioned. The general secretary casts the block vote, but he does not necessarily decide which way to cast it: that rests with his delegation.

Delegations are normally free to decide how to cast the block vote in elections at the congress, but in voting on motions they respect policy decisions taken by their own union's conferences. They cannot reverse a specific policy agreed by their own conference, but they can and do reverse decisions taken at their own executives. Thus, at the 1975 conference, the delegation of the builders' union, UCATT, narrowly voted to oppose the £6 pay rise limit even though the union's executive had approved it. So the union's general secretary, George Smith, had to cast the block vote against both his own and his executive's wishes.

Each union chooses its TUC delegation in a different way. Most delegations are formed of a mixture of rank-and-file members elected by branch ballots, plus a few members of the union executive, plus a selection of full-time officers including the general secretary. But in most delegations the rank-and-filers form the majority – a notable contrast to many foreign congresses, such as Germany's – which are dominated by full-time officers.

There is strong competition for the rank-and-file places, but voting turnout is tiny. The turnout for elections for the 1975 AUEW delegation, for example, varied from one per cent to four per cent. To illustrate the variety of selection procedures, here are some examples of how unions choose their delegations:

TGWU   Rank-and-filers, chosen by branch ballot in regions, form three-quarters of the delegation. The rest are chosen from full-time officers in rota together with three men from the thirty-eight-strong executive.

AUEW   Each of its four sections chooses delegates separately. All twenty-six delegates from the engineering section are elected by branch ballot in the regions (officers attend the conference, but do not vote). The seventeen delegates from the other sections are elected at each section conference.

NALGO   The union's twelve districts all elect delegates by branch ballot. Five officers attend, plus up to thirty-nine mem-

bers of the union executive. But, to avoid conflict between the
delegation and the executive, the union always holds a joint
meeting of the two groups on the first Saturday in August.

NUPE The regions elect twenty rank-and-filers, who are
joined by four members of the executive and five full-time
officials in rota, always including the general secretary and his
deputy.

NUM Unlike most unions, it sends its entire executive in its
delegation. A handful of officers, plus a rank-and-filer from
each region make up the delegation.

UCATT It also sends its full executive, plus five representatives from its rank-and-file general council, plus twelve rank-
and-filers elected by branch ballot.

The choice of delegation has a crucial influence on the power
of the general secretary to determine how the delegation votes.
Most rank-and-filers tend to submit to the 'experience' of their
general secretary and most full-time officers who are in their job
by appointment rather than election (and so are in the general
secretary's patronage) also tend to follow the general secretary's line. The tendency to accept the view of the general
secretary is most obvious in the two big general unions. The
leaders of the TGWU and the GMWU can in practice decide
themselves how to cast the block vote. By contrast, in the
AUEW the general secretary and president have little
influence.

Each delegation occupies specially allotted seats in the congress, while the TUC general council leaders sit on the platform
(although often migrating to and fro between the platform and
their delegation). The congress is chaired by the TUC president, who is elected each year according to seniority. Unlike the
TUC general secretary who sits on his (or her) left, the president has little power – except to resolve the frequent pro-
cedural wrangles.

The main task of each congress is (a) to review the past year
and debate the general council's annual report, (b) to determine new policy, through motions, and (c) to elect next year's
general council. Few of the motions are opposed, although
acceptance of many motions leads nowhere. The TUC leaders
often reckon it is simpler to accept a motion and then do
nothing rather than to oppose it and create an unnecessary row.
Any union can submit motions for debate, but many are with-

drawn or composited with other motions on the same subject, so that only sixty-odd motions are debated. Many of these are carried after a single speech.

Every congress is now televised. This adds a little drama and much heat and light. Both BBC and the ITV companies began the televising of TUC congresses as part of their campaign to televise parliament: but the audience is invariably small.

The general council is elected by vote of the delegations, and the results are usually announced on the Tuesday afternoon of each congress. There are thirty-eight seats on the council, allocated according to industry. Thus the railway workers get two seats, the miners two, the electricians one and so on. These divisions are occasionally revised to reflect the expansion or contraction of industries – but such changes are made with the greatest reluctance. In 1975, the Civil Service unions complained that their section (which includes the postmen) only provided two representatives for 775,000 members, although the average number of members per general council place was only 279,000. Their complaint was rejected.

Most of the council places are not seriously contested. The big unions can effectively nominate who they choose – knowing that other unions will back their nominee for fear of offending them and losing votes for their own candidate(s). In 1975, the AUEW nominated the Maoist Reg Birch. Most of the big unions, including the TGWU, did not approve of the choice but felt bound to support him. Birch got nearly three million fewer votes than most of the AUEW candidates, but was still elected by a comfortable margin.

Once elected, it is rare for a general-council man to lose his seat: only two men have done so since 1970. In 1972, Jack Peel, the right-wing pro-Europe leader of the Dyers, Bleachers and Textile Workers, was defeated because unions like the TGWU disapproved of his views on Europe and incomes policy. He was replaced by the almost equally right-wing Joe King. In 1975, Roy Grantham, another right-wing pro-European, was also beaten, although partly because his union had been involved in a dispute with Clive Jenkins' union, ASTMS, and had been reluctant to accept a ruling of the TUC disputes committee.

Because the changes in the composition of the general council are infrequent and based mainly on chance personal factors, the political balance does not reflect trends to left or right – except over a long run. When the views of the council change, this is usually because the views of its existing members change. The table shows the rough split between left and right after the congress of 1975.

The balance of power

Members of the TUC general council
(dates show year of first election)

Left	Unpredictable	Right
Hugh Scanlon (Engineers) 1968	George Smith (Construction) 1959	Alf Allen (Shopworkers) 1962
Len Edmondson (Engineers) 1970	Glyn Lloyd (Construction) 1973	Cyril Plant (Taxmen) 1963
Ken Gill (Engineers) 1974	David Basnett (Municipal) 1966	Audrey Prime (NALGO) 1965
Reg Birch (Engineers) 1975	Reg Bottini (Farmworkers) 1970	Tom Jackson (Postmen) 1967
Alan Fisher (Public employees) 1968	Charlie Grieve (Tobacco workers) 1973	Jack MacGougan (Tailors) 1970
Terry Parry (Firemen) 1970	Jack Jones (Transport) 1968	Frank Chapple (Electricians) 1971
Alan Sapper (Film technicians) 1970	Harry Urwin (Transport) 1969	Alex Donnet (Municipal) 1972
Lawrence Daly (Miners) 1971	Marie Patterson (Transport) 1968	Jack Eccles (Municipal) 1973
Les Buck (Sheet metalworkers) 1971	Dan McGarvey (Boilermakers) 1965	Joe Gormley (Miners) 1973
Ray Buckton (Train drivers) 1973	John Morton (Musicians) 1975	Geoffrey Drain (NALGO) 1973
Jim Slater (Seamen) 1974		Fred Jarvis (Teachers) 1974
Clive Jenkins (ASTMS) 1974		Sid Weighell (Railwaymen) 1975
Stan Pemberton (Construction) 1974		Bill Sirs (Steelworkers) 1975
Bill Keys (SOGAT) 1975		Fred Dyson (Textiles) 1975

The council tends to be more conservative than the rest of the labour movement because (a) it is filled by general secretaries who are older than the average and are more aware of industrial and economic realities, and (b) it gives disproportionate voting weight to smaller unions, who are usually less militant. In 1975, there was only one Communist Party member on the council – Ken Gill, who was elected in 1974. For the previous half-dozen years there was no communist on the council.

The general council meets on a Wednesday morning every month at the TUC's modern headquarters in Great Russell Street. Much detailed work is left to the numerous committees, but the two that matter most are the finance and general purposes committee – which often serves as a kind of inner cabinet – and the economic committee. The economic committee has masterminded most of the talks and discussion between the TUC and governments, and was instrumental in devising the terms of the £6 pay policy introduced in August 1974.

Every member of the general council can sit on a committee, but the two important committees are filled by the most senior men on the TUC. Like the general council, the committees meet monthly. But all major policy decisions must be referred to the general council for approval. This hierarchical structure does not suit those unions who are either too small to be represented or who are led by junior men. John Lyons, for example, of the power engineers, bitterly complained to the 1975 congress that neither he nor his union had been consulted on major issues of policy including such vital issues as the £6 pay limit. A typical example of how out of touch TUC policy can become was provided by the TUC's 1975 evidence on workers' participation in the power industry. The TUC blithely recommended full support for participation – although all the main unions in the industry were opposed to it (the EEPTU, the EPEA and the AUEW).

Much TUC advice to government is not based on detailed consultation with unions. Policy tends to spring either from the TUC's own tiny backroom staff or from general political themes laid down by the general council.

The staff are overworked and underpaid. But in return for this, they can enjoy the knowledge that they each have the power of a permanent secretary, at least when a Labour government is in power.

The power of the general secretary

The top job in the TUC is that of general secretary. The general secretary is elected for life by the congress, but the election is normally not contested. The last three general secretaries were all previously assistant general secretaries and rose from the bureaucracy.

This method of election provides the holder of the post with no special legitimacy and most have regarded themselves as civil servants ruled by the general council, rather than as politicians in their own right. The general secretary has no vote in any of the TUC's forums and so, technically, is quite powerless. That is why recent general secretaries, like Vic Feather and Len Murray, have had to carry out policies in which they did not believe. Both Feather and Murray were keen on British entry into Europe – but neither could admit as much in office, although Feather campaigned for the EEC during the 1975 referendum, after he left the TUC. Both Feather and Murray, at different times, realised the need for incomes policy. Feather, for example, was prepared to do a deal with the Heath government in the autumn of 1973, and Murray made repeated attempts to toughen the flaccid social contract of 1974-5, which were rebuffed by other union leaders (e.g. in February 1975).

Yet power is a subtle quality. George Meany, the veteran head of the American AFL-CIO, has little more formal power than the general secretary of the British TUC, yet by force of personality he came to dominate the American Labour movement. Len Murray, elected in 1974, has a possible fourteen more years in the job and could, if he chose, establish himself as a British Meany. This would be hard for him to achieve, because he has no deep roots in the union movement. He is an intellectual, with no experience of manual work, unlike George Meany who once was a plumber. That is a profound weakness in any labour movement. But already Murray has begun to show that he intends to bend the TUC more to his will than Vic Feather ever dared to do. He presides over committees and the general council with purpose and is prepared to fight over policy. Murray was born to a humble background (his father was a farm worker in Shropshire) but he quickly moved up the ladder. He got to grammar school and thence to London University. He was called up to the army during the war, and made a lieutenant. He landed in France on D-Day, but after two weeks of action he returned home, and he left the army in 1944.

He joined an engineering company in Wolverhampton. At

the same time he joined the Communist Party, although he left it soon after. Then he decided to complete his education by studying politics, philosophy and economics at New College, Oxford, just as George Woodcock had done before him (although Murray only got a second, while Woodcock got a first).

After leaving Oxford, he briefly became a trainee restaurant manager before successfully applying to join the TUC. The menu at Congress House proved tasty, but he stayed hidden in the depths of the TUC economics department until he was elected assistant general secretary in 1969, and then general secretary in 1973.

Murray, like Woodcock, seems aloof from the rest of the trade union movement. He has few close friends on the general council – perhaps the intellectual gulf is too great. Many members of the TUC general council left school at the age of fourteen, and a mere handful went to university. Murray is more left-wing than Feather, but more cynical. Yet his intellect and logic have won him respect from both the Heath and Wilson governments. He has taken good care to keep the TUC and government in close touch.

Vic Feather had less formal education but was more folksy and had a cheerful sense of humour; Murray is altogether a more serious man. Feather was born the son of a french polisher in Bradford. He left school at the age of fifteen to begin work as a flour boy in the Co-op. He attracted the attention of Sir Walter Citrine, the TUC general secretary, and became an enthusiastic activist in the Yorkshire labour movement. Feather won his spurs as a bouncy soap-box speaker and an acid journalist. He was also a talented cartoonist (he once drew a cover for *Punch*).

Although he also spent most of his career in the anonymity of the TUC bureaucracy, Feather was never one of the faceless faithful of Congress House. He was a dedicated socialist, but he also believed in democracy and freedom. After the war, he led the campaign against the attempts by communists to infiltrate the trade-union movement.

Feather also led a later and much more important crusade against communism at the turn of the 1950s, in the battle over corruption inside the ETU (see Chapter 7). At one stage, he wrote an exposé for the *Sunday Times*, under a pseudonym.

Other journalists leaked the fact that he had written it, and there was a moment when Feather's future in the TUC seemed to be threatened by his courageous action. Fortunately, he survived.

Feather was TUC general secretary for only four and a half years, one of the shortest terms of office this century. Under Feather's leadership, the TUC moved sharply to the left. This was despite, not because of, Feather's leadership, and was a result of the reasons explained in Chapter 2. Feather tried hard to mould the TUC into a new form, but the forces that opposed him were too great.

Feather allowed himself virtually no private life. He had little time to spend in his modest Hounslow home. He worked long hours and never took a holiday. He did not over-indulge and was a teetotaller until he was forty.

The impotent giant

The TUC is a highly effective lobby of governments of either party, because governments feel that they must please the TUC in order to avoid TUC unions going on strike. But the TUC is seldom master in its own house: its ability to control or direct member unions is highly limited, most obviously on issues of wage policy.

The best example of this is the collapse of the 1974-5 social contract. The TUC agreed to issue bargaining guidelines, which were overwhelmingly approved by the 1974 congress at Brighton. They provided that most wage deals in the coming year should only seek to maintain rather than improve real incomes, i.e. that the percentage wage rise should equal the percentage price rise over the same period (see Chapter 4). These guidelines were ignored from the start: the very next month one million workers in local government settled for a rise of over thirty per cent, although the retail price index was only 17.1 per cent higher than the year before. The TUC tried hard to reduce the most extreme wage claims, and in private it summoned union leaders to explain to other union leaders why their claim was so high. But these pleadings had little effect. The seamen's union, which had asked for a rise of eighty-one per cent, was quite able to fend off TUC criticism when its leaders were summoned to see Len Murray, Jack Jones and others. It eventually settled for thirty-seven per cent, without a word of public criticism from the TUC.

Equally, the TUC has shown no ability to coordinate strike action. It has only really tried once: in 1926, when it called the general strike. This was an ignominious failure. It did call a one-day general strike on 1 May 1973, to protest against the Heath incomes policy, but only fifteen per cent of union members obeyed the call (seven per cent of all workers). Many of the weaker unions, like the postmen in 1971 and the hospital workers in 1973, have sought support for their strikes from the TUC but never got any more than pious waffle.

This inherent weakness of the TUC is not matched by most foreign trade-union centres in Europe, especially in Scandinavia. Scandinavian TUCs directly supervise all the major wage bargains and specify the allowable range of wage bargains in the biennial central bargaining. They can call general strikes – as the Danes did in 1973 – but equally they can impose wage agreements on their members. They are quite willing to expel dissident unions – as the Swedish TUC did to its dockers' union – and to impose other sanctions on member unions. Even the Irish TUC has been able to enforce central wage agreements on its member unions by the use of expulsion threats, and also by the use of its power to regulate picketing. Countries like the United States where the union centre is weak also tend to be countries where bargaining is so fragmented that there is no demand for centralised wage bargains. The problem in Britain is that the unions are so strong that a centralised wage bargain is vital but seemingly unenforceable.

In July 1975, the TUC did sign a central wage bargain with the government, but the sanctions against those who broke it were directed exclusively at employers, and the TUC did not take any measures to enforce it on its own members. Such a formula could only work in the short-run.

But it would be wrong to assume that the TUC could not take power if it chose. The battle between 1970 and 1974 over the Tory Industrial Relations Act revealed the TUC's political power. The TUC adopted a policy of total non-cooperation, including instructing unions not to register under the new law.

This policy was only carried by a narrow margin, and as we saw in Chapter 5, was expected to collapse. But it did not collapse. Why? There were two reasons: !rst, the biggest and most powerful unions, like the AUEW and the TGWU, wanted to make their policy stick; and second, the TUC was prepared to discipline unions who would not toe the line. At its 1972 congress in Brighton, the TUC expelled thirty-two unions. This threat of expulsion persuaded many unions to deregister in the shadow of the gallows. One day, the TUC will have to adopt this kind of measure to enforce a central wage bargain.

15　Three faces of the TUC

This chapter looks at three other central issues which caused heated debate inside the unions in the 1970s. Each casts some light on the attitudes of the new (and old) unionism. First we shall look at the row over the legal rights of pickets – an indicator of the unions' growing presumption of immunity from the law: second at the debate over entry into the EEC – an indicator of the odd mixture of socialism and chauvinism within the unions: and third at the debate about workers' participation – an indicator of the unions' essentially conservative approach to the development of their industrial power, and of their deep-rooted belief in the inevitability of conflicting interests in industrial relations.

Picketing: the rule of what?

The use of physical violence in strikes is not new. The most violent strikes took place during the nineteenth century when trade unionism was in its infancy. The burning of haystacks and the destruction of farm equipment was a regular feature of the early farm strikes, and in the 1860s militants resorted to a variety of violent tactics including the use of bombs. The emergence of powerful trade unions generally acted as a force against violence, and the leadership made every effort to control excesses among their members.

The use of violence, or the calling of strikes which might lead to loss of life, have nearly always been opposed by union leaders. For example, in 1973 the Fire Brigades' Union firmly opposed a strike called by Glasgow firemen, and in the same year the GMWU insisted that its gas strike should be conducted so as to avoid any risk of explosions.

However, the unions have been notoriously tolerant of the development in the 1970s of semi-violent picketing. This was most marked in the 1972 dock, coal and building strikes. As a result, the Tory government asked the TUC to cooperate in drawing up a code to guide picketing tactics, but the TUC refused. Indeed its only reaction was to ask for liberalisation of the existing picketing laws to allow pickets more rights and freedoms. The issue, however, is not simply about whether picketing is 'peaceful' or 'violent'.

The police tried to enforce the law in the 1972 miners' strike. Some two hundred and sixty-three pickets were arrested (although none received serious punishment), but the police were unable to control several critical confrontations.

In Ipswich, for example, up to six hundred men picketed the local power station. This clearly constituted an obstruction and an intimidation. But the police arrested only four men there during the entire course of the strike.

The most serious flouting of the law, however, was at the massive Saltley coal depot in Birmingham. Here a crowd of six thousand men (mainly, but not all, miners) forced the police to close the gates of the depot. The picketing was accompanied by a variety of aggro. Reports of the time catch the flavour:

> The reinforcements today were matched by 300 policemen, two of whom were hurt. One had hospital treatment for rib injuries. The whole of the Birmingham force was put on two 12-hour shifts instead of the usual three shifts.
>
> In one incident, pickets let down the tailboard of a loaded lorry and about three tons of coke poured on to the road. Policemen had to shovel it on to the lorry to clear the way. Other miners continually used pedestrian crossings to stop traffic. Bottles, stones, fruit and meat pies were thrown during the fighting. Some miners lay in front of the lorries and were dragged clear by police . . .
>
> Arthur Osman, *The Times*, 8 February 1972

The miners' leaders found themselves swept off their feet, so that the moderate Mr Gormley told miners at Pendlebury: 'There are going to be casualties as in any other battle and people are bound to be hurt.' That was not the language of 1926.

One of the new tactics devised by the miners was the use of 'flying pickets'. In the past, strikers only picketed their place of work. Now the miners despatched teams of men to picket the power stations, many of which (in London) were miles away from any coalfield.

Other unions copied the flying-picket strategy, particularly in the long building strike in the summer of 1972. This time, most of the flying-picket squads were organised, not by the union, but by the unofficial groups of militants.

These flying pickets had a major impact. Without their efforts, the 1972 building strike might have easily folded up. At first, only a few London hotel sites had been affected, but by late August most major building sites in the country were at a standstill.

The more worrying development was the outbreak of violence. Threats and acts of personal violence by pickets were so widespread that the employers (the National Federation of Building Trades Employers) began to collect a dossier of incidents. When the strike was over, it was submitted to the Home Secretary. Its contents were frightening. Below is a selection of incidents reported to the NFBTE in August:

9 August: Two coachloads of pickets closed down a large site on the outskirts of Sheffield. Twelve operatives on the job abused and threatened with violence. 'One man who was excavating was told that if he didn't come out of that so-and-so trench he would never come out again. A joiner threatened that if he didn't pack his tools immediately, they would be packed for him and the new door he was hanging would be wrenched off.'

12 August: Police started arson enquiry at Dowsett Engineering Construction road link site, Sheffield. Three huts and an excavator caught fire soon after men ignored calls by pickets to stop work.

16 August: Traxcavator driver asked to strike on site at Sowerby Bridge. Querying consequences if he did not, he was asked if he had 'ever had his teeth kicked out'.

16 August: Workers and families threatened by a mass picket with violence if work continued on sewerage scheme at Padeswood, Buckley, Flintshire. Touring pickets involved. Threats to burn down caravan homes on the site.

18 August: Building firm's coach overturned in Birmingham; in another incident in the city a site office burned down.

19 August: Thirty-five cars have tyres punctured by tacks scattered on road at Laing Pipelines offshore site at Greythorpe near Hartlepool. One hundred and forty men picket.

21 August: Young apprentice had front teeth knocked out on site. On another siteagent locked in his hut which was set on fire.

21 August: Building worker in Glasgow followed home and told: 'If you are out at work tomorrow, it is not you who will suffer. It is your wife and kids.'

The police decided to prosecute twenty-four building workers after the building strike on charges arising out of the violent picketing. Several of the twenty-four were fined, but two of them, Dennis Warren and Eric Tomlinson (the Shrewsbury Two) were sentenced to three years' and two years' jail respectively, on charges of conspiracy to intimidate their fellow workers.

At first these sentences did not spark any major reaction in the unions except among the leaders of the far left. But the Building Workers' Charter, the Marxist splinter group in the builders' union, UCATT, began to turn the heat on. It eventually managed to win support from the UCATT executive, who in turn put the heat on the TUC. The TUC soon agreed with the far-left view that the sentences had been politically motivated and that both pickets ought to be freed immediately. Throughout 1974 and 1975, while the pickets were in jail, the TUC led a series of delegations to ministers to demand the pickets' release. In the meantime, the case was taken to the Court of Appeal where Lord Widgery confirmed the sentences and agreed on the need to deter violent picketing. He told the court 'If it is known tomorrow that these sentences should have been reduced or set aside, the effect must be to destroy the deterrent effect.' Later, the Home Secretary, Roy Jenkins, observed that 'The rule of law and the independence of the courts could be seriously undermined were governments to presume to re-judge the merits of cases decided by the courts.'

Yet the unions seemed unworried by this argument and by the violence that had originally prompted the sentences. Inside the TUC, only the EEPTU agreed with the jailing of the pickets – although when Tom Breakell of the EEPTU defended this view at the 1975 Trades Union Congress he was drowned by hecklers.

It is natural for unions to defend the rights of pickets, but the TUC's happy-go-lucky attitude to violence and the due process of justice suggested that increasingly unions felt that no law should limit their ability to maximise their industrial power.

The campaign against the EEC

The TUC has always been an international organisation,

aware of the need to maintain contacts and friends all over the world. Every year the TUC sends delegations abroad, and in London runs a lively international department. It is perhaps a little curious that so much of its work in recent years has been concerned with the communist bloc countries (there were sixteen separate trips to East Europe by British union delegates in 1974 – far more than were made to former Commonwealth countries, for example), but none the less no one can deny the TUC's enthusiasm for foreign involvement. Its attitude towards entry into the EEC was therefore oddly isolationist.

The TUC took an anti-market stance along with Hugh Gaitskell and the rest of the Labour Party when Harold Macmillan's Tory government applied for membership in 1961, but it switched to support entry when Harold Wilson applied for membership again in 1967. The unions' support for the EEC was given at a time when relations with the Wilson government were still good and when there was all-party support for entry. Successive TUC conferences supported British entry, although each contained caveats about the need to get the right terms.

The anti-marketeers in the TUC did not gain the upper hand until the Tories were returned to power. When Ted Heath negotiated entry, the upper hierarchy in the TUC were still sympathetic to entry. Vic Feather and Len Murray were both pro-market in private and there were many pro-marketeers on the TUC general council.

The switch of policy was spearheaded by the TGWU. It was firmly anti-market on principle by the end of 1970. Its executive foresaw 'great hardships for ordinary families, great increases in prices and a substantial loss of jobs. No small handful of politicians has the right to inflict such changes on the people.' This was the theme that union after union was to adopt in the round of summer conferences in 1971.

In 1970, the TUC conference had stalled on the issue. But by the autumn of 1971 the terms negotiated by the Government were known and the TUC could stall no longer. A straight anti-entry motion was proposed by Jack Jones and carried overwhelmingly. A pro-entry motion backed by Roy Grantham was voted down by a majority shout.

The unions' reversal on the Europe issue was a disappointment to social-democrat unions and politicians in Europe. The TUC was the only social-democrat union group in Europe to oppose entry. In the old Six, both the Christian and the social-democrat unions were enthusiastically in favour of the common market and had long been in favour of more integration (i.e. more supranationalism and less national sovereignty) as well as British entry.

The communists in France and Italy remained opposed to the EEC, because it was a capitalist plot and because it was a western anti-communist alliance. Even so, they recognised that in material and economic terms the EEC had improved their members' living standards.

The TUC's attitude came as a particular disappointment to the continental unions, because they had hoped that the presence of the TUC in Brussels would strengthen the unions vis-à-vis the institutions of the EEC.

In 1972 the TUC went even further than it had in 1971. It then decided that entry into the EEC was undesirable on any terms at all. The reasons were similar to those advanced by the French and Italian communists: but with this addition – the British unions regarded the loss of sovereignty as an important argument against the EEC on principle. It also voted not to participate even in those institutions within the EEC which had seats for unions, such as the Economic and Social Committee and the Standing Committee on Employment.

But the TUC non-participation decision meant not only that no British union voice was heard but that the employers' block on the council got more votes than the unions. This enraged the European unionists still further.

Meanwhile, Vic Feather was working hard to set up a new European trade union confederation. British entry into the EEC meant that there was a need to shake up the international trade-union structure in Europe. Previously, the social-democrat unions in the Six had banded together to form an organisation to represent union interests in Brussels. Meanwhile the unions of EFTA (the European Free Trade Area, which embraced Britain and Scandinavia) had also set up a smaller organisation, based in the same building in Brussels.

In 1972, it was decided to unite the two. Many of the unions in the Six, especially the Dutch and German, thought this plan was crazy. They pointed out that since most of the work of the new organisation would be lobbying in Brussels, it was idiotic to make the organisation embrace unions in countries which did not belong to the EEC. But the TUC would not budge. And it insisted that the new grouping should include unions from other neutral European countries like Switzerland. It would have nothing to do with an 'inward-looking' EEC union group. The new confederation was officially founded in February 1973, and Vic Feather was elected president. But the TUC still refused to cooperate with the EEC.

Many union pro-marketeers hoped that the TUC would be drawn into the EEC by stealth. Several unions, including the miners and the steelworkers, took their seats on EEC committees despite the official TUC boycott of all EEC institutions. At the 1973 conference a motion urging an end to the TUC boycott was narrowly defeated by 4.9 million to 4.5 million votes, and the TUC's total opposition to the EEC was reaffirmed.

In 1974 the Labour government began renegotiating the terms of British membership of the EEC, but the majority of the unions still wanted Britain to withdraw regardless of any new terms that might be obtained. When the referendum was held on the new terms obtained by Labour, the TUC continued its opposition without even bothering to hold a special congress – because it knew that few union leaders had changed their minds.

When the referendum produced the decisive majority in favour of entry, the TUC reluctantly agreed to start participating in the institutions of the EEC although, as Jack Jones made clear at Blackpool in September 1975, their opposition to the principle was still as great as ever.

Two cheers for industrial democracy

Workers' participation (or industrial democracy as it was called by the unions) developed as a major political theme in the 1970s. The concept, of course, was hardly new. In the late nineteenth century, the South Metropolitan, Commercial and South Surburban gas companies all provided for profit-sharing and for the worker-shareholders to elect a director to their boards. (Oddly, this form of democracy was abolished when the gas industry was nationalised in 1948.) In the early twentieth century, the left-wing radical syndicalists championed the need for workers' control. But their ideas soon died. Private industry saw no reason to share its managerial power, and the new nationalised industries made little or no attempt to involve the workers in decision-taking. The years of nascent union power were thus pathetically wasted by private and state capitalists alike.

Meanwhile, elsewhere in Europe industrialists were more imaginative. In West Germany, the post-war governments legislated to give unions representation on the supervisory board of every major public company with one-third of the seats on the board, and in the coal and steel industry half the seats on the board. The worker-directors were also given the power of veto over the appointment of the labour relations director on the main board. Other social-democrat countries like Holland, Norway, Sweden and Denmark followed Germany's example, although much later. In France the theme of workers' control was espoused by the CFDT, the socialist (and former Christian) union federation who adapted the slogan of 'auto-gestion' (i.e. self-management) – a theme that was dramatised by the occupation of the watchmaking factory of Lip at Besançon in 1973.

In Britain, the unions have shown little enthusiasm for legislation to extend participation. Most of them see nationalisation as a solution to industrial problems of every kind (in 1975 the unions wanted to nationalise ports, shipbuilding, aircraft, oil, banks, insurance, mining equipment and chemicals among others). They are always keen to extend collective bargaining to cover new issues like redundancy or pensions, but few are keen to assume managerial responsibilities which undermine their 'conflict' approach to industrial relations. But in 1973 the TUC produced a report on industrial democracy which recommended support for the reform of company law to provide for supervisory 'boards with fifty per cent worker-directors – although the TUC insisted that all directors should be appointed through or by trade unions. This report, however, did not win universal acceptance in the TUC. At the 1973 congress, left and right-wing unions combined to modify the official TUC line: insisting that unions should be free to choose whether they wanted to seek worker-directors in their industry. The right-wing opposition included those like Frank Chapple who reckoned that unions should stick to bargaining pay and conditions, and David Basnett who reckoned that industrial democracy should be confined. to an extension of collective bargaining. On the left, the opposition came from those like Ken Gill and Hugh Scanlon who saw industrial democracy as a compromise with capitalism. Scanlon wrote in the AUEW journal in 1973: 'Trade unionists who are appointed to such boards will always find themselves in a situation where they have conflicting loyalties. It is a dilemma within the capitalist system that cannot be solved and is probably likely to increase tension and frustration rather than improve relations in industry.' Some left-wingers, notably the theoreticians of the Institute of Workers Control, are enthusiastic for a more dramatic extension of workers' power but they are still a distinct minority.

The advocates of industrial democracy, however, got a shot in the arm when Tony Benn ran the Department of Industry from March 1974 to June 1975. Benn was an enthusiast for every type of workers' control and saw an opportunity in the rash of company collapses and bankruptcies of the great slump to provide for direct workers' control. He ordered his civil servants to prepare plans to finance workers' cooperatives in three major experiments: in Glasgow where a cooperative briefly created the *Scottish Daily News* to preserve the jobs of the printing workers (who used to produce the *Scottish Daily Express* which closed its operation in 1974), in Meriden where a cooperative started to produce motor cycles, and in Kirby, Lancashire, where a cooperative took over the old Fisher-Bendix plant. He also encouraged a major extension of worker control in state rescues for companies like British Leyland.

Benn was a popular figure in the unions, but there was a mixed reaction to his support for worker cooperatives. Several major unions were asked to help provide finance for the *Scottish Daily News*, but none showed the slightest interest and there was an equal lack of enthusiasm for the other cooperatives. Indeed, one major left-wing leader in the AUEW told me that he regarded the Meriden cooperative as 'the lump of the motor-bike industry'.

The problem for the unions was that the cooperatives made trade unionism redundant. If workers became their own managers, what need did they have for a trade union? Worse still, the new cooperatives allowed workers to earn wages well below the going rate and encouraged massive leaps in productivity which seriously embarrassed those who worked at the old rates.

Such was the great irony of the 1970s: the unions thrived on their new political power but many shied away from accepting for themselves or their members an increase in managerial power in industry – the very power which had first triggered the formation of unions. Meanwhile, companies who understood the paradox lined up to surrender their power. Chrysler, the car giant, which suffered a series of painful strikes, decided that industrial democracy was the best method to cut strikes, and in the summer of 1975 offered its unions seats on the board and shop stewards seats on a series of committees to frame company policy. Characteristically, the unions reacted with a shrug of indifference. The top union leaders left the discussion to shop stewards, who were intensely suspicious of the company's motives.

The one major experiment with worker-directors in nationalised industry produced little joy for the unions. In 1967, the newly formed British Steel Corporation decided to appoint worker-directors to its divisional boards. These were chosen by the BSC from a list of names approved by the steel unions and were paid £1,000 a year for part-time work. The experiment got off to a disastrous start. When the BSC commissioned an independent survey, it found that only half the workers thought the scheme was proving a success and half of the BSC managers were also opposed. This forced the BSC to modify its system (for a start, it changed its rule that no worker-director could be a union member), but not with any marked effect.

Both the Heath and the Wilson governments proclaimed themselves as enthusiasts for industrial democracy, but postponed any decision on policy. Although Tony Benn pioneered his own forms of workers' control, the central issues of union involvement in management were again postponed when Peter Shore, the trade secretary, set up a committee of inquiry in the summer of 1975.

British unions' ambivalent approach to industrial democracy was one of the saddest features of the new unionism and in direct contrast to social-democrat unions throughout the rest of western Europe, who regarded the growth of such democracy as a top political priority. In West Germany the unions pressed hard for an extension of worker control throughout industry, and in Scandinavia the unions championed a variety of

PART THREE
The way ahead

16 A policy for democracy

The trade unions' role as mere industrial groupings has long since died. Today the trade unions have become one of the major political forces in Britain: like modern-day barons they are perhaps more influential than political parties in determining the government of the country. In February 1974, a single union defeated a Tory government by the direct use of industrial power. The Labour government which came into office was committed to a range of policies with the common intention of winning sympathy and support from the trade unions. As a result, the unions now enjoy a major role in the determination of public policy on a vast range of issues. In 1974-5, for example, the TUC advised government on the following issues: industrial law, employment law, wage policy, price policy, food subsidies, taxation, manpower policy, income distribution, workers' participation, energy, education, social services, pensions, industrial health and safety, sex discrimination, race relations, standards of public life, prisoners' earnings, social science research, abortion, picketing law, opinion polls, cycle tracks, pollution, waste and reclamation, the arts, nuclear weapons, civil aviation, forestry, tourism, the EEC, Chile, Ulster, Ethiopia and Vietnam – to name but a samplemf ggovernments have no alternative but to take these union submissions seriously, if they do not want to alienate trade-union support – or at least acquiescence – for their central economic policy. The last two governments which tried to resist union pressure were defeated (Wilson 1970, Heath 1974).

But if unions are to exercise this degree of influence, it is important that they should be genuinely representative of their members. Are they?

Union elections: the rule of the activists

The system of elections used by unions varies widely. Most general secretaries are elected by a ballot of all union members, except in NALGO, NUPE and the ISTC where the general

How union elections work – Present systems in major unions

Union	General secretary	Other full-time national officers	Executive	Conference	Independent check in key elections
TGWU	Individual ballot Distributed by branches	Appointed by executive	Individual ballot Distributed by branches except for trade reps	Branch vote Show of hands	No
AUEW	Postal ballot	Postal Ballot	Postal ballot	Divisional vote Appointed by divisional committees	No
GMWU	Block branch vote Show of hands	Appointed by executive Subject to re-election	Regional appointment	Branch vote Show of hands	No
NALGO	Appointed by executive	Appointed by executive	Individual ballot Distributed by branches	Branch vote Show of hands	No
NUPE	Appointed by executive	Appointed by executive	Block branch vote Show of hands	Branch vote Show of hands	Yes
EEPTU	Postal ballot	Appointed by executive	Postal ballot	Branch vote Show of hands	Yes
USDAW	Appointed by executive	Appointed by executive	Block branch vote Show of hands	Branch vote Show of hands	No
ASTMS	Appointed by executive	Appointed by executive	Individual ballot Distributed by branches	Branch vote Show of hands	No
NUT	Appointed by executive	Appointed by executive President elected by national individual ballot	Individual ballot Distributed by branches	Branch ballot Various systems	Yes
NUM	Pithead ballot	Appointed by executive President elected by pithead ballot	Branch vote Some areas appoint representatives	Branch vote Usually show of hands, but varies	Yes
UCATT	Branch vote Show of hands	Appointed by executive	Branch vote Show of hands	Branch vote Show of hands	No
CPSA	Appointed by executive	Appointed by executive	Conference vote	Branch vote Show of hands	No
UPW	Branch block vote Show of hands	Appointed by executive	Conference vote	Branch vote Show of hands	Yes

secretary is appointed by the executive. But every general secretary is elected for life – except in UCATT, the EEPTU and the AUEW where he has to submit himself for re-election after a fixed term. This means that there is little electoral control over a general secretary once he is elected. Most union rulebooks provide that the general secretary can be sacked – but this power has never been used, except in extreme cases of fraud.

The general secretary has a major political influence in most unions and is normally the officer in the union who has been elected with the highest turnout: but most union rules still treat the general secretary as a mere civil servant. Few general secretaries (including Len Murray at the TUC) have a vote on their executive.

General-secretary elections are perhaps the most democratic forms of election in the unions: but, even so, only a small minority of union members vote. Many of the recorded figures are highly dubious, especially in the general unions. The TGWU claim that 36 per cent of members voted in its last general-secretary election – but this is almost certainly an exaggeration, although this cannot be checked because no detailed voting figures are published. The last GMWU election showed that 85 per cent of members voted: but this was a complete illusion. In GMWU elections, each branch casts its votes in blocks so that three members, say, can cast votes for a branch's total membership of, say, three hundred, as though they had three hundred votes. So, in fact, the actual numbers of members who voted may be well under 5 per cent. In the AUEW, branch-ballot turnouts used to average around 10 per cent, but under the postal-ballot system turnout has soared to 30 per cent. The NUM achieves a high turnout in its general-secretary election by using a pithead ballot: last time it was over 60 per cent. Some unions do far worse: the National Union of Seamen, for example, elected its present general secretary, Jim Slater, on a 2 per cent turnout. All elections held under branch ballots produce exceptionally low turnouts of 10 per cent or less (no figures are published). In some unions, the branch ballots are actually distributed among members at work for them to fill in and return to the branch secretary or (as in the NUT) to return by post to union headquarters. This can often be as unreliable a process as the more obviously undemocratic

show-of-hands vote where the ballot is not even secret. In the
1950s, Joseph Goldstein, an American researcher, published a
study of one TGWU branch picked at random. (*The Government
of British Trade Unions*, Allen & Unwin, 1952). He recorded
what happened on one occasion when branch officials received
a thousand ballot papers to hand out to their 950 members:

> A few packets were distributed to shop stewards, who might
> have been suspicious if they had not received them. A group
> of shop stewards, all members of the inner cabinet, gathered
> round a table one evening and with varied coloured pencils
> proceeded to place crosses by the names of the communist
> party candidates, Papworth and Jones [not Jack Jones] . . .
> This deceptive record indicated that approximately 95% of
> the eligible membership participated in the election, while
> close to 1% would be a more accurate figure.

According to Goldstein, only nine per cent of the branch's
members ever saw a ballot form. The TGWU indignantly
denied that Goldstein's researches were typical, then or now,
but there is no check on the union's ballots and there has been
no major independent investigation since Goldstein's work.

Goldstein also graphically exposed how a TGWU branch's
policy was generally determined by a small group of about one
per cent of the branch's membership. The average attendance
at union meetings was four per cent, but two-thirds of all
resolutions put to the branch were proposed by one of eight
people. Goldstein identified these as the 'hard core centre'. Six
of the eight were or had been members of the Communist Party.
It was hardly surprising that the officers of the branch managed
to hold on to the reins of power because five elections out of six
went uncontested. Goldstein concluded that 'officials are
elected by, and from, the self-appointed members of the inner
circle'. He also found that the vast majority of members of the
branch had no idea what was being done in their name. Over
ninety per cent of the branch's members did not even know the
name of the branch chairman. When an election was held in
1947, eighty-one per cent of those who did not normally attend
branch meetings did not even know an election was taking
place. As Ernie Bevin once put it, addressing a TGWU conference, 'Let us be quite frank with one another. Trade-union
ballots do not reach the standard of a parliamentary election.'

Even when the turnout is high, left-wingers tend to win a disproportionate share of the votes. This is because most union members know virtually nothing about the character or politics of the candidates. Their only sources of advice and information are the shop stewards or branch officials who do know the candidates. They, of course, are likely to advise support for left-wing candidates – which is why, for example, in the AUEW a Communist Party member, Les Dixon, could win an election (as he did in 1973) on a relatively high poll in a postal ballot.

Yet, whatever the shortcomings of the elections for general secretaries, they are more democratic than the elections for most union executives and union conferences: the bodies that determine union policy. As the table on union elections (p.214) shows, no union conference is elected on a postal ballot, and of the executives only the AUEW and the EEPTU are elected on a postal ballot. Nearly all are elected on a tiny turnout – except the AUEW and the EEPTU. This also applies to the elections for union delegations to the TUC. There is little published evidence on the level of branch turnouts, but as a rule-of-thumb, a branch turnout of over ten per cent is quite exceptional, a turnout of five per cent is average, a turnout of one per cent quite frequent.

A low turnout in elections to voluntary organisations is nothing unusual, and it is only a matter of concern where that organisation has political power. The voters in low-turnout elections tend to be activists, and in the case of the unions (and local political parties) highly politicised activists. This would not matter if their politics reflected the politics of union members – but this is inherently unlikely. The unions naturally attract left-wing activists (as industrial companies attract right-wing activists). That is why the candidates elected tend to be disproportionately left-wing.

Several unions ask candidates to submit an election address and personal details which are circulated to members or published in the union journal. But normally these contain no political views.

Only a handful of unions (see table) ask an independent agency to supervise their elections – although after the scandal of ballot rigging exposed by Goldstein in the TGWU, by Cannon and Chapple in the ETU, and more recently in the AUEW, it would be reassuring if more unions did so. The Electoral Reform Society counts the votes for the miners, teachers, public employees, tailors and several other unions.

But the central problem is not ballot rigging: it is that Britain's union leaders are elected by activists who form a fraction of the union's membership and whose views do not represent the majority of union members. Here are some examples of major issues on which the views of union leaders are quite out of touch with their members.

Incomes policy

The union leadership has consistently opposed statutory incomes policy since 1966. Frank Chapple of the EEPTU is the only major union leader who has publicly advocated statutory policy. Yet trade-union members have consistently been in favour. In July 1975, for example, a PEP poll showed that eighty per cent of Britons favoured a statutory policy (indicating support from a majority of trade unionists). Other polls back this up: (all asked only union members).

ORC February 1967: Do you think incomes policy is likely to help or harm the country's economy?

Help	53%
Harm	25%

Harris August 1972: Do you think the government should take legal action to curb wage increases?

Yes	62%
No	32%

ORC June 1973: Do you think that Britain should or should not have a system of controls on prices and incomes for many years to come?

Should	77%
Should not	16%

ORC November 1973: Is the TUC right to ask the government to end wage controls in the next phase?

Right	36%
Wrong	49%

ORC January 1974: Do you think incomes policy is likely to help or harm the country's economy?

Help 61%
Harm 17%

The unions also opposed voluntary cooperation with the Heath government on wage control. When Mr Heath suggested the £2 flat-rate pay rise in October 1972, he had overwhelming support from union members:

ORC October 1972: Should trade-unions cooperate to put this [£2 limit] plan into operation?

Yes 71%
No 17%

When Mr Heath introduced his statutory policy because the unions would not cooperate with the voluntary policy, he again faced union opposition. But union members did not back their leaders and when the TUC called a one-day strike on 1 May 1973, to protest at the policy, an ORC poll showed that seventy per cent of union members opposed the strike (March 1973).

Industrial relations law

As we saw in Chapter 5, the unions' opposition to legal reforms of industrial relations was total. But they were not supported by their members for most of the period – although after 1972 a small minority of union members agreed with opposing the IR Act, although not with non-cooperation. ORC (January 1969) found overwhelming support among union members for Mrs Castle's plans to take powers to impose secret ballots (62 per cent pro, 30 per cent anti) and to impose cooling-off periods (57 per cent pro, 36 per cent anti). There was also major support among union members for the key planks of the Industrial Relations Act:

ORC November 1970: Do you approve of the setting up of a court to deal with industrial disputes?

Yes 83%
No 11%

Harris March 1971: Do you support making union and employer agreements legally binding?

Yes	67%
No	20%

. . . and fines against companies or unions who break agreements?

Yes	64%
No	25%

* Harris November 1971: Do you think if the Industrial Relations Bill becomes law, it will be a good thing?

Yes	42%
No	31%

Gallup August 1971: In general, do you approve or disapprove of the government's Industrial Relations Act?

Approve	41%
Disapprove	39%

ORC December 1971: Do you approve of the Industrial Relations Act?

Yes	43%
No	43%

ORC September 1972: The trade unions should start using the new industrial relations laws for the benefit of their members.

Agree	58%
Disagree	32%

* In March 1971, the same poll showed 36% yes, 44% no.

The unions' policy of non-registration did not reflect members' views either. Every union which balloted its members found a majority in favour of registration.

Gallup July 1971: The TUC has advised trade unions not to register under the terms of the government's Industrial Relations Act. Do you think trade unions should or should not register?

Should   48%
Should not   29%

Entry into Europe

The unions steadily opposed entry into the EEC after 1970, but in the June 1975 referendum the total TUC opposition did not reflect their members' wishes, as a poll of union members immediately before the referendum showed:

Harris 5 June 1975: How will you vote in the referendum?
Yes   60%
No   25%

Eliminating the 15 per cent don't-knows, this suggested that 71 per cent of union members voted yes – almost the same figure as the national average in the referendum. An analysis of 1,022 trade unionists interviewed by Gallup from 7 May to 2 June found that 60 per cent intended to vote yes, 33 per cent no, and 11 per cent didn't know.

Nationalisation

As we have seen already, the trade unions' total support for socialist policies does not always reflect their members' wishes. Few detailed polls have been carried out on this subject. But an ORC poll of two thousand workers in January 1975 asked whether they supported or opposed nationalisation. The answers were:

Support   18%
Oppose   67%

Not only do union members hold different political views to their leaders on specific issues, but the majority reckon that the unions have too much power and do not help the country:

ORC 1971: Do you think that the way trade-union leaders behave is, or is not, a threat to the prosperity of the country?
Is a threat   68%
Is not   21%

ORC August 1972: Would you say that the trade-union movement has too much power, too little power or the right amount?

Too much	52%
Too little	11%
About right	32%

Industrial decisions

There is far less evidence to suggest that unions do not represent their members' views accurately in individual strike decisions – as the 1972 railway ballot and the 1973 and 1974 miners' ballots also demonstrated. But union members none the less see the unions' influence on companies as being generally harmful:

ORC January 1974: Which of these groups have too much power over British companies?

Workers	2%
Managers	5%
Unions	55%
Government	8%

There has been little detailed research on the relation of members' attitudes within an individual union since Goldstein's pioneering work. However, one study (*The Union of Post Office Workers* by Michael Moran, Macmillan, 1974) has produced some astonishing figures about attitudes inside the union of Post Office Workers. The UPW is one of the most moderate unions in the TUC – and so, supposedly, one of the most representative. Yet the study of a sample UPW branch in Colchester found that on almost every political issue the union's policy did not reflect members' views. For example, only twenty-one per cent thought the UPW should be affiliated to the Labour Party (although the union has been so affiliated for years), and over eighty-five per cent thought the union should not seek a closed shop (although the union has long campaigned for it). The degree of ignorance about the union was only matched by the degree of ignorance about themselves. Thus, only fifty-one per cent of members thought they paid the political levy although in fact ninety-five per cent pay it. The author of the study, Michael Moran, found that almost all the union's members joined for 'calculative' reasons – that is, because they saw material advantages from doing so – rather than political reasons. Moran noted that the UPW leaders did not feel they were out of touch with their members, but he reckoned that this was because they only come into contact with the activists.

Another measure of the unrepresentative nature of trade-union government is the party affiliations of members of union executives. At the October 1974 election, the Labour Party won 39.3 per cent of the total vote, the Tories 35.9 per cent, the Liberals 20.2 per cent, Nationalists 3.4 per cent and the Communists 0.057 per cent. There is no precise measure of how trade-union members vote, but a Gallup poll (June 1975) found that (at a time when the main parties were neck-and-neck on overall preferences) 49 per cent of union members intended to vote Labour, 25 per cent Tory and 10 per cent Liberal. Around 0.1 per cent normally vote Communist. Yet of the 345 members of the executive of Britain's largest thirteen unions, approximately between forty and fifty are Communist Party supporters (i.e. around 13 per cent), and almost all the others are Labour Party supporters (i.e. 87 per cent). If any of the 345 vote Tory, Liberal or Nationalist, they keep it to themselves. Thus the political colour of union executives bears a very indirect resemblance to that of their members.

Can union elections be reformed?

On the evidence above, there is a strong case for reforming union elections, but it is not easy to see how that can be done. Direct government intervention is likely to be counter-productive, as the experience of the Industrial Relations Act demonstrated. Trade unions are voluntary combinations and their rules of behaviour cannot be unilaterally determined by government. Yet government can provide finance and encouragement for reform – and might one day provide penalties (like the withdrawal of tax privileges) for unions who persist in undemocratic elections. The reforms that government and moderates inside the unions should seek might include:

Support for the postal ballot. Postal ballots do increase turnouts, as experience in the AUEW and the EEPTU has amply demonstrated, and they do help the chances of moderate candidates. They also make fraud and intimidation far harder. The main snag for most unions is that they are an expensive form of ballot especially since the sharp rises in postal charges in 1975. But it would cost a government a trivial amount to meet the cost of union postal-ballot elections. Suppose, for example, that every union held a postal ballot each year and all members voted, the cost in 1975 prices would have been £1.1 million in postal charges. But the net resource cost to the government would have been infinitely smaller – since it would hardly be necessary to open new post offices or employ extra post-men – perhaps only £100,000 (roughly ten per cent of the *daily* cost of state subsidies to British Leyland). The Tories made an attempt during the passage of the Employment Protection Bill in the summer of 1975 to insert a clause to provide for such subsidies but this was rejected by the government, although Harold Wilson told the Commons that he was personally in favour of postal ballots. Most union leaders (except Hugh Scanlon) have no objection to the provision of such subsidies. But the postal ballot by itself will not solve the problem.

Better information. More unions need to be encouraged to distribute election addresses and all ought to insist that party affiliations should be declared on addresses. It is a nonsense that Communist Party candidates for the AUEW have to declare how long they have been members of the union on the ballot form, but not that they are members of the Communist Party. The media also have an important role to play in pub-licising the character and politics of union candidates. In the 1974-5 round of AUEW elections, widespread publicity in newspapers undoubtedly helped the moderates. (As Hugh Scanlon explained in September 1975 on television: 'The left generally are opposed [to the postal ballot] because they know the influence of the media . . . they know how they interfere in our elections.'

Factory meetings. Employers should be compelled to provide unions with facilities to hold meetings during working hours. This would ensure higher turnouts for key policy decisions. In the civil service, the CPSA has been allowed to hold such meetings which helped to elect more moderates to the 1975 CPSA conferences which in turn elected a right-wing president, Kate Losinska.

Independent counting. Unions ought to be encouraged to ask the Electoral Reform Society to count their votes and supervise their elections. This would make any ballot fraud much harder to perpetrate. Alternatively, it might be wise to create a new agency to monitor elections.

One man, one vote. Those unions which do not use postal ballots should be encouraged to reform their procedures in other ways. The system of block branch voting (used, for example, in the GMWU) in which one individual can cast votes for hundreds of absent members, should be scrapped.

Secret ballots. All ballots ought to be secret – for the same reasons that all parliamentary ballots are secret: to avoid any prospect of intimidation. Many unions still vote in branches by show of hands (see the table at the beginning of this chapter).

Regular elections. Executive members ought to have to submit to regular re-election – say once every five years. Re-election ought not to be too frequent, because that tends to induce too much short-term politicking. Most executives do hold frequent elections, but general secretaries are normally elected for life.

Referenda. Unions ought to consult their members on major issues like incomes policy, the EEC, and industrial law reform. Several unions, like the NGA and the EEPTU, already do this. It is not a complicated process once all members are registered, together with addresses, at the union headquarters (which is also a prerequisite for the postal ballot). These referenda might also include wage and strike decisions. The NUM's use of regular pithead ballots on wage deals and national strikes is an excellent example (although, as these have shown, union members are often as industrially militant as their leaders). In Germany, most rule books provide that no strike can be called without a seventy-five per cent vote by union members.

If these reforms can slowly be implemented, the unions are likely to become more representative, but not wholly so: that would be impossible, because unions will naturally reflect a more radical and left-wing ethos than their members. But there is no reason why British unions should not come closer to the pattern of other unions in northern Europe – with more social democrats and fewer Marxists.

It would be wrong to impose a standard pattern on all unions: as we have seen, many of the variations suit different unions better. For example, it would probably be wrong to compel unions to elect all their full-time officers who do not serve on the executive because that would make it harder to promote younger able men. But the general standards outlined above might provide a general basis for reform.

Reform government, too

The danger in promoting electoral reform in trade-union elections is that it will increase the trade unions' claim to be as legitimate a political representative as a parliamentary politician – a claim which any anti-corporatist will naturally wish to avoid. However, this danger can partially be met by improving the legitimacy of parliamentary politicians. There are two important ways in which this might be achieved.

The first is to introduce electoral reform into parliamentary elections by the use of some form of proportional representation (PR) – probably by list voting in multi-member constituencies. The advantages of electoral reform have frequently been rehearsed, but it has particular application to the view trade unionists take of parliamentary politicians. Under a reformed system, the unions would normally face a coalition government. Such a government would be able to claim (a) that it had the support of more than fifty per cent of the voters (unlike previous post-war governments), (b) would not be dominated by Labour left-wingers or Tory right-wingers, and (c) would not be faced by an opposition which could expect to win a majority by itself in any ensuing election. In such a situation, the unions would be more careful to win public support for their policies – because it could never expect a government wholly committed for or against union policies. The unions would also know that there was a constant risk of an election. If PR had operated in February 1974, the miners would not have been able to claim such a signal victory – firstly, because the Tories would have emerged with more seats, and secondly, because the succeeding government would in any case have depended on MPs who did not believe that the incomes policy should have been abandoned.

The second way is to be less reluctant about the use of referenda. The 1975 Europe referendum showed (a) that the majority of voters will normally identify with causes supported by politicians in the middle ground, almost regardless of the specific issue (until the referendum, most voters told opinion polls they were anti-EEC), and (b) that it provides almost irrefutable evidence of the public will: thus the TUC immediately ended its boycott of the EEC, because it was impossible to argue that the referendum verdict was not a democratic decision.

Many of the political problems of the last ten years have arisen because trade unions refused to accept the legitimacy of parliamentary decisions: notably on such issues as trade-union law reform, incomes policies, and entry into the EEC. But unions would find it much harder to refute decisions taken by parliament and backed by referenda. Thus any government in the future which wishes to legislate on issues that may cause direct union opposition, like an incomes policy, would be well advised to first submit that policy to a referendum.

Anti-democrats might reply that this would run the risk that 'sensible' policies might be rejected by a 'short-sighted' electorate. The answer to this is (a) if the majority of the country is opposed to the policies that are necessary, then they probably cannot be successfully implemented anyway, (b) the evidence on most recent issues is that the public support commonly agreed 'sensible' policies (like incomes policy) by a greater majority than MPs and trade-union leaders, (c) in an advanced democracy, voters have more rights than choosing an MP once every five years, and (d) referenda are common in nearly every other democracy in the west.

The combination of more democratic trade unions, more democratic parliamentary elections, and more democratic public policy should provide for a more stable and acceptable government in Britain.

17 Resolving the wages war

The central issue that now confronts any British government is how to counter the inflationary consequences of free collective bargaining. As we saw in Chapter 3, the evidence that wage inflation has been one of the major causes of price inflation over the last decade is overwhelming. It is imperative that action is taken to conquer inflation, even at a high price in terms of other economic and social objectives. If no action is taken, all other objectives will be swept away in the hyperinflationary flood that will surely follow. Nor is it enough to produce some mild slowing down in inflation: for that would only be a prelude to another, yet faster, burst of inflation in the following boom.

There are broadly six approaches that need to be examined:

1 *Monetarism:* keeping money supply stable and letting unemployment rise until inflation stops.

2 *Social contract:* accepting every union demand on politics and hoping for lower wage demands in return.

3 *Corporatism:* a milder version of socialism – appointing union leaders to powerful political positions to induce moderation.

4 *Legalism:* direct legal restrictions on the right to strike designed to undermine union bargaining power.

5 *Incomes policy:* a continued, but refined, repeat of the pay controls used over the last decade.

6 *Heathism:* direct confrontation with a major union in which government or employer 'wins' a strike to deter excessive wage claims. This may or may not be combined with an incomes policy.

Let us look at each in turn.

Monetarism: uncertain and temporary

The increasingly influential money-supply school holds that the cause of inflation has been excess money supply, produced by the efforts of government to lower unemployment by excess government spending and budget deficits. This school, whose leading exponent in Britain is the Tory MP, Sir Keith Joseph, sees the solution to inflation in greater control of the money supply. In practical terms, this simply means more unemployment. This does not imply that governments would deliberately create unemployment, but that they would not take the traditional Keynesian countervailing action when unemployment started to rise. When I was writing this book (late 1975) this was precisely the policy being pursued by a Labour Government although it could hardly admit as much.

The first fallacy to be disposed of is that the monetarist solution is bound to work. This can be seen in terms of the quantity theory of money (see Chapter 4): P (prices) × V (velocity) = M (money supply) × T (number of transactions). According to this, prices will move in direct proportion to the money supply only if the velocity of circulation is constant and if the number of transactions in the period is also constant. But if the money supply is held constant, the result may simply be to cut the number of transactions (i.e. to lower the level of demand and to raise unemployment), or to increase the velocity of circulation (i.è. the speed at which money changes hands). That is why it was possible in 1974-5 for money supply to rise by only 8.4 per cent while prices rose by 24.8 per cent. It seems to be true that the velocity of circulation is stable over the long run, but we may not be able to wait for the long run. In all hyperinflations, the velocity has altered sharply. (In the Indonesian inflation, for example, the velocity doubled from 16.7 to 32.2 between 1964 and 1966 when people realised that they needed to spend money fast.) Thus there can be no guarantee that a money-supply policy will cut inflation, however high unemployment goes.

Yet it may be true that, in practice, higher unemployment will affect union bargaining behaviour, and it will, of course, eliminate most of the inflation due to excess demand. The evidence on the effect of unemployment on union bargaining is mixed. The surge in wage demands began in 1972 just as unemployment hit a post-war peak. The next biggest surge took place in 1974-5, when unemployment was also rising sharply. Between August 1974 and August 1975, unemployment rose by 374,000 (+59 per cent), yet in the same period average wage rates rose by a record 27.2 per cent.

Unemployment, however, did appear to have a moderating

influence in 1974-5 in wage settlements in those industries where it was a real and immediate threat – like the building industry. But unemployment is unlikely to be regarded as a major threat in most industries where wages are determined by collective bargaining. For a start, roughly half all nationally-bargained wage deals are in the public sector. Civil servants or miners, for example, do not feel threatened by unemployment and are unlikely to be constrained by fear of it. Some Tories argue that unemployment ought to be used as a deliberate weapon in public-sector industries so that, for example, miners are given the option of an inflationary wage rise only if, in exchange, pits are closed down and miners are made redundant. But, oddly, they do not seem to see that if a union has the industrial strength to achieve an inflationary wage rise, it also has the industrial strength to resist redundancies – unless the country can entirely dispense with the work done by that union (so that a strike inflicts no damage).

In private industry, the growing willingness of governments to rescue bankrupt companies has removed yet another sanction. Many unions believe that by the use of sit-ins – a weapon of growing importance since it was successfully pioneered at Upper Clyde Shipbuilders in 1971 – they can force a factory or company to stay in business or force government to rescue them. At British Leyland, for example, the threat of bankruptcy did not moderate wage deals in 1970-75. As one Cowley shop steward put it to me: 'My job is to get the maximum for my members. It's not my job to stop it going broke: that's management's job.' In 1975, when a government takeover was agreed and when production had plummeted by thirty per cent, the unions in British Leyland agreed to wage rises only marginally below the going rate.

But the major objection to the high-unemployment solution is that even if it works, the wage-restraining effect may only be temporary. As soon as unemployment ceases to rise, or starts to fall again, all the 'benefits' may be lost. It may be possible (although politically very difficult) to maintain high unemployment for a period, but it is certainly impossible to keep it rising. Once unemployment stabilises, the fear of job losses begins to recede and it is the fear that determines the effect on wage bargains. Those already unemployed, after all, cannot bargain. In the eight years to 1966, the average unemployment rate in Britain was 1.7 per cent. In the eight years after 1966, it averaged 2.7 per cent. Yet this change appears to have had no long-term effect on wage bargaining.

Unemployment is not only a gross human waste and one of the surest mechanisms for maximising misery and social discontent (regardless of the level of unemployment pay), but it is also a sure way of reducing economic growth. In periods of high unemployment, training is cut and thus investment in new manpower falls dramatically. (For example, in the 1970-71 slump, the annual number of trainees fell by twenty-five per cent in one year.) It also provides every incentive for the maintenance and extension of restrictive practices. Ever since the last war, Britain has suffered from restrictive practices which were created in the 1930s to protect jobs. Is it really wise to pursue the one policy which will help perpetuate restrictive practices into the 1980s and 1990s?

The political effect of unemployment is uncertain. It could well help the Marxist left – for it certainly seems to provide *a priori* evidence of the failure of capitalism and democracy. This effect could be most dramatic among the young school-leavers, who will suffer disproportionately. If they cannot find a decent job, what reason have they to identify with the economic system? In the trade unions it could help to breed a generation as embittered as some of the present generation of union leaders. Of course, high unemployment may lead to an apparent moderation in the unions as it did in 1975, but the underlying effect may not be moderating. In the 1930s the unions were not militant, but it was the period when the future leaders of unions in the 1970s were joining the Communist Party. There can be no certainty about the political consequences of a repeat of the 1930s – but at the very least it would be wrong to suppose that unemployment is bound to moderate the unions.

Unemployment is already being used as an anti-inflationary weapon, but it is unlikely to provide a total cure for the disease, and might infect us with yet worse diseases.

The social contract: how it failed

The argument sounds persuasive: the unions say they cannot restrain their wage demands because Britain is an unequal society. Therefore, create an equal society and then the unions will have no case for not restraining their demands. This was

the basis of the 1974 social contract. The Labour Party reckoned that by accepting – almost *in toto* – the TUC's socialist
programme of nationalisation, higher taxes on the rich, more
legal freedom for unions and higher taxes on industry, they
could expect a 'response' in terms of wage demands from the
unions. The Labour Party was as good as its word. In the
following eighteen months, it implemented all the policies the
unions had backed and which had been put forward in its
manifesto. Yet the 'response' from the unions was to casually
check in with the highest wage claims ever recorded. In the
following year, Britain's inflation doubled and wage inflation
topped thirty per cent. This hardly suggested that the dawn of
socialism had had significant effect on wage claims. Indeed, the
most inflationary wage settlements were signed in the most
socialised industries, i.e. the public sector (according to a survey by Incomes Data, average wage settlements in the first half
of 1975 were 39.7 per cent in the public sector, and 33 per cent
in the private sector).

Another measure of the benefits of socialism is to compare
the incidence of strikes under Labour and Tory governments. A
study of strikes between 1950 and 1967 showed that there were
on average only two per cent fewer strikes in a year of Labour
government than in a year of Tory government – hardly of
great significance.

Britain has steadily become a more egalitarian society since
the war. Thus the top one per cent of income-earners who
received twelve per cent of after-tax incomes in 1938-9 only got
four per cent in 1972-3 (according to the Royal Commission on
the Distribution of Income and Wealth, 1975). Since then,
massive inflation plus high marginal tax rates has cut their
share even further. Yet it has been in the last decade when the
move to egalitarianism has been most intense that trade-union
militancy has also been at its most intense. It might, of course,
have been even more intense if there had not been a move
towards egalitarianism, but there is no evidence to suppose that
this is so.

Other socialist policies – such as further nationalisation of
private industry – are only likely to strengthen the power of the
unions and the inflationary consequences of free collective
bargaining.

If Britain's unions were wholly Marxist, then their power

and militancy might be controlled by the introduction of socialist policies. But they are not, and most of their attitudes and structures are primarily devoted to maximising the wages and conditions of their members: so that their behaviour is unlikely to be altered by further steps on the road to socialism.

Corporatism: so what's new?

A simple remedy for the inflationary clash of state and union power is not just to make the state's policies more socialist, but also to surrender more state power to the unions. This essentially corporatist solution has become increasingly popular among thinkers in both major parties.

This thesis is an attractive one at first sight: it is a traditional solution to a challenge to state power. But it is based on a fundamental misunderstanding about the nature of British unions. As we have seen, the union barons – the men who sit on the TUC general council – have already been given a major role in the determination of government policy. Under a Labour government, the barons enjoy more influence than most Labour MPs. They influence policy both by direct representation and through the organs of the Labour Party which they control. Even under a Tory government, the barons have been granted an ever-increasing policy role. Yet this transfer of power to the barons has not, apparently, modified union attitudes. Why not?

The reason is simple: it is no use modifying the attitudes of the barons without also modifying the attitudes of the hundreds of men who sit on union executives and attend union conferences, not to mention the 300,000 odd shop stewards – for they are the men who ultimately determine union policy. If the barons are sucked into the establishment, the main consequence will be to discredit them inside their unions. So, since the war, the TUC general council's policy has often been overturned by the full congress (1951, on incomes policy; 1967 on incomes policy; 1971 on registration) so that the barons' support for responsible policies has been of little avail – especially on wage demands.

This is not to say that corporatism cannot help: in unions where the general secretary is all-powerful, involvement in major government decisions may well be a moderating force. Jack Jones, for example, was strongly influenced by the power given to him by ministers, in his swing towards moderation, and thanks to the structure of the TGWU he was able to carry the union with him. But even in the TGWU the general secretary cannot control many of the industrial decisions. Mr Jones made every effort to stop the national dock strike of 1972 and the London dock strike of the spring of 1975 – but he was sharply rebuffed.

Corporatism has more application in the day-to-day operation of industry through the extension of industrial democracy. There is no doubt that greater worker involvement has helped to break down the traditional class hostility between worker and boss in many industries, but success is not automatic. As we saw in Chapter 11, extensive workers' control in the printing industry has brought no benefits at all.

The corporatism that produces the greatest gains is the corporatism of attitudes, not the corporatism of institutions. Thus, attitudes (and wage militancy) of working people are not greatly influenced by inviting TUC leaders to Downing Street, or by electing workers to company boards, but they are influenced if the foremen stop being dictatorial and if plant managers spare the time to talk and listen.

Legalism: a cul-de-sac

One method of restraining the power of free collective bargaining is to limit the right to strike: a weapon which has been used in wartime in a direct way and which was employed in a more subtle way in the Industrial Relations Act. The right to strike is not a fundamental right. It is a fundamental right of an individual to withdraw his labour (i.e. quit his job), but it is not a fundamental right to combine to withdraw labour. Certainly this is the view of the majority of the population as evidenced by a Gallup poll. In 1970, for example, Gallup found that only twenty-four per cent thought that the right to strike was an essential freedom in a democracy, and another poll in 1968 found that sixty-six per cent would approve if all unofficial strikes were made illegal, and only twenty-two per cent would disapprove. Of course, it is a feature of most free democratic societies that the right to strike exists, but in most of these societies those who exercise that right have to face the consequences if, by so doing, they infringe the rights of others: for example, the right of an employer to enjoy the benefits of a contract freely entered into, the right of workers in other industries dependent on the strike-hit industry to carry on working, the right of consumers to expect a reliable flow of goods, and so forth.

Yet the history of the Industrial Relations Act (which imposed relatively limited restraints on the right to strike) demonstrates that unions do not, at present, accept the right of any government to legislate to restrict strike rights, and are prepared to flout any law passed to achieve this. In other words, the law cannot alter union behaviour unless a means can be found to give that law a special legitimacy in the eyes of the trade unions. This could conceivably be achieved by a referendum on a new Industrial Relations Act – but the obstacles to winning such union acceptance now seem immense. Since the unions were successful in defeating the Industrial Relations Act, they will be all the more confident of defeating any future attempt to legislate and would probably oppose it with considerably more venom than they displayed between 1971 and 1974. The passage of another such act would also embitter relations between government and unions with little benefit. The law can play an important role in reforming the relations between government and unions, but it can best be deployed as an economic weapon in the form of a statutory incomes policy.

Incomes policy: awful but inevitable

Incomes policy is unpleasant, messy, unjust, hard to prolong and the cause of much distortion. Yet it probably must remain the central approach to the control of free collective bargaining, for the reasons I outlined in Chapter 4.

There are various ways in which future incomes policies might proceed. The most obvious is a repeat of the pattern of the last decade, with alternating periods of incomes policy interrupted by periods of free collective bargaining. The advantage of this is that the periods of free collective bargaining iron out some of the more ridiculous distortions caused by incomes policy, yet need not be long enough to accelerate inflation too far. The trouble is that the more this process is repeated, the more predictable it becomes. As a result, the unions increasingly tend to rush in with excess wage demands to beat the next incomes policy. This process would almost certainly accelerate, if unchecked. One possible policy would be to legislate for continuous incomes policy broken by, say, a three-week gap for free collective bargaining: all settlements which were not agreed in this period would then be subject to the legal limit. Then the threat of a strike would no longer be a central influence on wage bargains because it would not be worthwhile for a union to strike. But in the future some more permanent form of incomes policy will be required.

The enforcement of incomes policy is also a central problem but, curiously, the statutory sanctions for excessive wage rises provided by most incomes policies have seldom been used. But it might be more effective to control pay rises through a tax system. This could be done by imposing a penal hundred-per cent rise in national insurance contributions on employers or employees who pay or receive excess wage rises. This is not administratively impossible, and has the great attraction that it would be almost impossible to strike against: the only danger would be a purely political strike to demand the end of the imposition. The imposition of such an 'excess wage tax' would help to make the operation of incomes policy more obviously permanent – but the rates could be varied in each budget.

Every effort must be made to regularise the formulation of incomes policy, and to involve the unions in that process. It would be highly desirable if Britain moved towards the Scandinavian system of central wage bargains: a system ideally suited for countries where unions exert major power.

The two political features of the Scandinavian system are (1) that unions and employers (or government) agree a wage norm and then enforce that norm on their members: (2) that all major collectively-bargained wage deals start on the same date ('synchropay'). Variants of the system operate in Denmark, Norway, Sweden, Finland, Holland, Ireland and Japan. In Scandinavia, the central bargain is usually signed between the employers' federation and the national TUC – although governments have been playing an increasingly important part in the process. In Norway, a committee of experts from both sides meets before talks start to agree on the relevant economic facts and figures. This helps to establish a basic consensus before the hard bargaining gets under way. The final deal lays down the norm for wage rises – a flat-rate increase, a percentage increase, or more often a mixture of the two. This is then quickly followed by industry-by-industry deals which keep closely to the terms of the central deal. All deals normally start from the same date and provide phased rises through the period agreed.

The synchronisation of pay deals would have major attractions for Britain. Much of Britain's wage inflation is caused by leapfrogging wage claims in which unions try to match earlier wage claims in the year and outgun subsequent claims. Union leaders have shown little enthusiasm for synchropay in public: some of them fear that it might make it easier for governments to control wages (it would) and also that it would over-concentrate the time of union bargainers – (it would, but many unions, like the miners, manage all right, although wage bargains are only struck once a year). However, in private they are not so hostile. Ray Buckton of ASLEF argued at a TUC general council meeting in the summer of 1975 that if there was to be any general wage restraint, all wage bargains should be struck from, say, November, so that everyone would suffer or gain by the same amount. The notion of synchropay was also considered by the Heath government as a possible basis for stage three of its pay controls – but the principle has never been properly debated in public.

Synchropay could be operated within a statutory or a voluntary incomes policy, but it would probably have to be initially introduced via a statutory policy in order to force all bargainers to start on the same date. This would not be hard to do, although there would have to be carefully designed transitional arrangements to take account of the dates of each group's previous settlement.

The danger of synchropay is that by combining all pay agreements into a single period it would increase the threat of several parallel major strikes – or even a general strike. This is a risk that has to be faced. In Denmark in 1973, central wage talks broke down and were followed by a thirteen-day general strike. In Finland in 1971, the communist unions refused to agree to a central deal and led a seven-week strike throughout the engineering industry, but they were decisively beaten and the policy survived. It is probably better to run the risk of a major strike and to know when it might come, if this means relative peace for the rest of the year (or two years).

Centralised bargaining (which is not necessarily a concomitant of synchropay) works well in Scandinavia because both the employers' and the unions' central organisations are so strong. Most Scandinavian employers banded together around 1900 at the same time that the unions combined. By contrast, not only is Britain's TUC weak, but the main employers' group (the CBI) is even weaker. It was not formed until 1965 and only represents a minority of industrial companies. Both will need to acquire much greater control powers if a system of central bargains is to work in Britain. Scandinavian employers have used lock-outs as freely as the unions have used strikes, which has helped to maintain a better balance of power between the two. If unions in one industry call a strike, the employers are quite happy to hit back in other industries with lockouts. Norwegian employers, for example, can lock out up to twenty-five per cent of all Norwegian workers with a seventy-five per cent majority vote on their governing board.

Both employers and union centres are able to enforce the central bargain on their members (a) by careful policing and monitoring of all collectively bargained industrial deals, and (b) by ruthlessly expelling those who do not toe the line. Both maintain central strike (and lockout) funds, and members, who may need access to these funds, do not want to be expelled and left alone to the mercy of the opposition. In Britain, employers hardly ever group together or collect strike funds (although the Engineering Employers' Federation successfully raised a £1 million strike fund to beat the AUEW's sit-in campaign in 1973). In Norway no union can end a contract, make a wage claim, or call a strike without getting approval from the union centre.

Central wage bargaining has not dramatically reduced inflation in Scandinavia below average world levels – partly because low levels of unemployment have caused persistent wage drift on top of the centrally agreed wage rises (i.e. demand-pull inflation). But it has cut strikes and averted British levels of inflation. The clearest example is in Norway, which has experimented with both central deals and decentralised free collective bargaining. There have always been far fewer strikes in central-bargain years. Thus in 1961, 1962 and 1974 (free-bargain years) an average of 240,000 days were lost in strikes each year, while in the ten central-bargain years between 1963 and 1973, the average days lost per year were only 13,500. Between 1964 and 1974, Britain lost an average 63.3 days in strikes per hundred workers, while Norway lost 1.1 days and Sweden 4.3. Finland and Denmark have not scored so well (77.2 days and 48.4 days), but most of these were lost in one major conflagration. In eight out of the ten years, they each lost fewer days than the British.

Scandinavian unions have been enthusiastic for central bargains because they reckon that it is the only practical way to help the lower paid. The 'solidarity' principle (as it is called) of giving the biggest pay rises to the lowest paid has been a feature of the bargains in every Scandinavian country. This has partly been counteracted by wage drift in the best-paid industries, but even so there has been a substantial redistribution. One of the astounding consequences of this is that Sweden, which is twice as rich as Britain, pays its managers far worse. In April 1975, the average Swedish managing director was earning nearly forty per cent less than his British equivalent – taking account of prices, taxes and currency movements. But there has also been a marked redistribution within the working class. In 1961, for example, 22 per cent of workers in Sweden's engineering industry earned less than 85 per cent of the average wage, and 21 per cent earned more than 115 per cent. By 1974 these proportions had dropped to just 13 per cent and 12 per cent.

It may be that in Britain redistribution might be the carrot to tempt the unions to sign central bargains but, as we have seen, socialism by itself has not so far proved a useful moderating force.

The concept of an annual share-out of national income was developed by Harold Wilson in an interview in 1975, although it has never been properly investigated. But there would be many attractions to a system which could combine synchropay, central wage bargains, and direct state-TUC bargaining. It could work like this: in his annual budget, the Chancellor would map out possible economic developments in the coming year on varying assumptions about wage rises and tax changes. He could warn the unions that if they insisted, say, on a twenty per cent rise in wages, that would mean a postponement of a rise in old age pensions or an extra hundred thousand unemployed or whatever. Thus the unions would be forced to bargain and express choices. In the past the unions have been allowed to demand extra wage rises without having to consider the consequences for national economic policy.

Then the bargaining would start between government, unions and CBI. If an agreement was reached on, say, a £3 plus five per cent formula, all wage rises starting on the following 1 June would have to conform to this formula. Any union which demanded more would risk expulsion from the TUC just as any employer who conceded more would risk expulsion from the CBI (which would require considerable reform of the powers of both). The bargaining might be extended to cover prices (so that the CBI could agree a price rise limit to match the TUC's wage-rise limit) – although this would be a mainly cosmetic exercise.

When no agreement could be reached, the government would normally impose a statutory incomes policy and, perhaps, tight price control. The threat of this would be another factor inducing the CBI and TUC to reach agreement. All wage restrictions would normally apply only to major collective bargains (involving, say, over five thousand workers). This would make the policy easier to monitor and would also stop unnecessary interference with smaller and thus normally less monopoly-dominated wage bargains. There are plenty of variations that can be worked out on these themes, but it should not be beyond the wit of British governments to devise a new style of regularising incomes policy along these lines.

Heathism: the coming confrontation

Governments can create conditions for moderates to win power in the union, they can legislate to prevent excess pay rises, they can increase unemployment or they can implement incomes polices demonstrably based on public consent and support. All these may help to moderate the rate of inflation and to reduce the toll of strikes, but they are unlikely to alter one critical presumption: namely, that major unions (like the miners, power workers and railwaymen) can always 'win' if forced to go on strike.

This assumption was challenged by the 1970-74 Heath government but the challenge failed, most dramatically in the winter of 1973-4. The government decided to resist the miners' excess wage claim with every weapon in its armoury, including a direct appeal to the electorate in a general election: Heath's policy was not aimed at producing confrontation (if it

had been, why did he make such special concessions to the
miners in the framing of the stage-three policy?) but his policy
was not to avoid confrontation in the face of a direct challenge
to the government's central policy. Nor did the majority of the
NUM executive (excepting the Scargill-McGahey axis) seek
confrontation. And yet it came. And when it was over, it
seemed to show that the assumption that a union like the NUM
was unbeatable was indeed right. The direct confrontation not
only failed in its immediate aim of keeping the miners' pay rise
within the stage-three limits, but it destroyed both the policy
and the government itself. So it was no wonder that many
people drew the conclusion that the policy of confrontation – simply refusing to concede excess wage demands even
under the threat of a strike – was both sterile and useless.

But the paradox of February 1974 is that the failure of the
Heath government to win the confrontation with the miners
makes another such confrontation between government and a
major union almost inevitable. Why? Because trade unions
exist to maximise the pay and conditions of their members.
Every wage deal a trade union signs involves a calculation of
the costs and benefits of going on strike. If it is generally
believed that a union can always expect to 'win' if it strikes, this
must induce the union to put a higher price on a peaceful
settlement. Moderate and well-meaning men may lead the
union and may be able to persuade their executive and activists
not to push their power on a particular occasion – perhaps to
help a Labour government. But such moderation cannot pre-
vail for ever, when it is believed that the union could achieve a
higher wage rise without enduring a long and painful strike.
The union will, sooner or later, push for a higher wage rise.
This is a situation that is bound to lead to accelerating wage
inflation, because each union will naturally strive to utilise its
industrial power to win a wage rise a little above the going rate.

In many foreign unions, moderate anti-inflationary trade-
union leaders can ignore the union's potential power because
the activists have no means of rejecting their leaders' policy.
But in Britain, most union general secretaries only enjoy
limited scope – especially on wage policy. Joe Gormley, the
miners' president, did not want to strike in either 1972 or 1974,
but that did not stop the strike. Frank Chapple, the power
workers' leader, believes in tough incomes policy, but yet had

to lead his men into battle in 1970.

Sid Weighell, the railwaymen's leader, did not want to use strike threats in June 1975, but was forced to do so by a militant executive. All these men are moderates, yet none could stop the dyke with his finger. All have a job to do – to maximise their members' wages – and none can ignore the most obvious means of achieving that. If they do, they put their reputation and influence inside the union at risk. There will always be men inside the union to put the case for militancy – be it Arthur Scargill in the NUM or Dave Bowman in the NUR – and these men will win support from activists as long as they are right in arguing that militancy pays off.

So it appears that we face two stark choices: either we accept a steadily accelerating rate of inflation, or we accept the need to change that critical assumption about union power: namely, that the benefits of strikes or strike threats nearly always exceed the costs for major unions.

If the first choice seems unacceptable for anyone who wishes to see the survival of democracy and the mixed economy, then it follows that policy must be geared to alter the great, dehabilitating assumption about society's inability to resist strikes. How? Perhaps it can be done by less drastic policies, but I cannot see any alternative to the restaging of a major confrontation or a series of confrontations in which government reasserts its power.

A better, more coherent organisation of employers on the Scandinavian model might help to restore the balance of power in private industry. More direct appeals to the electorate for support, in referenda, might make it harder for major public-sector unions to strike against government policy. But some dramatic sign of a new order in industry will be needed to mark the change.

The 'reality' of trade-union power is not an arithmetical fact: it is a reflection of the attitudes and preferences of industry, of society, of the public and of government. As long as these preferences favour stable production more than stable prices, the unions can naturally enjoy increased power. But if those preferences change, so too does the 'reality' of trade-union power. So what is required is a clear demonstration of the change in society's preferences. This can be done by government withstanding a long and damaging strike and 'winning' – the measure of the victory being whether other unions will then wish to imitate the striking union or not. In recent times, there have been two 'defeats' for major union strikes: the London busmen in 1958 and the postmen in 1971. Both defeats were followed by a period of decelerating wages and falling inflation, few strikes and rising production. Yet neither defeat was significant enough to affect the long-run balance of expectations about the balance of power in industry. The last time that balance was decisively changed was in December 1926 when the miners' strike collapsed in ignominy. In 1926, 162 million days were lost in strikes after an eighteen-year period when an average twenty-five million days were lost in strikes each year and union power grew immeasurably. Yet in 1927 the total number of days lost in strikes was a mere one million. Before 1926 the leadership of the trade union movement was moving rapidly·to the left. After 1926 it moved rapidly to the right. It was not the Great Depression that cut strikes and boosted the moderates: it was the traumatic defeat of the most powerful and independent union in the country.

It is a common fallacy to suppose that inflicting a defeat on a union will strengthen the militants because the union will become 'embittered'. Defeated unions do indeed become embittered, but their bitterness is more often directed not towards the government but towards the militancy that led them into battle. The UPW, for example, used to be a union in the middle left of the TUC. Yet after 1971, when it was so decisively defeated, it moved swiftly to the right – embittered both by its own militants and by the system of free collective bargaining from which it had suffered.

No one in his right mind would wish to repeat the misery and the humiliation of 1926: yet some such confrontation is the only way in which the balance of power can be restored and the anti-strike arguments of the moderate union leaders can be supported by 'reality'.

It is hard to predict the circumstances in which this confrontation will happen, or when, or with what union. But happen it will – and probably sooner than anyone expects. The union may, of course, win that confrontation, and even perhaps the one after that. But each time the politicians and the public will learn to understand a little better. Each time their resolution will grow. And – if inflation does not explode – then inevitably one confrontation will end in a decisive victory for government. If there is the will to suffer a major loss in production in one year, anything can be achieved. If the political will exists. During the 'great confrontation' between Heath and the miners, industry was put on a three-day week and yet industrial production for the first quarter of 1974 was only 6.1 per cent less than in the last quarter of 1973; the gross national product (at constant prices) only fell by 2.0 per cent in the same period and all the fall was recovered in the following quarter, so the real economic damage was negligible. What was missing was not economic power but political power.

When the next unpleasant and ugly confrontation (or confrontations) has passed, a new era can start in union-government relations and a new era for Britain's predominantly social democratic and moderate trade-union movement.

Whither the unions?

I have argued above for the need to contain union power – at least as it has been exercised over the past decade. But nothing will have been achieved by the application of the policies I suggest, unless the politicians who battle for supremacy have some conception of the eventual stable state for which they should be aiming.

Britain's trade-union movement will always have innate aggression, but this can be channelled into productive conflicts. In recent years, it has primarily been engaged in escalating wage demands. Government has to stop that by the means I suggest, but this same pressure could easily re-establish itself unless the thrust of union power can be directed elsewhere.

West Germany has shown how this can be done through the development of co-determination: giving unions a say in industrial policy. In Britain, so far, workers' participation has been a mixed success. As we saw in Chapter 16, the unions have been suspicious and hostile. Yet in the last five years the attitude of the TUC has begun to shift – aided perhaps by the philosophy espoused by Tony Benn.

So far the issue has been needlessly confused. Too often, attempts to introduce workers' participation have only been attempted to 'save' lame-duck companies. The use of participation by the unions has too often been directed in totally negative directions: to stop redundancies and closures, and to block technological advance.

Equally, the unions have been misled if they imagine that participation implies the right to a political veto on government policy on non-industrial issues. This should not be conceded and in any case would do little to help for the reasons I have given in the argument against corporatism.

What needs to be achieved is full co-determination in industry not just on negative issues but on positive issues. Unions should be consulted not simply about closures but about opening new plants, developing new machinery and increasing profits. The formal structure for achieving this is not so important. Most advances in British history have been piecemeal and it is probably best that this should be so. In some industries, worker-directors may be the best spur to participation. In other industries, the mere change in managerial systems may suffice.

Len Murray has often remarked that those who are first to criticise the unions for behaving irresponsibly are the last to advocate giving them more responsibilities. If unions can be given responsibility, it will not only divert pressure from the function of wage determination – which cannot ever again be left to free collective bargaining – but it will open up endless possibilities for overcoming union resistance to industrial change. Several industries (like ICI) have experimented with this philosophy and been amazed by the results.

In Britain's classbound society, the suspicion between the working and managerial classes is bound to make all progress to participation difficult. Yet unless this suspicion can be extinguished, and unless the differences between the two classes can be narrowed, there is no hope of any progress. Britain will be doomed to spiral downwards: steadily redistributing a smaller and smaller cake of national wealth as the means of investment and technological change are destroyed.

After the trauma of the necessary confrontation on wages, it may also be necessary to recreate a new legal structure to define the limits and rules on strikes and other forms of industrial action. But this will never be of critical importance. Even the best legal structures can be swept away when industrial forces become too great. For years, the Australians boasted that their system of compulsory arbitration explained their notable record on industrial relations. It was totally swept away by the inflation of the 1970s and strikes soared to British levels. The government which has the power to impose a new legal structure on Britain's unions will also be a government which is strong enough not to have to do so.

Index

Index